1/22/12
$75.00

Educating Democracy

Educating Democracy

Alexis de Tocqueville and Leadership in America

Brian Danoff

Published by
State University of New York Press, Albany

© 2010 State University of New York

For information, contact State University of New York Press, Albany, NY
www.sunypress.edu

Production by Cathleen Collins
Marketing by Anne M. Valentine

Library of Congress Cataloging-in-Publication Data

Danoff, Brian.
   Educating democracy : Alexis de Tocqueville and leadership in America /
Brian Danoff.
      p. cm.
   Includes bibliographical references and index.
   ISBN 978-1-4384-2961-8 (hardcover : alk. paper)
   ISBN 978-1-4384-2962-5 (pbk. : alk. paper)
   1. Citizenship—Study and teaching—United States. 2. Democracy—Study
and teaching—United States. 3. Civics—Study and teaching—United States.
4. Education—Aims and objectives—United States. 5. Political leadership—
United States—History. 6. Tocqueville, Alexis de, 1805–1859—Influence.
I. Title.

   LC1091.D26 2010
   320.973—dc22   2009012996

10 9 8 7 6 5 4 3 2 1

Contents

Acknowledgments

I am greatly indebted to the late Wilson Carey McWilliams, who served as advisor for the dissertation that grew into this book. Carey once wrote that W.E.B. Du Bois "was always an 'elitist,' even at his most radically democratic . . . because he was convinced of the need for exceptional individuals . . . who see beyond the practical and the possible, exerting the *pull* of high culture and theory." A modest man, Carey was, nevertheless, precisely one of these exceptional individuals, and I am so grateful to have known—and to have learned from—this exemplary scholar, teacher, citizen and friend. I miss him dearly.

I am also grateful to the other members of my dissertation committee. Dennis Bathory, Dan Tichenor, and Bruce Miroff each provided stimulating comments, criticisms, and suggestions that were crucial for the development of my ideas on Tocqueville, leadership, and American political thought. While earning my PhD at Rutgers, I also learned a great deal about political theory in seminars with Benjamin Barber, Gordon Schochet, and Stephen Bronner. Thanks also to Clayton Sinyai, my fellow graduate student, for being a formidable intellectual sparring partner as well as a source of moral support.

My passion for political theory was first inspired and nurtured by three outstanding teachers—Peter Euben, Jack Schaar, and David Thomas—at U.C. Santa Cruz, where I was an undergraduate. I am indebted to them and also to Jim Miller, who was a wonderful mentor when I was an MA student in the liberal studies program at the New School for Social Research. As an MA student, I was also fortunate to learn from Nancy Fraser and George Shulman.

Portions of this manuscript have been previously published as journal articles. I am grateful to the journals' editors and anonymous reviewers for spurring me to think through my ideas in a more thoroughgoing manner. I also owe a major debt to Cheryl Welch and Bob Putnam for offering comments and encouragement after reading some of the material that has been incorporated into this book. Thanks are due as well to all of the discussants who provided feedback on my research at professional meetings. In addition to making presentations at the annual meetings of various political science associations, I also presented some of the ideas in this book at a conference on Tocqueville convened by the Workshop in Political Theory and Policy Analysis at Indiana University. I am grateful to Aurelian Craiutu and Elinor Ostrom for providing me with this opportunity. I also received valuable comments when I presented some of my research on Tocqueville at a faculty research seminar held by the political science department at Miami University. I thank all of my colleagues in the political science department for providing a supportive environment for my research and teaching in political theory.

I am very grateful to Michael Gibbons, Marc Landy, and another anonymous reviewer at State University of New York Press for providing enormously helpful comments that pushed me to improve the book manuscript in a number of ways. For all of their support and assistance with the publication process, I also thank Michael Rinella, Cathleen Collins, Anne Valentine, Andrew Kenyon, Amanda Lanne, and Gary Dunham, the executive director of State University of New York Press.

Miami University provided me with a research leave for one semester, which gave me the time to finish the book. Miami also provided me with material support in the form of a summer research grant for work on the manuscript. At Rutgers, a Louis Bevier Fellowship facilitated the completion of the dissertation stage of the work.

I am truly blessed to have such supportive and loving parents, and I owe them each so much. My mother helped spark my interest in politics at a young age; I am grateful to her for that, and also for being a careful reader of much of my work. My father helped hone my critical thinking skills throughout my childhood by doing such things as requiring family members to write reviews of the movies we watched on cable. (The rule wasn't followed for long.) Other beloved family members—Sharon, Jim, Taffy, Jo, Orna, Sam, Ronny, and my grandparents—have also been a great source of every kind of support. A very special thanks goes to my son, Julian. Since he was born two years ago, he has brought me immeasurable joy, every single day.

Finally, I am deeply grateful to my wife, Donna. Without her love, grace, patience, humor, wisdom, and unflagging encouragement, I could never have completed this book. I cannot thank her enough for her support, and for reminding me of all that is important in life. With great love, I dedicate this book to her.

Significant portions of chapter 1 and chapter 5 appeared in Brian Danoff, "Asking of Freedom Something Other than Itself: Tocqueville, Putnam, and the Vocation of the Democratic Moralist," *Politics and Policy* XXXV:2 (June 2007): 165–90. I thank the editors of *Politics and Policy* for permission to reprint this material.

Significant portions of chapter 1 and chapter 3 appeared in Brian Danoff, "Lincoln and Tocqueville on Democratic Leadership and Self-Interest Properly Understood," *The Review of Politics* LXVII:4 (Fall 2005): 687–719. I thank the editors of *The Review* for permission to reprint this material.

A brief portion of chapter 3 appeared in Brian Danoff, "Lincoln, Machiavelli, and American Political Thought," *Presidential Studies Quarterly* XXX:2 (June 2000): 290–311. I thank the editors of *Presidential Studies Quarterly* for permission to reprint this material.

Significant portions of chapter 2 appeared in Brian Danoff, "Political Thought in the Early Republic: The Federalist-Antifederalist Debate," in *A History of the U.S. Political System: Ideas, Interests, and Institutions*, ed. Richard A. Harris and Daniel J. Tichenor (Santa Barbara: ABC-CLIO, 2009). I thank ABC-CLIO for permission to reprint this material.

Introduction

Alexis de Tocqueville is widely considered to be one of the greatest analysts of American political life, and his writings on America have been endlessly interpreted and reinterpreted. But, remarkably, there have been few, if any, sustained analyses of Tocqueville's ideas on leadership, and the relevance of these ideas for American political theory and practice.

The argument of this book is that the best way to approach the problem of democratic leadership in America is through Tocqueville. This is not to say that Tocqueville provides us with a definitive and final account of democratic leadership. Indeed, while I use Tocqueville to set the theoretical terms for this book, I also show how certain American thinkers have built on, contested, and sometimes even improved upon these terms. Although I do not always embrace Tocqueville's understanding of democratic leadership, I focus on Tocqueville because no one else so brilliantly analyzes the American character, and no one else so effectively raises the important questions that we need to ask regarding the role of leadership in America. My analysis of Tocqueville centers on *Democracy in America*, but at times I turn to Tocqueville's other writings in order to gain a more complete understanding of his ideas on leadership.

In recent years, "democratic theory" has been one of the dominant areas of inquiry for political theorists. The role of leadership within democratic theory, however, has been somewhat neglected. Of course, there have been some important exceptions to this general neglect. Although he believes that strong leadership has a tendency "to undermine civic vigor," Benjamin Barber has sought to find forms of leadership that are consistent with his vision of "strong democracy."[1] Moreover, there is a group of presidency scholars—namely, James MacGregor Burns, Bruce Miroff, Marc Landy, and Sidney Milkis—who have explored the relationship between leadership

1

and democracy. Most political scientists who study the presidency have followed in the footsteps of Richard Neustadt and have focused their work, as Jeffrey Tulis has pointed out, on "presidential effectiveness"—that is, on the capacity of the president to successfully impose his will onto the political landscape.[2] Although it may be useful for the study of political power, this focus on "effectiveness" tends to obscure the question of how different presidents have strengthened or weakened democratic citizenship. In contrast to this dominant approach, Burns, Miroff, Milkis, and Landy have thoughtfully explored the question of whether or not "democratic leadership" is an oxymoron.[3] If democracy means rule by the people, then is a democratic regime threatened by the rule of strong leaders? As Miroff puts it, "Leadership has rarely fit comfortably with democracy in America. The claims of leaders to political precedence violates the equality of democratic citizens. The most committed democrats have been suspicious of the very idea of leadership."[4] Kenneth Ruscio has noted that leadership is in tension not just with the democratic value of *equality*, but also with the value of *liberty*, for "[l]eadership often means persuading people to do something they originally may not have wanted to do or perhaps even fashioning policies that may require them to do something they will never want to do . . ."[5] Miroff and Ruscio thus prompt us to ask, does leadership inevitably threaten democratic citizenship, or are there types of leadership that enhance rather than diminish democracy?[6]

In my view, a critical engagement with Tocqueville's writings can yield crucial insights into precisely this question. Perhaps more than any other political theorist, Tocqueville's writings can reveal to us the rich problems and possibilities that arise from the effort to combine leadership with democracy. Oftentimes, defenders of strong leadership are suspicious of participatory democracy. By the same token, participatory democrats are often hostile toward leadership. In contrast to both of these views, Tocqueville embraces participatory democracy *and* leadership in a single, complex vision.

Tocqueville's approach to the problem of democratic leadership—and to the problem of democratic authority—is thus different from both conservative scholars who fear participatory democracy, such as Samuel Huntington, and radical scholars who fear strong leadership, such as Robert Paul Wolff. In *The Crisis of Democracy*, Huntington suggests that "the vitality of democracy in the United States in the 1960s" led directly to "a substantial decrease in governmental authority."[7] In order to restore the proper balance between democracy and authority, Huntington hopes that democracy will somehow be restrained, and authority somehow revitalized. Wolff, for his part, argues that "authority" and "autonomy" are inherently in conflict with one another; in a modern state, the best way to safeguard autonomy would be to minimize authority by creating an "instant direct democracy."[8] Huntington and Wolff disagree, of course, over how much emphasis should be placed on authority versus democracy. But for all of their differences, conservatives such as Huntington and radical democrats such as Wolff both agree that authority and democracy are involved in a kind of zero-sum game. In contrast to both Wolff and Huntington, Tocqueville argues that certain forms of authority—and leadership—can augment rather than weaken democratic self-rule.

Throughout this book, my focus will be on the concept of *leadership*, but at times I will discuss the closely related concept of *authority*. Some clarification of these terms is thus in order. Wolff defines authority as "the right to command, and correlatively, the right to be obeyed."[9] But, as Joseph Raz suggests, Wolff's definition is too narrow. Raz argues that a better "explanation of authority is that offered by John Lucas: 'A man, or body of men, *has authority* if it follows from his saying "Let X happen," that X ought to happen.'"[10] For Lucas and for Raz, authority is thus the power to generate an "ought." This means that authority is closely related to what Raz calls "normative power."[11] Raz is helpful here insofar as he points toward the notion that authority is not merely the right to command, but rather authority is that which shapes norms. Drawing in part on Raz's insight, in this book I define authority as that which *educates*. As Sebastian de Grazia usefully puts it, "authority . . . is responsible for the setting up of values. . . . By observing man grow into the citizen we learn that authority is a creative, a cultivating force. Far from being merely restrictive, it forms his character, upholds the things worth loving, and teaches him to see." Whereas scholars such as Wolff suggest that freedom is always at odds with authority, de Grazia writes that, "authority is a necessary condition of freedom, for freedom apart from values or goals or morals makes no sense."[12] My understanding of authority in this book is also informed by the work of John Schaar. Much like de Grazia, Schaar suggests that, "Authority and authorities form our values and goals, show us what is admirable, and uphold us in the pursuit of ideals."[13] Authority, in short, attempts to offer "a conception of what freedom is *for*," as Schaar puts it.[14] With this definition of authority in mind, one can now see that by "leaders" I refer to political actors who seek to shape the norms—and thus seek to educate—their fellow citizens.

To be sure, education is not the only task of leadership; for instance, leadership also entails the coordination and organization of collective action. Following Tocqueville, though, I suggest that education is the most important task of the democratic leader. As we shall see, instead of emphasizing the issue of "effectiveness," Tocqueville's conception of leadership focuses our attention on the question: How can leaders educate their fellow citizens so that they are more fit for democratic self-rule?

Tocqueville's approach to leadership thus differs not only from the approach favored by presidency scholars who focus on the effectiveness of leaders. Tocqueville's approach also differs from that of Robert Faulkner. In *The Case for Greatness: Honorable Ambition and Its Critics*, Faulkner offers an account of statesmanship that is inspired by Aristotle's concept of the great-souled man. Faulkner argues—as I also do in this book—that the "service" of great leaders "is at least as necessary in democracies as in other political orders."[15] However, Faulkner does *not* emphasize—as I, following Tocqueville, seek to do—that a key part of what makes a democratic leader great is his or her ability to educate, elevate, and empower the citizenry. Faulkner celebrates the "superior powers" and "superior character" of great statesmen, but he does little to suggest that great democratic leadership involves empowering *other* citizens and elevating their character.[16]

Tocqueville teaches us that democratic leadership must, above all, be *educative* leadership when he writes in the Introduction to *Democracy in America* that,

> The first duty imposed on those who now direct society is to educate democracy; to put, if possible, new life into its beliefs; to purify its mores; to control its actions; gradually to substitute understanding of statecraft for present inexperience and knowledge of its true interests for blind instincts; to adapt government to the needs of time and place; and to modify it as men and circumstances require.[17]

In this book, I put Tocqueville into dialogue with key American thinkers on the subject of how leaders can best "educate democracy." In chapter 1, I provide a critical interpretation of Tocqueville's understanding of the relationship between leadership and democracy. Then, in the light of Tocqueville's theory of leadership, I examine the Antifederalists (chapter 2), Abraham Lincoln (chapter 3), Woodrow Wilson (chapter 4), and Robert Putnam as well as Robert Bellah (chapter 5). As we shall see, these American thinkers each strived to think through the supposed opposition between leadership and democracy in ways that resemble, in important respects, Tocqueville's political theory.[18] These thinkers thus contribute to an important but insufficiently examined strain within American political thought according to which leadership—and authority—are crucial for the full flowering of democracy. Although only the first chapter is focused solely on Tocqueville, each of the later chapters helps us further understand Tocqueville's political thought. In other words, Tocqueville's ideas on leadership and democracy can illuminate the American figures that I examine, but these American figures also help to illuminate Tocqueville. For the most part, these American figures help to confirm Tocqueville's theoretical claims, but sometimes these figures expose important shortcomings in Tocqueville's theory of leadership.

If leaders are defined as those who shape norms, then parents, schoolteachers, and members of the clergy can all rightly be considered leaders. However, my focus in this book is primarily on *political* leaders—one can also call them statesmen—who seek to guide and educate the polity as a whole. In *Ruling Passions: Political Offices and Democratic Ethics*, Andrew Sabl argues that Tocquevillian leadership in America can be discerned largely in the activities of the "moral activist" and the "community organizer," both of whose "sphere of activity is civil society rather than the state."[19] Although often very illuminating, I think that Sabl's emphasis on community organizers and moral activists as Tocquevillian leaders does not do justice to Tocqueville's interest in how "men in power" can educate democracy.[20] By considering statesmen such as Lincoln and Wilson in the light of Tocqueville's theory of leadership, my book returns attention to the key Tocquevillian question of how governmental leaders—called by Tocqueville "men in power" as well as "those who now direct society"—can best educate the citizenry.

That said, like Sabl, I do not confine myself in this book solely to the study of elected leaders. For in the book's final chapter, I turn to an analysis of Robert Putnam and Robert Bellah. This chapter considers the leadership role played by "public intellectuals." By including public intellectuals such as Putnam and Bellah within my analysis of democratic leadership, I follow Tocqueville's lead. For when Tocqueville discusses the education of American democracy, he usually has in mind governmental leaders (those who "direct society," as he puts it), but he sometimes has in mind those whom he calls "moralists." Tocqueville never defines the term "moralist," but with this term he seems to refer to writers of a philosophical bent who have a wide audience, and who try to shape the values and goals of the citizenry. According to Tocqueville, both governmental leaders *and* moralists should seek to educate democracy, often in similar ways. For instance, in Volume II of *Democracy*, Tocqueville suggests that in an era of restlessness and skepticism, the "duty of rulers" is precisely the same as the task of "moralists," insofar as both should seek to uphold "distant goals" in the minds of the citizenry.[21] Because Tocqueville sometimes includes moralists (or public intellectuals, to use a more current term) as well as power-holders in his discussion of democratic leadership, I do the same in this book.

By seeking to elucidate how Tocqueville and certain American theorists understand the problem of democratic leadership, my work can be viewed as part of a wider post-Hartzian effort to depict the richness and complexity of American political thought. In *The Liberal Tradition in America*, Louis Hartz argued that American political thought and culture is predominantly "Lockean," by which he meant it is marked by individualism, the pursuit of self-interest, and materialism.[22] According to Steven Dworetz, Locke's original theory was actually *not* intended simply to promote self-regarding behavior.[23] In Dworetz's interpretation, Locke was a "theistic liberal" who was concerned with God's law and the salvation of the soul.[24] Dworetz is no doubt correct that Locke himself did not intend to promote the pursuit of radically selfish behavior; after all, Locke himself insists in the *Second Treatise* that "a *State of Liberty*" is "*not a State of Licence.*"[25] Nevertheless, I believe that Lockean liberalism *does* lead toward the pursuit of raw self-interest if it is not complemented by republican and religious ideals. As Robert Bellah and his co-authors point out, "The essence of the Lockean position is an almost ontological individualism. The individual is prior to society, which comes into existence only through the voluntary contract of individuals trying to maximize their own self-interest."[26] Lockean theory, then, encourages us to think of human relationships as purely voluntary relationships which are based on nothing more than utility.

Hartz's masterpiece successfully demonstrated the dominance of Lockean liberalism in American political thought, but later political scientists—such as Wilson Carey McWilliams and Michael Sandel—have shown that there are highly valuable minor chords in American thought as well. In *The Idea of Fraternity in America*, McWilliams argues that while America's "public institutions" are based on "Enlightenment liberalism," American thinkers have also often given voice to an older conception of politics, a conception that is rooted in the Judeo-Christian tradition.[27] In *Democracy's Discontent*, Michael Sandel argues that while America is today dominated by procedural liberalism, American political thought also contains a significant republican tradition.[28] It is my hope that this book will be viewed as complementary to the works of these post-Hartzian scholars, for my aim is to demonstrate that American thinking on leadership has often sought to transcend the liberal individualism that Hartz found to be so widespread in America. As we shall see, the Tocquevillian understanding of leadership that is articulated in this book resonates with McWilliams's understanding of "the political order" as "an educative community," and it also resonates with Sandel's insistence that democratic politics must be a "formative politics."[29]

Unlike the dominant liberal tradition, the Tocquevillian conception of leadership that I trace in this book emphasizes the pursuit of the common good over the pursuit of self-interest, and it emphasizes society's need for character-formation over the individual's desire for unrestrained private freedom. According to Tocqueville, then, it is the task of leadership to shape character and to point the citizenry toward higher ideals than materialism and individualism. As John Diggins and Mark Kann have noted, "America was born in an act of resistance to constituted authority," and Americans have long been wary of strong leadership.[30] According to Tocqueville, however, leadership is in fact necessary to restrain and elevate the citizenry. Upon this view, leadership is not simply charged with the task of setting up and maintaining procedures that allow each individual to pursue his or her own good; instead, leadership is charged with the task of educating democratic citizens, and providing their understanding of freedom with a sense of purpose, a sense of "what freedom is *for.*"

All of these ideas about leadership can be found, in a particularly compelling fashion, in the political thought of Tocqueville. Moreover, we shall see how the American thinkers examined in this book each have their own distinctive version of these ideas. I have chosen these particular American thinkers primarily because their ideas resonate with—and sometimes productively challenge—Tocqueville's ideas on leadership. I have also chosen them, however, because they allow us to consider the relevance of Tocqueville's ideas on leadership during four key periods of American history: namely, the period of the Founding (chapter 2), the period that culminated in the Civil War (chapter 3), the Progressive period (chapter 4), and, finally, the present era, a time when civil society is widely thought to be in decline (chapter 5).

In his important book on *Leadership*, Burns writes that after the intellectual and political upheavals of the seventeenth and eighteenth century,

> the doctrine of authority came into the modern age devitalized, fragmentized, and trivialized; it became a captive of the right, even of fascism. Mussolini substituted authority, order, and justice for liberty, equality, fraternity. . . . [Authority] was not transformed into a doctrine suitable for the new age. No new, democratized, and radicalized doctrine arose to salvage the authentic and the relevant in authority and link these strengths to a doctrine of leadership that recognized the vital need for qualities of integrity, authenticity, initiative, and moral resolve. . . . *The resulting intellectual gap . . . was especially evident in America.*[31]

Like Burns, my goal is to articulate a theory of leadership that is conducive rather than hostile to democratic politics. But I believe, unlike Burns, that the resources for carrying out this project already lie largely *within* American political thought (at least in an inchoate form), particularly when complemented by Tocqueville's ideas. Through a critical appropriation of the American canon that has been inspired by Tocqueville, then, my most ambitious goal in this book is to help pave the way toward a theory of leadership that is appropriate for democracy in America.

Chapter 1

∗⟱⟱∗

Tocqueville on Leadership
and the Education of Democracy

In this book, I explore the concept of democratic leadership, using Tocqueville's ideas not as a source of definitive answers, but rather as a starting point and source of inspiration. To set the stage for the rest of the book, this chapter offers an analysis of Tocqueville's views on leadership in democratic times.

As noted in the introduction, Tocqueville asserted that the "first duty" of modern leaders "is to educate democracy; to put, if possible, new life into its beliefs [and] to purify its mores. . . ."[1] By arguing that a key task of leadership is the moral education of the citizenry, Tocqueville invokes an idea that reaches back at least as far as Plato and Aristotle. For Plato, the leader should be a kind of "moral artist" who improves the souls of his fellow citizens. The leader should be concerned with "the engendering of justice in the souls of his fellow citizens and the eradication of injustice, the planting of self-control and the uprooting of uncontrol, the entrance of virtue and the exit of vice."[2] As I will discuss later in this chapter, Tocqueville does, to be sure, share with many other modern liberal theorists the fear that governmental efforts to shape the souls of citizens may end up violating individual rights. But, on the whole, Tocqueville agrees with the ancients that every political regime must concern itself with shaping "the character of human souls," as Harvey Mansfield and Delba Winthrop put it in an article that links Tocqueville's ideas to those of Aristotle.[3]

Tocqueville and the "Democratic Turn" in Leadership Studies

But if Tocqueville's ideas on educative leadership point back to the ancients, they also point forward, to the influential theory of leadership offered by James MacGregor Burns. Indeed, one of my primary claims in this book is that Tocqueville anticipated many key aspects of what one might call the "democratic turn" in recent leadership studies. By the "democratic turn," I refer to the work of such scholars as Burns, Bruce Miroff, Sidney Milkis, and Marc Landy. All of these authors argue that political scientists should cease to understand leadership primarily as command, coercion, manipulation, or domination; rather, leadership should be viewed as a process through which leaders help to empower, educate, and invigorate citizens.[4] Tocqueville, I suggest, deserves to be viewed as a key precursor to this contemporary understanding of leadership.

This contemporary understanding of leadership was inaugurated largely by Burns's *Leadership*. In this work, Burns famously distinguishes between two types of leadership, transactional and transforming. According to Burns, "transactional leadership" involves mere brokerage; it seeks to satisfy the self-interest of leaders and followers through an exchange of such goods as "jobs for votes, or subsidies for campaign contributions." Although Burns believes that transactional leadership has its proper place, he far prefers "transforming leadership." Transforming leadership is "elevating." It leads "people upward, to some higher values or purpose or form of self-fulfillment." Transforming leaders try to foster "moral development;" ultimately, the transforming leader inspires people to pursue "the universal values of freedom, equality, democracy, and justice." Through transforming leadership, "people can be lifted *into* their better selves. . . ."[5]

Tocqueville understood leadership in similar terms, for he often criticized what one might call the transactional leadership that was prevalent in France during his lifetime. Tocqueville complained that French leaders were concerned solely with gaining political office, and in order to win elections they simply exchanged patronage for political support. Clearly, Tocqueville hoped that a kind of transforming leadership could inspire people to pursue higher values and purposes. The transforming leader, according to Burns, "looks for potential motives in followers, seeks to satisfy higher needs, and engages the full person of the follower."[6] In his famous speech of 1848 in the Chamber of Deputies, Tocqueville denounced his fellow French leaders precisely for abandoning this noble conception of leadership. Tocqueville complained that French politicians only engaged the citizenry's "evil, not their honest side, appealing to their passions, weaknesses, interests, and often to their vices." Instead of elevating people, as Burns suggests leaders should do, French politicians simply "play on the chord of private self-interest in men."[7] According to Burns, "The result of transforming leadership is a relationship of mutual stimulation and elevation."[8] In contrast, by focusing on the petty pursuit of self-interest, France's rulers abandoned any higher purposes, and thereby debased themselves and their followers. Lacking any inspirational leadership, the people of France "hope for nothing except to profit at the stock exchange," as Tocqueville put it in 1858.[9]

Tocqueville told Arthur de Gobineau that there is "only one human species, all resembling each other, all of whose members were equally capable of perfecting themselves."[10] It is the task of democratic leadership, in Tocqueville's view, to elevate people toward this (never fully attainable) perfection. As Tocqueville puts it in *Democracy*, "It would seem that sovereigns now only seek to do great things with men. I wish that they would try a little more to make men great."[11] Tocqueville and Burns suggest that in order to "make men great," the leader must not simply appeal to what is lowest in people (self-interest), but to their higher moral impulses.

Because he wanted leaders to try to "make men great," Tocqueville did not depart from the classical tradition as much as Martin Zetterbaum has suggested he did. Zetterbaum argues that Tocqueville "strives to erect his system upon what is operative in most men most of the time, and this turns out to be what is lowest rather than what is highest in man. As in Machiavelli, we take our bearings from what men are, not from what they may become."[12] In contrast to Zetterbaum, I would argue that Tocqueville was *always* thinking about what people "may become," and it was his hope that leaders could inspire and lift up the people. In fact, Tocqueville rebuked Gobineau precisely for focusing on what people are rather than what they may become. As Tocqueville put it: "You consider the men of our days to be big children, very degenerate and very poorly raised. . . . Like you, I believe that our contemporaries are rather poorly raised which is the first cause of their miseries and their weakness; but I believe that a better upbringing could redress the evil that a bad upbringing has accomplished."[13] Instead of basing his system on what is lowest in human beings, Tocqueville's theory was thus based on a cautiously optimistic faith in human potential, and the conviction that "one must not despise man, if one wants to obtain great efforts from others and from oneself."[14]

The Doctrine of Self-Interest Properly Understood: Necessary, but Incomplete

Like Burns, Tocqueville believes that democratic leadership must aim at the moral elevation of the citizenry. But how, in Tocqueville's view, is this task to be accomplished? A part—*but only a part*—of Tocqueville's answer is that leaders should elevate people through what he calls "the doctrine of self-interest properly understood."[15] To understand Tocqueville's theory of democratic leadership, a careful analysis of his ideas on the "doctrine" is crucial. As we shall see, despite his apparent endorsement of the doctrine in *Democracy*, Tocqueville remained ambivalent toward it. For Tocqueville, leaders should, indeed, sometimes strive to educate their fellow citizens through appeals to self-interest properly understood. However, Tocqueville also believed that if republican government is to endure, leaders must at times seek to cultivate norms of commitment and obligation that transcend self-interest altogether.

Tocqueville's measured praise for the doctrine of self-interest properly understood appears in Volume II of *Democracy*, in the context of his discussion of "individualism." Tocqueville argues that in the post-feudal era, when ties between people and between generations have been cut, most people will focus their thoughts on themselves. In short, people will succumb to individualism, which Tocqueville defines as "a calm and considered feeling which disposes each citizen to isolate himself from the mass of his fellows and withdraw into the circle of family and friends; with this little society formed to his taste, he gladly leaves the greater society to look after itself."[16] Disconnected from his or her fellow citizens, the individualist cannot truly be free, for in Tocqueville's view, freedom entails joining with others to shape the common world. Granted, Tocqueville never offered one precise definition of what he meant by "freedom." At times, such as when he worried about the tyranny of the majority in Volume I of *Democracy*, he thought of freedom as being left alone to act and think for oneself. Most often, though, he associates freedom not with being left alone to determine one's own destiny, but rather with participation in one's community. For instance, when Tocqueville wrote that "nothing is more fertile in marvels than the art of being free," he is referring to the freedom that arises when "each man in his sphere takes an active part in the government of society."[17]

After describing the problem of individualism in *Democracy, Vol. II, Part II, Chapter 2*, Tocqueville devotes the next six chapters to explaining why the democratic vice of individualism has been largely avoided in the United States. One might have expected Tocqueville to conclude that individualism is *more* prevalent in the United States than anywhere else, given his view that more than any other country, the United States lacks aristocratic institutions. In Tocqueville's view, while aristocratic institutions are unjust in the sense that they violate our natural equality, they are, nevertheless, valuable to freedom insofar as they prevent individualism by connecting people to their fellows and to past and future generations.[18]

Although the United States lacks these feudal institutions, Tocqueville suggests that individualism is warded off in America for a number of reasons. In chapter 4 (and then later in chapter 7), Tocqueville argues that America's participatory political institutions help keep individualism at bay. Such institutions "bring men constantly into contact, despite the instincts which separate them, and force them to help one another."[19] Then, in chapter 5 (and also in chapter 7), Tocqueville suggests that Americans also battle individualism by participating in civil associations that are not explicitly political; these civil associations help teach "habits of acting together in the affairs of daily life."[20] Next, in chapter 6, Tocqueville discusses how the problem of individualism is further mitigated by the prevalence of newspapers, which help make associations possible.

Finally, in chapter 8, Tocqueville suggests that the Americans also "combat individualism by the doctrine of self-interest properly understood." In this chapter, Tocqueville argues that in the democratic era, "moralists" have recognized that "the forces driving man in on himself are irresistible." Because "every man's thoughts are centered on himself," moral leaders have found it futile to try to inculcate an ideal of virtue according to which it is one's duty to make sacrifices for the common good. Instead, in democratic times moralists seek to persuade the public "that by serving his fellows man serves himself and that doing good is to his private advantage."[21] A key task of leadership in America, then, is to teach people to be virtuous. But people should be urged to love virtue not just for its own sake, but also for the benefits it brings them. Tocqueville makes it clear that "self-interest properly understood" not only teaches us to be good in our private lives, but it also leads us to be good citizens insofar as it induces us to participate in communal life. Tocqueville concludes that, "Contemporary moralists . . . should give most of their attention to" this doctrine of self-interest properly understood, because it is "the best suited of all philosophical theories to the wants of men in our time" and is "their strongest remaining guarantee against themselves."[22]

In *Democracy*, then, Tocqueville expresses some optimism that the doctrine of self-interest properly understood can succeed in the task of morally educating a democratic citizenry. And yet, upon closer examination, Tocqueville's political thought as a whole reveals that he held significant reservations about the doctrine.

Tocqueville's doubts about the long-term efficacy of the "doctrine of self-interest properly understood" are evident in a notebook entry of May 29, 1831. The notebook entry is titled: "General Questions: Contrast of Ancient Republics as Virtuous vs. the United States as Based on Enlightened Self-Interest."[23] Tocqueville writes that one can distinguish between "the principle of the republics of antiquity," on the one hand, and "the principle" of the United States, on the other. The principle of the former called on citizens "to sacrifice private interests to the general good. In that sense one could say that they were virtuous." In contrast, the principle of the United States is "to make private interests harmonize with the general interest. A sort of refined and intelligent selfishness seems to be the pivot on which the whole machine turns. These people here do not trouble themselves to find out whether public virtue is good, but they do claim to prove that it is useful."[24] But Tocqueville then immediately adds: "If the latter point is true, as I think it is *in part*, this society can pass as enlightened, but not as virtuous."[25] The words "in part" indicate that Tocqueville rejected the idea that service and commitment to the public is *always* of instrumental value to the citizen, which means that arguments based on self-interest properly understood are likely to be insufficient. In the same notebook entry, Tocqueville goes on to ask: "But up to what extent can the two principles of individual well-being and the general good in fact be merged? How far can a conscience, which one might say was based on reflection and calculation, master those political passions which are not yet born, but which certainly will be born? That is something which only the future will show."[26] This passage indicates that in Tocqueville's view, utilitarian arguments for civic commitment may, over time, fail to rein in, or "master," the destructive passions of the human soul. If a commitment to the common good is rooted only in "reflection and calculation"—if it is rooted, in short, in the doctrine of self-interest properly understood—then the likelihood of its maintenance over time is highly precarious. As early as 1831, then, Tocqueville worried about the long-term ability of the doctrine of self-interest properly understood to sustain a republican government.

Perhaps the most striking instance where we can see Tocqueville's deep reservations about leaders' use of the doctrine of self-interest properly understood is found in *The Old Regime and the French Revolution*. In *Democracy*, Tocqueville had optimistically argued that if they are taught that civic virtue is "useful" rather than "beautiful," the Americans can manage to avoid the "shameful troubles" that might befall an otherwise self-interested people.[27] In *The Old Regime*, however, one finds a very different argument, for in this work Tocqueville argues that participatory freedom must ultimately be loved not for its usefulness, but for its intrinsic beauty. As Tocqueville put it, "What has made so many men, since untold ages, stake their all on liberty is its intrinsic glamour, a fascination it has in itself, apart from all 'practical' considerations. . . . The man who asks of freedom anything other than itself is born to be a slave."[28] In *Democracy*, Tocqueville had suggested that the doctrine of self-interest properly understood can actually help *preserve* freedom, for he notes that "freedom . . . will not be able to last without education"; the doctrine of self-interest properly understood, he suggests, should be a key part of this education.[29] In *The Old Regime*, however, Tocqueville implies that this doctrine is not linked to the preservation of freedom at all, but rather to its ultimate loss. If it is to be preserved, participatory freedom must be loved for *intrinsic* reasons, Tocqueville now suggests. In *The Old Regime*, Tocqueville concedes that, "in the long run freedom always brings to those who know how to retain it comfort and well-being, and often great prosperity." However, Tocqueville then notes that in the short-term, free and virtuous peoples might lack "amenities of this nature," and, in the end, "those who prize freedom only for the material benefits it offers have never kept it long."[30]

There is thus a tension in Tocqueville between his apparent endorsement of the doctrine of "self-interest properly understood," on the one hand, and the reservations that he expresses about leaders' use of this doctrine at certain moments, on the other hand. What are we to make of this tension, or ambivalence, in Tocqueville's thought? There are a few possible ways that we might attempt to solve this puzzle.

One possible way to address the puzzle would be to note that ambivalence is a theme that runs throughout Tocqueville's political thought. Tocqueville was, of course, simultaneously "full of fears and of hopes" when he considered the rise of democracy as a whole.[31] From this perspective, it is not surprising that Tocqueville expresses both fear and hope when he considers the democratic doctrine of self-interest properly understood. Upon this view, the apparent contradiction in Tocqueville's thought surrounding the doctrine actually cannot be resolved, because this contradiction, or tension, is an expression of Tocqueville's deep ambivalence about democracy as a whole.

Another possible way to address the puzzle would be to argue that, over time, Tocqueville changed his mind about "self-interest properly understood." After all, Tocqueville's writings, letters, and speeches on France reveal a deep disgust with interest-based politics.[32] For instance, in 1833 Tocqueville complained that in France, "Everyone is focusing more and more on individual interest. It is only those who want power for themselves, and not strength and glory for their homeland, who rejoice at the sight of such a symptom."[33] According to Melvin Richter, "There is good reason to believe that Tocqueville's qualified optimism about the possibility of a democracy based upon the principle of interest rightly understood did not long survive his return to France and his entry into political life."[34] Perhaps, then, Tocqueville was ambivalent about the doctrine of self-interest properly understood in the 1830s, but by the time he wrote *The Old Regime*, he had simply abandoned any hope that this doctrine could preserve and promote participatory freedom. This would help explain why he praises the doctrine of self-interest properly understood in the 1830s, but then insists in the 1850s that loving freedom for anything other than itself dooms one to slavery.

Neither of the preceding attempts to solve the puzzle of Tocqueville's ambivalence is fully satisfactory. The first argument assumes that Tocqueville's ideas are contradictory, but gives up too soon on any attempt to resolve the contradiction. The second argument suggests that Tocqueville's ideas in *Democracy, Vol. II, Part II, Chapter 8*, are superseded by his later ideas. This is not fully satisfactory, in part because of Tocqueville's explicit claim in the foreword to *The Old Regime* that his ideas on freedom have actually not changed in the years that separate the publication of *Democracy in America* from the publication of *The Old Regime*.[35]

In my view, a more fully satisfactory solution to the puzzle can be derived from a remark made in *Democracy, Vol. II, Part II, Chapter 8*. Tocqueville here writes of the doctrine of self-interest properly understood: "Though [contemporary moralists] may well think it incomplete, they must nonetheless adopt is as necessary."[36] Tocqueville here suggests that the doctrine of self-interest properly understood is *necessary* but *incomplete*. This means that democratic leaders should appeal to "self-interest properly understood," but civic virtue and participatory freedom cannot ultimately be maintained solely on this basis. Tocqueville's long-standing ambivalence about the doctrine can be explained, then, by the fact that sometimes Tocqueville is emphasizing the necessity of the doctrine, and sometimes he is emphasizing that the doctrine is incomplete, insofar as it cannot, on its own, preserve freedom in democratic times.

More evidence for this interpretation can be found in *The Old Regime*. As we have seen, Tocqueville wrote that, "those who prize freedom *only* for the material benefits it offers have never kept it long."[37] The word "only" suggests that it is actually perfectly acceptable for citizens to love freedom for utilitarian purposes, but this must not be the *only* foundation of their love. Taken as a whole, then, Tocqueville's various thoughts on "self-interest properly understood" suggest that his true teaching is: Love participatory freedom for its effects, but love it, in the final analysis, for its own sake, and because of a genuine commitment to civic virtue.

For Tocqueville, this genuine commitment to civic virtue can be fostered by the "spirit of religion."[38] In Volume II of *Democracy*, Tocqueville argues that religion combats individualism by inculcating a sense of duty to one's fellows. "Every religion," he writes, "imposes on each man some obligations toward mankind, to be performed in common with the rest of mankind, and so draws him away, from time to time, from thinking about himself."[39] Earlier, we saw Tocqueville's fear that "a conscience . . . based on reflection and calculation"—in other words, a conscience based on self-interest properly understood—might not be able to restrain the dangerous passions of Americans.[40] We can now see that for Tocqueville, religion is thus needed to help shape the conscience of Americans.

In Tocqueville's view, a genuine commitment to civic virtue is fostered in America not only by "the spirit of religion," but also by what one might call the spirit of republicanism. According to Michael Sandel, American political thought contains a "republican tradition;" according to this tradition, citizens should actively participate in public affairs, and care deeply about the common good.[41] That Tocqueville also finds in America a republican tradition is evidenced by such passages as the following: "if an American should be reduced to occupying himself with his own affairs, at that moment half his existence would be snatched from him; he would feel it as a vast void in his life and would become incredibly unhappy."[42] In this passage, Tocqueville suggests that Americans do not love public liberty simply because of its extrinsic effects on their well-being; rather, they love it because public liberty *itself* directly constitutes their happiness. As Dana Villa notes, this and other passages suggest that "Tocqueville did not think either the public spirit or the 'free *moeurs*' of the Americans could be reduced to modalities of self-interest."[43] In other words, Tocqueville *did* sometimes detect genuine republican virtue in America. Indeed, a footnote to the above-quoted passage suggests that Tocqueville saw in America a republican spirit that harkened back to the republican values of ancient Rome. After noting the unhappiness of a hypothetical American confined to "his own affairs," Tocqueville writes in the footnote: "The same fact was already noted at Rome under the first Caesars. Montesquieu remarks somewhere that nothing equals the despair of certain Roman citizens who after the excitements of a political existence suddenly return to the calm of private life."[44] By explicitly comparing the Americans to the ancient Romans, Tocqueville suggests that it is not only the "spirit of religion," but also the spirit of republicanism, which can help move the Americans toward a deep commitment to civic virtue. Self-interest properly understood has its place, but Tocqueville thought it was insufficient unless it was supplemented by both religion and republicanism.[45]

My interpretation of Tocqueville can help shed light on a thorny question asked by a number of Tocqueville scholars: namely, how much weight should be given to Tocqueville's ideas on self-interest properly understood when assessing Tocqueville's political theory as a whole? Roger Boesche seems to deemphasize the significance of Tocqueville's apparent endorsement of self-interest properly understood; in Boesche's view, "Any detailed study of Tocqueville's letters and notebooks should cure the temptation to see Tocqueville as championing a politics based on interest. Once his concentration on American democracy had subsided . . . he wrote scarcely a word that would countenance any kind of politics based on self-interest."[46] In contrast to Boesche, Harvey Mansfield and Delba Winthrop give greater weight to Tocqueville's statements on self-interest properly understood. According to Mansfield and Winthrop, Tocqueville's "disdain of the pettiness of the bourgeois," as expressed in his private letters and other writings, should not lead us to underestimate Tocqueville's attachment to "the 'doctrine of self-interest well understood,'" for the latter was "intended for the public and [is] therefore a truer statement of his teaching" than his privately expressed disgust with "the bourgeois way of life."[47] If my interpretation is correct, then Boesche goes a bit too far in downplaying the significance of the doctrine of self-interest properly understood in Tocqueville's thought. After all, there is no getting around the fact that Tocqueville described the doctrine as "the best suited of all philosophical theories to the wants of men in our time." On the other hand, while we should agree with Mansfield and Winthrop that "self-interest properly understood" is a key part of Tocqueville's teaching, we should never forget that Tocqueville saw this doctrine as a *necessity*, and never as a positive good. Moreover, Tocqueville considered the doctrine to be *incomplete*. Mansfield's and Winthrop's statement that Tocqueville "apparently welcomes the American doctrine of 'self-interest well understood'" should not lead us to conclude that Tocqueville's admiration for the doctrine was by any means unequivocal.[48]

Tocqueville on Religious Authority

I have suggested that for Tocqueville, the doctrine of self-interest properly understood should be supplemented, in part, by religion. In today's context, this is, to be sure, a highly controversial claim, for the contemporary landscape is marked by far greater religious, ethical, and cultural pluralism as compared to Jacksonian America. Because Tocqueville's claim about the necessity of religion is controversial, and because this claim plays an important role in his understanding of both leadership and authority, a more detailed discussion of his views on religion is warranted here.

In *The Republic*, Plato calls democracy a regime "without rulers."[49] In such a regime, total freedom leads to the eventual collapse of all social and moral order. Tocqueville agreed with Plato that in a democracy the danger of fragmentation looms large. However, Tocqueville believed that certain forms of authority just might be able to tame the passions of the *demos* and allow them to make good use of their freedom. Authority could shape the habits and mores of the people so that their lives would be marked by ordered liberty rather than license. Tocqueville summed up his understanding of the relationship between authority and liberty in *Democracy* by quoting John Winthrop's "fine definition of freedom":

> There is a *liberty* of corrupt nature, which is affected by *men* and *beasts* to do what they list; and this *liberty* is inconsistent with *authority*, impatient of all restraint. . . . But there is a civil, a moral, a federal *liberty*, which is the proper end and object of *authority*; it is a *liberty* for that only which is *just* and *good*; for this *liberty* you are to stand with the hazard of your very *lives*. . . . This *liberty* is maintained in a way of *subjection* to *authority*; and the *authority* set over you will in all administrations for your good be quietly submitted unto, by all but such as have a disposition to *shake off the yoke*, and lose their true *liberty*, by their murmuring at the honour and power of *authority*.[50]

Like the ancients, Winthrop here argues that authority is necessary for true freedom because true freedom involves the taming of the passions. This was precisely Tocqueville's conviction. He wrote that, "Desires are masters against whom one must fight." In Tocqueville's view, "independence" without self-mastery can be a "heavier burden than slavery itself," for the former entails being dominated by one's petty and ever-changing desires.[51] Tocqueville agreed with Winthrop and the ancients that, in Aristotle's words, "doing what one likes" is a pernicious notion of freedom, for this type of freedom quickly degenerates into slavery—the slavery of the self to the passions.[52] If people are to be genuinely free, then, they need to master their own desires. And, it is the task of authority to facilitate this self-mastery.

Tocqueville believed that one of the most important forms of authority in America was religious authority. Democracies in particular need religion, because democracies do not contain the ordering institutions that once existed in aristocratic ages. Once the people are free of feudal ties, and to a large extent free of the past, what is to stop them from over-running all limits? What is going to stop a democratic people from trampling over private rights and the common good? The answer, for Tocqueville, is *morality*, and morality, according to Tocqueville, is best instilled by religion.

In Tocqueville's view, religion gives democratic citizens a salutary sense of limits. Without religion, the American may be tempted to believe that he is "master of the universe, that he can fashion it to his liking." The American has, after all, radically transformed his environment: "In his life-time rivers have changed their courses or diminished their flow, the very climate is other than he knew it, and all that is to him but the first step in a limitless career."[53] Tocqueville certainly finds something grand and noble in these transformative accomplishments, but he is also worried that these very successes may lead Americans into holding the dangerously hubristic idea that anything is possible and everything is permitted. It is the religious heritage of the Americans that rescues them from this potentially destructive belief. As Tocqueville puts it: "While the law allows the American people to do everything, there are things which religion prevents them from imagining and forbids them to dare."[54] Religion, Tocqueville similarly wrote in June of 1831, "arrests the wanderings of the innovating spirit; especially does it make very rare that moral disposition, so common with us, to launch oneself through all obstacles, *per fas et nefas* [by fair means or foul], toward the chosen goal."[55] Tocqueville, then, greatly esteemed "the bridle of religion" because it restrained people's desires.[56]

Yet Tocqueville did not admire religious authority solely because it checks and restrains, but also because it inspires and uplifts. Tocqueville believed that in the democratic era, people tend to be led by the low values of materialism and individualism; religion is particularly needed in such an era, because religion can help guide democratic nations toward nobler ideals of brotherhood and compassion for one's fellows. Religion teaches that freedom should not be used merely to fulfill the "passion for well-being" that Tocqueville found rampant in America.[57] Rather, for Tocqueville, religious authority teaches that freedom should be used in the service of certain lofty principles, principles that include "neighborly love, pity, leniency" as well as "the equality, the unity, and the fraternity of men."[58] For all of these reasons, Tocqueville writes that in democracies, "it is ever the duty of lawgivers and of all upright educated men to raise up the souls of their fellow citizens and turn their attention toward heaven . . . and with one accord to make continuous efforts to propagate throughout society a taste for the infinite, an appreciation of greatness, and a love of spiritual pleasures."[59]

We have seen that in Tocqueville's view, religious authority is necessary for the proper use of freedom. In the absence of authority, people will succumb to the tyranny of the passions, and their lives may very well be dedicated merely to the satisfaction of materialistic and self-interested pleasures. But in addition to saving people from the tyranny of the passions, Tocqueville believed that religion can help ward off another kind of tyranny—namely, the tyranny of majority opinion. In *Escape from Authority*, John Schaar writes that "when authority is lacking fashion reigns." Without the guiding ideals of authority, people will likely submit to "the slavery of the social," to "the tyranny of the neighbors."[60] Schaar echoes

Tocqueville, for Tocqueville believed that if they lack traditional forms of authority such as religion, a democratic people will blindly accept the authority of public opinion. Schaar writes that in the absence of salutary authority, "The man of today is led, to be sure, but he is led by fashion and opinion, by the taste and desire of the many at the moment."[61] Similarly, Tocqueville writes: "somewhere and somehow authority is always bound to play a part in intellectual and moral life. . . . The independence of the individual may be greater or less but can never be unlimited. Therefore we need not inquire about the existence of intellectual authority in democratic ages, but only where it resides and what its limits are."[62] Tocqueville worries that in the democratic age, intellectual authority will reside not in salutary forms of authority such as religion, but rather in the debased form of authority called public opinion. Tocqueville suggests that those who are guided by religious authority just might have the courage to resist the prejudices of the many, since they will hold justice and goodness in higher regard than the current dictates of fashion. For example, a Christian conscience just might induce a person to resist racial intolerance or the mob, described by Tocqueville, which attacked journalists who were opposed to the War of 1812.[63] In the absence of religious authority, the prejudices and the passions of the majority may have freer reign.

Tocqueville makes some powerful arguments for why religion can be valuable in democratic times. His analysis, though, also raises some troubling questions. Perhaps most problematic is his suggestion that the United States requires consensus on the truths of Christianity. Tocqueville argues that, "without ideas in common, no common action would be possible, and without common action, men might exist, but there could be no body social."[64] Tocqueville fears that in the democratic age, public opinion is all too often the source of these "ideas in common." Public opinion, he worries, can "confine the activity of private judgment within limits too narrow for the dignity and happiness of mankind," leading to a kind of "slavery" with a "new face."[65] Tocqueville is pleased to find, though, that in America, Christianity also serves as a source of authoritative "ideas in common" that bind citizens together. When Tocqueville discusses the limits that Christianity places on private judgment, he does not express the kind of fears that he expresses when considering the constraints imposed on free thought by the power of public opinion.[66] Tocqueville writes, with approval, that in America, "Christianity . . . is an established and irresistible fact which no one seeks to attack or to defend." By "accept[ing] the main dogmas of the Christian religion without examination," Tocqueville believes that the Americans submit to a salutary form of moral authority that instills in them a valuable sense of limits, as well as a valuable sense of unity.[67] As Hanna Pitkin puts it, *Democracy in*

America "tied free citizenship to a universally shared Christian faith and a Christian consensus on severe mores."[68] But today, in an era marked by pluralism, free citizenship must be based on something other than shared religion. I will argue in chapter 3 that Abraham Lincoln improves upon Tocqueville, in part because Lincoln suggests that American citizenship should be based not on shared Christianity, but rather on shared adherence to the broad principles of the Declaration of Independence. Lincoln would agree strongly with Tocqueville that "ideas in common" are crucial for a democracy; however, Lincoln suggests that Americans should be bound together not through religion, but rather through a shared "dedicat[ion] to the proposition that all men are created equal."[69]

Tocqueville's analysis raises another difficult question: is it really true that religion works to combat individualism? William Galston, a political theorist who generally praises the role of religion in America, notes that there is certainly no "guarantee that the kinds of individuals we tend to become under the influence of various faith traditions will embrace the requirements of citizenship." After all, "Theorists as diverse as Machiavelli and Rousseau saw an outright contradiction between the teachings of Christianity and devotion to civic life."[70] On the other hand, there is empirical evidence that religious Americans *are*, in fact, more likely to be active citizens than nonreligious Americans. In 2001, a report by the Saguaro Seminar on civic engagement concluded that,

> Involvement in communities of faith . . . is strongly associated with giving and volunteering. . . . Even holding other factors constant (comparing people of comparable educational levels, comparable income, and so on), religiously engaged people are more likely than religiously disengaged people to be involved in civic groups of all sorts, to vote more, to be more active in community affairs, to give blood, to trust other people (from shopkeepers to neighbors), to know the names of public officials, to socialize with friends and neighbors, and even simply to have a wider circle of friends.[71]

There is, then, considerable evidence that Tocqueville was correct when he suggested that religion can serve as an antidote to individualism.

But if religion may sometimes work to erode individualism, it has also, of course, led to intolerance and repression. As James Morone puts it in *Hellfire Nation*, while religious-based "moral fervor stirs our better angels," it also "spurs our demons." A double-edged sword, religious-based morality has, according to Morone, "inspire[d] the dreamers who turn the nation-upside down in the name of social justice," but it has also "unleash[ed] our witch-hunts and racial panics."[72] Indeed, Tocqueville him-self sometimes worried about the potentially repressive aspect of religion. For although he is generally admiring of the Puritans, he also criticizes their use of coercion to enforce church attendance and adherence to church doctrines. He rebukes the Puritans for thereby "invad[ing] the sphere of conscience" and for "completely forgetting the great principle of religious liberty."[73] Moreover, Tocqueville maintains that many of the Puritans' laws regulating social life (including sexual relations) were "ridiculous and tyrannical," and "bring shame on the spirit of man."[74]

Tocqueville's critical remarks on the Puritans' legal code and Morone's discussion of American history both remind us that religion in America has, at times, posed a threat to liberty and equality. On the other hand, Alan Wolfe's study of American middle-class attitudes suggests that most religious Americans today are, in fact, tolerant and moderate in their political and social views. Painting a very different portrait of American religion than the one found in Morone's book, Wolfe suggests that middle-class Americans tend to avoid "words like 'sin,' 'moral rot,' 'decay,' or 'Satan'"; instead, most Americans practice a "quiet faith" that abjures the notion "that religion should be the sole, or even the most important, guide for establishing rules about how *other* people should live."[75] If Wolfe is right, then Morone might overstate the danger posed by religion, at least in contemporary America.

Although the evidence is mixed, I find persuasive Tocqueville's claim that religion is, on the whole, beneficial for democracies. However, I would also suggest that in our era of religious pluralism, *political* leaders should seek to elevate and educate Americans not primarily through appeals to religion, but rather through appeals to what I call "the spirit of republi-canism," for the latter is potentially more inclusive than the former. As we have seen, Tocqueville detected a republican tradition in America, for he found that Americans were like the ancient Romans in their enthusiasm for "the excitements of a political existence."[76] The republican tradition suggests that to be a good citizen is to partake of the joys, but also the sacrifices, of an active political existence. Tocqueville, though, sometimes made the troubling suggestion that American identity should be based not on shared devotion to republican ideas and practices, but rather on shared adherence to Christian beliefs. Today, political leaders should focus on uniting citizens through republican ideals, for these ideals can be shared by people of many religious faiths (or of no religious faith). Consider the proposals, now growing in popularity, for a national service program; the idea of national service is that *all* young Americans—of every religion or of no religion—would be required to give some of their time and energy to the political community.[77] The concept of national service fits with the republican tradition identified by Tocqueville, and it is a proposal that suggests that American citizenship should be rooted in shared sacrifice rather than shared religious doctrines. To repeat, religion may very well be healthy for democracy, but this does not mean that it is the task of political leadership to educate democracy through religious appeals.

In fact, there is much evidence that Tocqueville himself did not believe that it was the task of political leaders to directly cultivate religion in the citizenry. Granted, Tocqueville does state, as we have seen, that "it is ever the duty of lawgivers . . . to raise up the souls of their fellow citizens and turn their attention toward heaven."[78] On the whole, though, he suggests that the role of political leaders in fostering religion must remain a very limited one. As noted earlier, Tocqueville criticizes the Puritans for attempting to impose religion through legal measures. In Volume II of *Democracy*, he further expresses his reservations about political leaders attempting to cultivate religion when he writes: "It is easy to see that it is particularly important in democratic times to make spiritual conceptions prevail, but it is far from easy to say what those who govern democratic peoples should do to make them prevail."[79] Tocqueville then explicitly rejects the notion of "state religions" as a way to promote religion.[80] Reprising an argument made in Volume I, Tocqueville suggests that state religions are actually *damaging* to religious belief, for "religion cannot share the material strength of the rulers without being burdened with some of the animosity roused against them."[81] But if church and state should remain separate, "What means are then left to the authorities," Tocqueville asks, "to lead men back toward spiritual opinions or to hold them within the religion thereby suggested?" Tocqueville's answer is "that the only effective means which governments can use to make the doctrine of the immortality of the soul respected is daily to act as if they believed it themselves. I think that it is only by conforming scrupulously to religious morality in great affairs that they can flatter themselves that they are teaching the citizens to understand it and to love and respect it in little matters."[82] In Tocqueville's view, then, political leaders should not actively seek to cultivate religion in the citizenry.[83] All they can do to encourage religion is to act as if they believe in the "immortality of the soul." This, in turn, appears to mean, for Tocqueville, that leaders should at times call on the nation to pursue lofty and future-oriented public policies that push people to move beyond "materialism"—that is, beyond "ephemeral and casual desires."[84]

To sum up, while religion has sometimes produced intolerance and repression, I concur with Tocqueville that, on balance, religion is valuable in democratic times, particularly as a potential antidote to individualism and materialism. Moreover, I agree with Tocqueville that although religion is desirable in democracies, political leaders should avoid attempts to promote religion directly. However, I depart from Tocqueville insofar as he suggests that Christianity should serve as the foundation of a shared American national identity, by providing people with the "ideas in common" that every "body social" requires. As we shall see in chapter 3, Lincoln avoids this mistake.

Tocqueville and Political Participation as Education

We have observed that for Tocqueville, democratic leaders should, at times, wield the doctrine of self-interest properly understood. However, Tocqueville believed that the doctrine of self-interest properly understood is "necessary," but "incomplete." This means that democratic leaders must also sometimes attempt to cultivate in the citizenry a form of civic virtue that points beyond self-interest altogether. Tocqueville believed that religion can help point people beyond self-interest, but he cautions governmental leaders against the idea that it is their role to directly foster religion. Tocqueville, though, does *not* warn leaders against directly fostering what I call "the spirit of republicanism." In fact, Tocqueville teaches that political leaders should try to build and maintain participatory institutions that allow citizens to practice behavior aimed at the common good.

Indeed, in Tocqueville's view, creating and nurturing participatory institutions is one of the key tasks of democratic leadership. For Tocqueville, democratic leaders must aim not at dominating and manipulating citizens ("do[ing] great things with men"), but rather at empowering citizens ("mak[ing] men great"). The democratic leader seeks ways of enhancing the dignity and power of citizens, and this is to be done, in large part, by finding ways to foster the direct participation of the people in political life.

Tocqueville believed that it was crucial for leaders to create participatory institutions for a number of reasons. First, the practical experience of local self-government is valuable because of the elevating effects that it has on people's mores. Most obviously, local participatory government instills habits of independence and self-reliance. Moreover, the experience of active self-government makes people less apathetic and individualistic. In the American townships, Tocqueville did not find self-reliant individuals who merely wanted to be left alone. Rather, he saw self-reliant and independent citizens who were at the same time very public-spirited and highly involved in governmental affairs. In short, he found "citizens" rather than "docile subjects."[85] In a draft for *Democracy*, Tocqueville wrote: "Administrative centralization works toward despotism and destroys *civic virtue*. People get used to living as strangers, as settlers (*colons*) in their own country, to saying: 'That does not concern me. Let the government look after that.'"[86] Because they were active political participants in a decentralized political system, the Americans were able to maintain a considerable measure of civic virtue.

Tocqueville argues in Volume I of *Democracy* that local participation can foster what he calls "reflective patriotism." Whereas in aristocratic ages one found an "instinctive patriotism," which was based on ancient memories of the land and one's ancestors, in democratic ages one could only hope for reflective patriotism. The latter type of patriotism arises when the individual citizen "understands the influence which his country's well-being has on his own."[87] Once he understands that the public interest affects his own private interest, he will strive to foster the common good, since he knows that this will lead to his own private good as well. The only way that the citizenry can reach this understanding, though, is to actually give them a share in government. As Tocqueville puts it,

> the most powerful way, and perhaps the only remaining way, in which to interest men in their country's fate is to make them take a share in its government. . . . [In America] how does it come about that each man is as interested in the affairs of his township, of his canon, and of the whole state as he is in his own affairs? It is because each man in his sphere takes an active part in the government of society.[88]

At first, then, people who participate will be patriotic because their head tells them that it is in their own self-interest to work for the common good. But in the end, patriotism will also become a matter of the heart and spirit. As Tocqueville puts it in Volume II of *Democracy*: "It would not be fair to assume that American patriotism and the universal zeal for the common good have no solid basis. Though private interest, in the United States as elsewhere, is the driving force behind most of men's actions, it does not govern them all."[89] Tocqueville here suggests that he was wrong when he wrote in Volume I that patriotism could only be inspired in democratic ages by calculations of self-interest. He now argues that patriotism may start out as mere self-interest writ large, but it soon grows into something nobler:

> The free institutions of the United States and the political rights enjoyed there provide a thousand continual reminders to every citizen that he lives in society. At every moment they bring his mind back to this idea, that it is the duty as well as

the interest of men to be useful to their fellows. Having no particular reason to hate others, since he is neither their slave nor their master, the American's heart easily inclines toward benevolence. At first it is of necessity that men attend to the public interest, afterward by choice. What had been calculation becomes instinct. By dint of working for the good of his fellow citizens, he in the end acquires a habit and taste for serving them.[90]

Americans might at first work for the common good out of a sense of self-interest (properly understood); however, participation in politics eventually changes them, at least to a degree, into a truly public-minded citizenry. As Richard Krouse usefully puts it, for Tocqueville, "Interest becomes, as it were, the mechanism of its own . . . self-transcendence: it is *aufgehoben*. In this way democratic man becomes more than mere *bourgeois*: he becomes, in part and on occasion, a genuinely public-spirited republican citizen as well."[91] Like Rousseau before him, Tocqueville believed that political freedom can modify the individual's tastes and desires and can thus allow him to attain his or her highest capacities. Echoing a passage in Rousseau's *Social Contract*, Tocqueville writes: "Feelings and ideas are renewed, the heart enlarged, and the understanding developed only by the reciprocal action of men one upon another."[92]

We have now seen that Tocqueville admired participatory freedom partly for its effects; that is, participatory freedom mitigates the modern vices of individualism and apathy, and thereby ultimately wards off despotism. Ultimately, though, Tocqueville admires participatory freedom not for its effects, but for its "intrinsic glamour," as he puts it in *The Old Regime*. In the end, then, Tocqueville believes that leaders should try to foster participatory institutions because the exercise of freedom has an intrinsic goodness. Like Aristotle, Tocqueville believed that without participatory freedom, people are somehow less than fully human. As he puts it in *Democracy*, a people without freedom "will slowly fall below the level of humanity."[93]

Certainly, the leader who desires only personal aggrandizement will not want to hand over to the people any freedom. But the leader who truly seeks national greatness and prosperity should remember, according to Tocqueville, "that a nation cannot long remain great if each man is individually weak, and that no one has yet devised a form of society or a political combination which can make a people energetic when it is composed of citizens who are flabby and feeble."[94] The best way to avoid "citizens who are flabby and feeble," in Tocqueville's view, is to empower them by giving them a share in self-government, particularly at the local level.

It can now be seen that my interpretation of Tocqueville differs somewhat from that of Patrick Deneen in his often profound book, *Democratic Faith*. For Deneen, Tocqueville is a "democratic realist" who rejects the "democratic faith" that democracy can "transform" individuals into something better than they are at present. I agree with much of Deneen's analysis, and Deneen is certainly correct that Tocqueville was often critical of the idea of human perfectibility.[95] But in contrast to Deneen, I have stressed throughout this chapter that Tocqueville *does*, at times, evince a faith that democratic political participation can elevate and educate (if not wholly transform) the individual. To be sure, Deneen is careful to note that even democratic realists such as Tocqueville have a "modest" version of democratic faith insofar as they have a "belief in, trust for, and confidence toward human ability and capacity for self-rule."[96] However, Deneen's emphasis on Tocqueville's moderation leads him, I think, to pay insufficient attention to those passages in which Tocqueville does have an optimistic belief, as Krouse puts it, that "democratic man" can become "more than mere *bourgeois*: he becomes, in part and on occasion, a genuinely public-spirited republican citizen as well." Moreover, while Deneen lays a great deal of stress on Tocqueville's criticisms of perfectibility, Deneen does not mention Tocqueville's comment to Gobineau that human beings are "equally capable of perfecting themselves," nor does Deneen mention Tocqueville's hope for leadership that can "make men great."[97] In short, I agree with Deneen that Tocqueville did not naively hope that democracy could produce perfect, God-like citizens; however, Tocqueville had, I think, greater hope in the transforming power of democratic politics—and of democratic leadership—than Deneen suggests.

The Continuing Necessity of Leadership

At times, Tocqueville suggested that the goal of the democratic leader (like the goal of a parent) is to gradually render oneself unnecessary. As Tocqueville put it, "The greatest care of a good government should be to habituate people, little by little, to doing without it."[98] Tocqueville therefore rejected paternalistic forms of leadership that aimed to keep the people in a permanent state of tutelage. This becomes clear in Tocqueville's chapter in *Democracy* on "What Sort of Despotism Democratic Nations Have to Fear." Tocqueville here foresees a new sort of despotic regime in which the people are so individualistic and so consumed with "petty and banal pleasures" that they have completely abandoned political activity—that is, they have given up on the effort to collectively control their own lives. Tocqueville writes:

Over this kind of men stands an immense, protective power which is alone responsible for securing their enjoyment and watching over their fate. That power is absolute, thoughtful of detail, orderly, provident, and gentle. It would resemble parental authority if, father-like, it tried to prepare its charges for a man's life, but on the contrary, it only tries to keep them in perpetual childhood.[99]

Tocqueville here makes it clear that while salutary forms of leadership aim to turn dependent subjects into independent citizens, debased forms of leadership intend to permanently infantilize the people. As Tocqueville put it in a draft for *Democracy*: "I can imagine making ourselves guardians to the *communes* if we want to emancipate them. That the government, if it wishes, may treat the local powers like *children*, I allow; but not like *fools*. Only fools are kept under supervision throughout their lives."[100] Tocqueville's theoretical claim, then, is that leaders sometimes need to initially guide their subjects, but they then need to empower them gradually and allow them to become independent citizens.

But does this mean that a democracy might reach a point when leadership is no longer necessary, because the citizenry will be so well educated that they can then dispense with the guidance of leaders? In fact, during his travels Tocqueville *did* once suggest that strong leadership may not actually be needed in America. Tocqueville saw a nation that already had many participatory institutions as well as the requisite mores for self-government, and so at times he was tempted to think that brilliant leadership was not generally necessary in America. As Tocqueville put it in an 1832 notebook entry, "The greatest merit of American government is to be *powerless* and *passive*. In the present state of things America needs, in order to prosper, neither skillful leadership nor profound plans, nor great efforts, but liberty and still more liberty. What a point of comparison between such a state of affairs and our own!"[101] But note that Tocqueville here refers to "the present state of things." What if conditions were to change? What if crises one day arose, sparked, for example, by the closing of the frontier, the concentration of capital, or conflict over slavery? Would America not then need "skillful leader[s]" who can formulate "profound plans" and inspire "great efforts" on the part of the citizenry?

In fact, Tocqueville came to believe that even though the Americans had the necessary mores and experience for self-government, there would, nevertheless, *always* be a need for skillful leadership. For Tocqueville, the education of democracy must be an ongoing process, for the dangers of individualism and apathy always loom large in an egalitarian

society. Tocqueville places particular emphasis on the enduring necessity
of moral leadership in Volume II of *Democracy*. He there writes that in
the democratic era, when people tend to be caught up in "ephemeral
and casual desires"—particularly the desire to make "sudden and easy
fortunes"—leaders are needed who can inspire people to work arduously
toward "distant goals" that are more noble.[102] For Tocqueville, then,
democratic leaders must promote the idea that political and social life
should be guided not by the pursuit of mere self-interest, but rather by
the pursuit of principle. Leaders must offer citizens an elevating sense of
purpose—a sense of what freedom is *for*—so that people will not become
engrossed solely in "caring for the slightest needs of the body and the
trivial conveniences of life."[103]

My claim that Tocqueville emphasizes the importance of moral leadership in America may initially appear to be at odds with Tocqueville's
analysis of "great" and "small" parties in Volume I of *Democracy*. According to Tocqueville, it is "great" parties that provide moral leadership.
As Tocqueville defines them, "Great political parties are . . . attached to
principles," whereas "small parties . . . are not enlarged and sustained by
lofty purposes. . . ." In Tocqueville's view, "Great parties convulse society;
small ones agitate it; the former rend and the latter corrupt it; the first
may sometimes save it by overthrowing it, but the second always create
unprofitable trouble." Tocqueville then observes that, "America has had
great parties; now they no longer exist. This has been a great gain in happiness but not in morality."[104] Because Tocqueville suggests that the decline
of great parties has augmented the "happiness" of America, one might
be tempted to conclude that he endorses a politics of interest—that is, a
politics characteristic of "small parties"—rather than a politics animated
by moral purpose. However, Tocqueville's discussion of great and small
parties should be read along with his chapter on "Why Great Revolutions
Will Become Rare" in Volume II. In the latter chapter, Tocqueville writes
that, "If the citizens continue to shut themselves up more and more narrowly in the little circle of petty domestic interests and keep themselves
constantly busy therein, there is a danger that they may in the end become
practically out of reach of those great and powerful public emotions which
do indeed perturb peoples but which also make them grow and refresh
them."[105] This passage suggests that Tocqueville would likely be inclined
to welcome parties (and leaders) that have within them an element of
greatness, for such parties could help elevate the nation, at least some
of the time, beyond a "petty" politics based on "interests."[106] Granted,
this might "perturb" the people and disrupt their short-term happiness,
especially if this so-called happiness is rooted in what Tocqueville calls "a
cowardly love of immediate pleasures."[107] Nevertheless, Tocqueville sug-

gests that this disruption of their happiness is worthwhile, if it ennobles the people by spurring their moral growth.

Moreover, in another chapter in Volume II, titled "Why There Are So Many Men of Ambition in the United States But So Few Lofty Ambitions," Tocqueville specifically calls on leaders to pursue "lofty" rather than "paltry" goals.[108] In short, he here calls on leaders to embrace a model of moral leadership reminiscent more of great parties than small ones. Explicitly rejecting the idea that happiness should be the highest goal of a society, Tocqueville now declares that, "the leaders of the new societies would do wrong if they tried to send the citizens to sleep in a state of happiness too uniform and peaceful;" instead, leaders "should sometimes give" the citizenry "difficult and dangerous problems to face, to rouse ambition and give it a field of action."[109] Tocqueville thus *does* clearly believe that leaders animated by moral purpose are necessary in the democratic age. Otherwise, Tocqueville writes, there is a danger "that men will wear themselves out in trivial, lonely, futile activity, and that for all its constant agitation humanity will make no advance."[110] Tocqueville, then, insists on the necessity of moral leadership, even as he acknowledges that principled leaders may, at times, stir people to act in ways that cause them to lose some of the short-term happiness that results from the narrow pursuit of material self-interest.

Tocqueville's Elitist Strand and his Departure from Burns

Tocqueville's belief in the continuing necessity of leadership in America is also evident in his discussion of representative government. While Tocqueville always advocated participatory democracy at the local level, he simultaneously believed that matters of great national importance, particularly foreign affairs, would need to be handled by an enlightened elite.[111] Tocqueville certainly had more faith in the transformative power of political education than did the authors of the *Federalist*. Nevertheless, Tocqueville actually agreed with Hamilton, Madison, and Jay that at the level of *national* politics, an elite body of statesmen should be in control, no matter how far advanced was the political education of the masses. Tocqueville thus heartily endorsed the mechanism of indirect elections for senators; sounding much like Madison in *Federalist* 10, Tocqueville suggests that when "the popular will has passed through" the Senate, it is "in some sense refined and . . . clothed in nobler and more beautiful shape."[112]

Tocqueville often emphasized that elected officials should not simply implement the will of their constituents, but should rather consult their own judgment in order to actively lead. Tocqueville found it deeply troubling that,

> in several Constitutions in the United States, recognition is given the voters' right to force their representatives to vote in a certain way. This principle is combated by the best minds. If it were adopted generally it would be a mortal blow to the representative system, that great discovery of modern times. . . . It would then be the people itself which acted, the deputies becoming no more than passive agents.[113]

In the same vein, Tocqueville argues that the president should try to "guide" the majority rather than "follow" it.[114] Indeed, in his notes for *Democracy*, Tocqueville suggests that George Washington was great precisely because of his "courage in fighting against popular passions."[115] Tocqueville does not suggest that Washington was also great because he embodied republican values that he shared with his fellow citizens.

Tocqueville's discussion of the Senate and the House in *Democracy* reveals some of Tocqueville's aristocratic prejudices. He asserts with disdain that because its members are directly elected by the people, the House of Representatives is made up of "vulgar elements" such as "village lawyers, tradesmen, or even men of the lowest classes."[116] Tocqueville assumed that great leaders would always come virtually exclusively from "the higher classes of society."[117] In part because of his aristocratic preconceptions, Tocqueville was unable to appreciate any of the merits of President Jackson's statesmanship. Tocqueville could see in Jackson only a vulgar demagogue, and he was insensitive to Jackson's skillful leadership during the crisis over nullification.[118] One wonders if Tocqueville would have been similarly blind to the greatness of Lincoln, an erstwhile village lawyer who came from the lower classes.

The most enduring elements of Tocqueville's thought are the elements that celebrate the ability of ordinary people, once they have the proper mores and enough practical experience, to successfully engage in the art of politics. Nevertheless, no discussion of Tocqueville's ideas on leadership would be complete without acknowledging that Tocqueville's thought simultaneously has a distinctly elitist strand running throughout it.

While Tocqueville anticipates, as we have seen, many of Burns's insights into the study of leadership, the elitist strand running through Tocqueville's political thought ultimately distinguishes it from the work of Burns, and also from the work of Miroff. For Burns and Miroff, "mutuality" is central to democratic leadership; leaders must remain close to the people and engage in dialogue with them.[119] In contrast, Tocqueville tends to conceive of leaders as distant from the masses of the people.

For Tocqueville, the greatest virtue of leaders in democratic times is "virile candor and manly independence of thought"; he thus reserves his highest praise for leaders who have the moral courage to defy the transient and unwise desires of the majority.[120] I would argue that a major problem with Tocqueville's conception of democratic leadership, however, is that while Tocqueville rightly notes the importance of moral courage, he fails to emphasize the other key virtue of democratic leadership—namely, closeness to the people. These two aspects of democratic leadership are in tension with one another, but this is a tension that the democratic leader must nevertheless negotiate. The democratic leader should respect, but not passively accept, public opinion. Tocqueville recognized that the leader should not passively *accept* public opinion, but he failed to emphasize that the democratic leader must at the same time always *respect* and listen closely to public opinion.

Tocqueville's rejection of mutuality is evident not only in his theory of leadership, but also in his own practice of leadership. Tocqueville wrote that when he ran for a seat in the Constituent Assembly after the 1848 Revolution, "Each little town had its club, and each club asked the candidates to give an account of their views and acts and imposed formulations of policy on them. *I refused to answer any of these insolent questions.*"[121] With his refusal to even engage in dialogue with his fellow citizens, we can see that while Tocqueville may have stressed the importance of moral courage in his understanding of leadership, he by no means stressed the importance of closeness to the people.

According to Burns, genuine leaders inspire "followers to act for certain goals that represent the values and the motivations—the wants and needs, the aspirations and expectations" that are "mutually held by *both* leaders and followers."[122] In contrast, Tocqueville praises the leadership of lawyers in America precisely because their values and aspirations are starkly *opposed* to the values and aspirations of the people. Tocqueville writes that "at the bottom of a lawyer's soul one finds some of the tastes and habits of an aristocracy. They share its instinctive preferences for order and its natural love of formalities; like it, they conceive a great distaste for the behavior of the multitude and secretly scorn the government of the people."[123] Tocqueville hoped that American democracy could be moderated by leaders who in a sense stand outside of and above the democratic citizenry. Lawyers in America, he writes, are "increasingly separated from the people, forming a class apart."[124] Tocqueville conceived of lawyers, judges, and senators as quasi-aristocratic actors who could provide a measure of order, stability, and wisdom to a regime dominated by the often impetuous democratic majority. In other words, Tocqueville usually celebrated leaders who had the courage to denounce the people from above, but he usually failed to celebrate leaders who remain close to their fellows and seek to persuade them as equals.

At one point in *Democracy*, Tocqueville does begin to develop a conception of leadership that combines both moral courage *and* closeness to the people, but he does not fully follow through with the idea. When discussing the American clergy in Volume II, Tocqueville notes that they do not denounce the materialistic behavior of the citizenry from a high and mighty stance; instead, the American clergy

> freely allow [the people] to give some of their hearts' care to the needs of the present. . . . [American clergy] take an interest in the progress of industry and praise its achievements; while they are ever pointing to the other world as the great object of the hopes and fears of the faithful, they do not forbid the honest pursuit of prosperity in this. . . . All the clergy of America are aware of the intellectual domination of the majority, and they treat it with respect. They never struggle against it unless the struggle is necessary. . . . [T]hey freely adopt the general views of their time and country . . . *They try to improve their contemporaries but do not quit fellowship with them.*[125]

According to Tocqueville, then, the American clergy generally embrace the values of the American people and respect their opinions, but when "necessary" they will reject majority opinion and will work to "improve" their fellows morally. In this passage on the American clergy, Tocqueville moves toward the idea that a democratic leader can effectively critique his or her fellow citizens while still remaining close to them. If he had followed the implications of his own analysis a bit further, Tocqueville perhaps could have seen in his description of the American clergy the starting-point for a more fully nuanced theory of democratic leadership. Instead, Tocqueville tended to hope for leaders who could bravely stand apart from the people and publicly "deplore the defects of the laws and the unenlightened mutability of democracy."[126]

Conclusion: Tocqueville and Liberal-Republican Leadership

We have seen that for Tocqueville, democratic leadership involves the education—and thus the moral elevation—of the citizenry. To educate and elevate, Tocqueville thinks that leaders should employ the doctrine of self-interest properly understood. At the same time, though, Tocqueville thinks that the religious and republican traditions are also needed in order to cultivate citizens who care, at least sometimes, about the common good. Although Tocqueville believes that both religion and republicanism can help lift people beyond self-interest, he suggests that *political* leaders should focus more on cultivating republicanism than religion. This means that democratic leaders must seek to build and safeguard institutions that promote participation in political life. Moreover, leaders should try to inspire a democratic citizenry to collectively pursue lofty and distant goals, even though this pursuit may not serve citizens' immediate self-interest. We have also seen that while Tocqueville celebrates leaders who possess the virtue of moral courage, he fails to suggest that in democratic times it is also important for leaders to remain close to the people. In the remaining chapters of this book, various American thinkers are examined in the light of Tocqueville's ideas on democratic leadership. We shall see how these American theorists (some of whom were also statesmen) worked with—and sometimes productively reworked—the ideas on leadership that I have identified as Tocquevillian.

Before concluding this chapter, it should be noted that Tocqueville's theory of leadership can be termed a "liberal-republican" theory. Drawing on the republican tradition that extends back to the ancients, Tocqueville believed that the task of authority is political and moral education. Citizen-formation is thus the most important task of leadership. The goal of leaders in democratic times, as Tocqueville puts it, is "to make men great." In order to become great, Tocqueville believed that people need to be guided by authoritative notions of the good life. This means that while Tocqueville may have been a "liberal" in certain respects, he was not the type of liberal who believes that "the right is prior to the good," to use Sandel's terminology.[127] He did not believe, that is, that a political community should be merely a "procedural republic" that allows each individual the freedom to choose his or her own notion of the good.[128] For Tocqueville, a political community must provide authoritative notions of the good life so that people have a salutary sense of "what freedom is *for*." And for Tocqueville, these norms come from both the republican and religious traditions.

It might here be objected that if people accept authoritative norms on the basis of trust, then they have lost the liberty that Tocqueville himself wanted to preserve. But Tocqueville would say that this is the objection of the lover of license, not the lover of liberty. Tocqueville writes: "It is true that any man accepting any opinion on trust from another puts his mind in bondage. But it is a salutary bondage, which allows him to make good use of freedom."[129]

As we have seen, Tocqueville in fact often rejected the idea that the absence of restraint is tantamount to freedom. If individuals are simply let alone, this "negative liberty" will tend to lead to the tyranny of base passions, or the tyranny of public opinion. True freedom, for Tocqueville, arises only when one masters one's passions, and this can only come about through the internalization of authoritative norms that originate outside of the individual. Once they have mastered their base passions (such as the passion for well-being), they will be genuinely free insofar as they can now fulfill their higher capacities.

Drawing on the republican and religious traditions, then, Tocqueville believed that authority was necessary in order to restrain and guide the citizenry. And yet, like many modern liberals, Tocqueville was simultaneously very *wary* of authority. For instance, even as he praises Winthrop's discussion of liberty and authority in Volume I of *Democracy*, Tocqueville also criticizes the Puritans, as we have seen, for "invad[ing] the sphere of conscience" and for "completely forgetting the great principle of religious liberty."[130] Tocqueville thus wants authority to provide people with a sense of the just and good, but he expresses reservations about the use of state power to ensure that citizens follow these authoritative norms. In other words, although Tocqueville believes that it is the task of leadership to shape the values and goals of the citizenry, Tocqueville remains a liberal thinker insofar as he does not want these values to be imposed by force. In short, when it comes to values and goals, Tocqueville wants leaders to educate, but not coerce, the citizenry.

Like the ancients and the Puritans, Tocqueville believes that authority is necessary to educate people and make them better. However, like modern liberals, Tocqueville also seeks to protect and promote individuality and individual rights. Indeed, on the very same page in which Tocqueville asks, in republican fashion, for leaders to try to "make men great," Tocqueville also asks, in liberal fashion, for the creation of "clear and fixed limits to the field of social power." He writes that, "Private people should be given certain rights and the undisputed enjoyment of such rights. The individual should be allowed to keep the little freedom, strength, and originality left to him."[131]

Did Tocqueville recognize that there may have been a tension between his desire for a republican politics of citizen-formation, on the one hand, and his admiration of rights-based liberalism on the other? In fact, it is not clear that Tocqueville did always recognize the tension, and one wishes at times that he had more explicitly discussed it. If the tension had been pointed out to him, though, he probably would have argued that a politics of citizen-formation needs to somehow be *combined* with a politics of individual rights. In his manuscript notes for his chapter "Concerning the Philosophical Approach of the Americans," Tocqueville wrote:

> In the Middle Ages we saw that all opinions had to flow from authority. . . . In the eighteenth century we arrived at the opposite extreme, that is, we pretended to appeal all things only to individual reason and to drive dogmatic beliefs away entirely. . . . In our times, the [18th century] movement still continues among minds of the second rank, but the others . . . admit that received and discovered beliefs, authority and liberty, *individualisme* and social force are all needed at the same time. The whole question is to sort out the limits of these pairs. It is to that [question] that I must put all my mind.[132]

Tocqueville believed, then, that a modern democratic polity needs to unite a respect for strong authority, on the one hand, with a respect for individuality and individual rights on the other. Tocqueville may not provide us with a blueprint for how to combine these two elements, but he convinces the careful reader that one of the most important tasks of politics in democratic times is to search for the proper combination, both in theory and in practice.

Chapter 2

⊷⇒○⇐⊶

The Antifederalists and Tocqueville on Democratic Leadership and Democratic Authority

In this chapter, I examine the Antifederalists in the light of Tocqueville's theory of leadership. I focus on the Antifederalists rather than the Federalists in part because I believe that the Antifederalists articulated a theory of leadership that has not been explored sufficiently by scholars. We shall see that on the subject of leadership there are important affinities between Tocqueville and the Antifederalists. Along with these affinities, we shall also see that in certain respects the Antifederalists depart from Tocqueville, in ways that are instructive to those who seek to understand the nature of democratic leadership.

In her seminal critique of the Antifederalists, Cecilia Kenyon asserts that, "What the Antifederalists lacked was a theory of leadership. . . . [T]hey [did not] produce anything comparable to *The Federalist* on the function of leadership in a representative government."[1] I will argue, though, that the Antifederalists *did*, in fact, offer an important theory of leadership. Kenyon is certainly correct to suggest that the Antifederalists disagreed with the authors of *The Federalist* on the subject of leadership, but this should not lead us to conclude that the Antifederalists did not have their *own* positive vision of leadership.

The interpretation of the Antifederalists that is offered here is in large part a new one. In my view, the Antifederalist rejection of the Constitution was rooted to a significant degree in their conviction that the Constitution

39

posed a threat to democratic leadership and, more broadly, to authority in America. My claim that the Antifederalists believed in the importance of leadership and authority might come as a surprise, given that many leading commentators have viewed them as hostile to both leadership and authority. Just as Kenyon has argued that the Antifederalists were hostile to the principle of *leadership*, Jackson Turner Main has suggested that they were opposed to the principle of *authority*. As Main puts it in his admiring study of the Antifederalists, "From the broadest point of view, the issue [during the ratification debate] was whether authority or liberty should be emphasized"; the Antifederalists, Main suggests, came down on the side of liberty, whereas the Federalists came down on the side of authority.[2] But in my view, this characterization of the Antifederalists is misleading. It is true that there were some libertarian Antifederalists who did believe that the relationship between liberty and authority was one of simple opposition. These Antifederalists did want to choose liberty over authority, as Main suggests. However, there was another important strand of Antifederalism that had a far more nuanced view of the relationship between liberty, on the one hand, and leadership and authority, on the other. By trying to combine liberty with leadership and authority, these Antifederalists had much in common with Tocqueville. Critics of the Constitution such as Mercy Warren and Charles Turner believed, as did Tocqueville, that authority was in fact necessary to prevent liberty from degenerating into mere license. These Antifederalists believed in the importance of *internalized* authority, and thus they believed in the importance of moral, political, and religious education.

Of course, anyone who writes on the Antifederalists must acknowledge that they were a diverse group of thinkers who often disagreed with one another regarding both theoretical and practical questions. As Main has rightly pointed out, "Antifederalism was not a single, simple, unified philosophy of government."[3] Given their large and varied output, my interpretation of the Antifederalists is necessarily selective. What I have done here is focus on those Antifederalists (probably representative of the majority) who reject libertarianism and who thus articulate a nuanced understanding of leadership and authority as necessary and healthy for democracy.

Main suggests that the Antifederalists wanted to "continu[e] the struggle for . . . individual freedom from restraint."[4] Although this is true for some Antifederalists, many others believed, like Tocqueville, that moral and religious authority were necessary to restrain the passions and to guide liberty toward what John Winthrop called the "*just* and *good*." These Antifederalists were indeed suspicious of strong centralized political authority, but at the same time they believed, as Mercy Warren put it, that "Authority and obedience are necessary to preserve social order, and to continue the prosperity or even the existence of nations."[5] No mere rebels against authority, the Antifederalists, like Tocqueville, thought deeply about the complex relationship between leadership, authority and democratic self-rule. If we are to better understand what types of leadership and authority are appropriate for a democratic regime, we would do well to carefully examine Antifederalist ideas; this examination can be fruitfully done through a careful comparison of the Antifederalists and Tocqueville.

Did the Antifederalists Lack a Theory of Leadership?

In Kenyon's view, the "lack of an adequate treatment of the necessary and positive role of leadership remains one of the gravest defects of Antifederalist thought."[6] But in making this claim, Kenyon gives insufficient attention to a number of ways in which Antifederalists *did* claim that leadership was valuable and necessary in a democratic regime. First, some Antifederalists emphasized that citizens need to be educated by moral leadership. Writing as "A Columbian Patriot," Mercy Warren, for instance, argued that virtuous statesmen should play a key role in preserving and promoting America's first principles, which for her were the principles of republicanism. Without virtuous leaders to educate the people and restore them to first principles, freedom will be lost: "The happiness of mankind depends much on the modes of government, and the virtues of the governors; and America may yet produce characters who have genius and capacity sufficient to form the manners and correct the morals of the people, and virtue enough to lead their country to freedom."[7] Warren here reminds one of Machiavelli, who wrote in *The Discourses* that a corrupt people can be restored to virtue if "some man of superior character arises amongst them, whose noble example and virtuous actions" will bring the people "back to themselves, so to speak."[8]

Warren warned that the character of leaders critically shaped the character of the citizenry. In a characteristic passage, Warren argues that infidelity arose in Europe when "the worst passions of men" were "let loose on the multitude by the example of their superiors."[9] Other Antifederalists shared this outlook. For instance, Philadelphiensis warned that, "under a tyrannical and unjust [government], the greater part of the people will . . . be wicked: The complexion of the *governing* is ever the colour of the *governed*."[10] When discussing leadership, the Federalists often emphasized the importance of "energy" as well as technical and administrative prowess; the Antifederalists, on the other hand, were more likely to emphasize the importance of *moral* leadership.[11]

As we have seen, Tocqueville also emphasized the importance of moral leadership. Tocqueville believed that mores are the key variable in politics; however, he also believed that leaders play an important role in *shaping* mores. As Tocqueville put it in an 1853 letter, "political societies are not what their laws make them, but what sentiments, beliefs, ideas, habits of the heart, *and the spirit of the men who form them*, prepare them in advance to be, as well as what nature and education have made them."[12] Like Tocqueville, the Antifederalists hoped that a vibrant, public-minded citizenry could rule itself at the local level; also like Tocqueville, though, Antifederalists such as Warren and Philadelphiensis believed that virtuous and skilled leadership was needed to create and maintain such a citizenry, a citizenry that would avoid the vices of materialism, individualism, and apathy. Because certain Antifederalists believed that virtuous leaders can help create a virtuous people, we can see that Kenyon understates the degree to which the Antifederalists acknowledged the importance of leadership.

The Antifederalists' distinctive understanding of leadership is further revealed by their frequently expressed desire for representatives who would remain close to the people, and thereby gain "the confidence of the people." Outstanding Antifederalist thinkers such as Brutus and the Federal Farmer argued that there are two forms of government—those that rest on the confidence of the people, and those that rest on "force." The former type of government is a government that rests on "persuasion." A government that rests on persuasion can be called a government with authority, because this type of government is freely obeyed by the citizenry. As the Federal Farmer put it,

> In viewing the various governments instituted by mankind, we see their whole force reducible to two principles—the important springs which alone move the machines, and give them their intended influence and controul, are *force* and *persuasion*: by the former men are compelled, by the latter they are drawn. We denominate a government despotic or free, as the one or other principle prevails in it.[13]

The Antifederalists believed that under the proposed Constitution the representatives would be so distant—both literally and figuratively—from the people, that they would not be trusted. Lacking the people's trust, representatives would not be freely obeyed. And without the freely granted support of the people, the government would resort to force in order "to compel obedience," as the Federal Farmer put it.[14]

According to Yves Simon, "coercion" and "persuasion" are the two main "instruments of authority."[15] But in the Antifederalist view, a government only genuinely has authority if it rests on persuasion rather than on coercion. The Antifederalists certainly wanted their representatives to be obeyed. Mercy Warren, for instance, spoke in no uncertain terms of "the indispensable subordination and obedience due to rulers" who have been chosen by the people.[16] However, Warren and other Antifederalists wanted to create a polity in which this obedience would be freely granted, and this would be unlikely to happen in a regime where the representatives were so distant from the people.

Much like Rousseau, the Antifederalists believed that people were not truly free unless they lived under laws of their own making. As Melancton Smith put it, "the fundamental principle of a free government [is] that the people should make the laws by which they [are] to be governed: He who is controlled by another is a slave; and that government which is directed by the will of any one or a few, or any number less than is the will of the community, is a government for slaves."[17] While the Antifederalists shared with Rousseau the idea that people are not free if the laws are not of their own making, they did not share in Rousseau's rejection of representation.[18] According to A [Pennsylvania] Farmer, "sovereignty . . . consists in the understanding and will of the political society, and this understanding and will is originally and inherently in the people." However, if sovereignty is "delegated to representatives chosen by the people from among themselves," the government can still legitimately be "called a democracy."[19]

The Antifederalists, then, accepted the principle of representation, as did Publius. However, the Antifederalists believed that representatives would only have the confidence of the people under certain conditions. Specifically, they believed that the representatives should be personally known to the people, and they should be numerous and diverse enough so that they genuinely mirror the people. As Smith put it, representatives should "resemble those they represent; they should be a true picture of the people; possess the knowledge of their circumstances and their wants; sympathize in all their distresses, and be disposed to seek their true interests."[20] Given that the new Constitution would create very large legislative districts, very few constituents could ever know their representatives well enough to establish a genuine relationship of trust. Moreover, in a large legislative district, hard-working middle-class citizens were unlikely to be elected. Congress would be dominated by the wealthy, for only rich and prominent men would have the resources and the name-recognition to win elections in districts of great size. The members of Congress would thus not be able to really know, nor give voice to, the concerns of people who "walk in the plain and frugal paths of life," as Smith put it.[21] The Antifederalists by no means wanted to bar the wealthy from having a voice in the government, but they wanted to ensure that the "poor and middling classes" had a prominent voice as well; this would be impossible, though, with such a small Congress. Because there would be "no genuine representation of the people,"[22] the proposed government would lack the confidence of the people, and would thus have to act not on the basis of authority, but on the basis of force. This would mean, for instance, that if the American people were asked to pay taxes to a federal government from which they felt estranged, they would do so only if compelled, as Brutus pointed out.[23]

Antifederalists sought to make representatives close to the people by having annual elections, small legislative districts, and mandatory rotation in office. As Ralph Ketcham notes, they favored these measures not simply because they wanted to keep a jealous watch over their representatives. Instead, these measures were designed to ensure that the citizenry were themselves active participants, in a sense, in their government. As Ketcham puts it,

> The anti-federalist ideal went beyond a close control of officials by the people. In a truly self-governing society, there would be such dialogue, empathy, and even intimacy that the very distinction between ruler and ruled would tend to disappear. Such a close link between the people and officials would embody the idea of liberty being both security of rights and effective voice in public affairs.[24]

Noting that the Antifederalists favored institutional mechanisms that would keep representatives close to the people, Kenyon writes that the Antifederalists "regard[ed] representatives as delegates bound by the instructions of constituents rather than as men expected and trusted to exercise independent judgment." This is highly problematic, she writes, "for representation of this kind makes difficult the process of genuine deliberation. . . ."[25] But is Kenyon correct that the Antifederalists simply wanted their representatives to slavishly follow the desires of the people? Kenyon fails to note that some Antifederalists suggested that representatives *should*, at times, depart from the wishes of the people. For instance, in an important passage, Brutus noted that under the proposed Constitution, "The representatives of the people cannot, as they now do, after they have passed laws, mix with the people, and explain to them the motives which induced the adoption of any measure, point out its utility, and remove objections or silence unreasonable clamours against it."[26] Brutus suggests here that one of the advantages of small districts is precisely that they more effectively allow representatives to vote *against* the people's wishes; for after the vote is cast, the representatives can then *educate* the people by engaging in dialogue with them, so that the people can understand why their initial view was mistaken. If, after this dialogue, the people are still not persuaded, they can vote the representative out of office. But, if districts are large, and the people do not truly know their representatives, then their legislative leaders will have no chance to persuade and to educate the people through dialogue with them. Kenyon accuses the Antifederalists of neglecting "genuine deliberation," but, in fact, they actively sought deliberation, not just between representatives, but, perhaps even more so, between leaders and citizens. Indeed, as Brutus suggests, without this dialogue, government by "persuasion"—that is, free government—would be lost. After all, inherent in the very notion of government by persuasion is the idea that leaders should engage in a dialogue with their fellow citizens in order to explain, convince, and educate. Government by persuasion, then, is decidedly *not* government by leaders who always slavishly follow the people.

The Antifederalists thus offer an important theoretical insight into the nature of democratic leadership. We have seen in chapter 1 that for Tocqueville, leaders should be distant from the people, so that they can bravely defy the people when necessary. But the Antifederalists teach us that if leaders remain close to the people's values and aspirations, this does not necessarily mean that the leaders will be unable to exercise independent judgment. On the contrary, closeness to the people might actually empower leaders to disagree with—but to then successfully *educate*—the people. As we shall see in chapter 3, Abraham Lincoln also theorized—and enacted—precisely a conception of leadership in which the leader is close to the people, but at the same time remains an independent-minded *teacher* of the people. Unlike Tocqueville, the Antifederalists and Lincoln were able to perceive that democracy can best be educated by leaders who are close to the people, and who engage with them in dialogue.

Force, Persuasion, and the Authority of Government

We have seen that the Antifederalists were by no means anarchists. What they were opposed to was not government *per se*, but rather governments that rest on force rather than on authority. But what exactly was wrong with a government that rests on force? The Antifederalists rejected such a government for two main reasons. First, they rejected such a government on moral grounds: A government based on force would mean the negation of liberty in its most basic sense. As the Federal Farmer puts it, "Government must exist—If the persuasive principle be feeble, force is infallibly the next resort. The moment the laws of Congress shall be disregarded they must languish, and the whole system be convulsed—that moment we must have recourse to this next resort, and all freedom vanish."[27] If freedom were to vanish, it would be the greatest of tragedies, since the Revolution itself was fought precisely for the sake of liberty.

As I discuss below, the Antifederalists believed in the importance of positive liberty—that is, the freedom to pursue not whatever one desires, but only the just and the good. However, they also believed in the importance of negative liberty—the freedom to make choices for oneself, free of coercion. These two notions of freedom may seem to be in tension, but this tension can be resolved, or at least eased, in the following manner: True freedom only comes when one pursues the just and the good. However, one's choice to follow the just and the good only has moral value if the choice is made *voluntarily*. Hence, negative liberty (freedom from coercion) is a prerequisite to positive liberty (the voluntary pursuit of the just and the good). A government with force rather than persuasion as its primary principle would mean the end of negative liberty, and hence ultimately the end of the human capacity to freely choose the just and the good.

The second, more practical, reason that a government resting on force was to be rejected is that such a government would not genuinely have the energy and vigor that its proponents claimed for it. Hamilton argued that whereas the government under the Articles was "destitute of energy," the new Constitution would create "a vigorous national government" that could "dictate the terms of the connection between the old and the new world."[28] As Jeffrey Sedgwick points out, in the view of Publius, "energy" in the government should come largely from the executive branch. Sedgwick notes that, "What is striking about [Publius's] discussion of executive energy is that Publius locates energy in the institutional or legal basis of the office, not in its popular support."[29] But in the view of the Antifederalists, it is only freely given popular support that makes a nation energetic and powerful. As Philadelphiensis put it,

> As to this government being efficient, or rather sufficient to protect the people from the violence of a foreign enemy; the idea is so absurd that it offends common sense; it can neither have strength, energy, nor respectability, in the great scale of nations. For a new country to become strong and energetic,

so as to be able to repel a foreign foe, . . . the people must be . . . *well-affected* to it. . . . Who in his senses could suppose that people, with their spirits broken by oppression, would voluntarily fight for that government, to which they are necessarily disaffected?[30]

As this passage reveals, the Antifederalists emphasized that citizens will not be willing to fight and die for a government that does not truly feel like their own. In a similar vein, Brutus wrote that, "The execution of the laws in a free government must rest on [the confidence of the people], and this must be founded on the good opinion they entertain of the framers of the laws." In the view of Brutus, the proposed Constitution does not "have a representation for the whole union sufficiently numerous to obtain that confidence which is necessary for the purpose of internal taxation, and other powers to which this proposed government extends."[31] Important governmental tasks such as taxation would thus have to be carried out through the use of force. The use of force might work to some extent, but Brutus wants to suggest that it is far better not only morally, but also practically, for taxes to be voluntarily paid. Governmental power is enhanced, then, when the government can rely on the free support of the people. As the examples of taxation and war suggest, successful government requires that the people sometimes sacrifice their own narrow self-interest for the general good. But if the people do not believe that their government truly expresses their "understanding and will," they will not be willing to make sacrifices for it. Only a government that truly has the confidence of the people—only, that is, a government that rests on genuine *authority*—will successfully persuade people to sometimes sacrifice their private interest for the common good.[32]

Hence, from the Antifederalist perspective, Hamilton's desire for a mightier nation would be self-defeating insofar as he sought to attain it though a government that was not genuinely close to the people. Hamilton himself tried to refute the Antifederalist claim that the new government would lack authority. He declared that,

> It was remarked yesterday [by Melancton Smith], that a numerous representation was necessary to obtain the confidence of the people. This is not generally true. The confidence of the people will easily be gained by a good administration. This is the true touchstone. . . . The popular confidence depends on circumstances very distinct from considerations of number. Probably the public attachment is more strongly secured by a train of prosperous events, which are the result of wise deliberation

and vigorous execution, and to which large bodies are much less competent than small ones.[33]

And in *Federalist* 27, Hamilton similarly wrote: "It may be laid down as a general rule, that confidence in and obedience to a government will commonly be proportioned to the goodness or badness of its administration."[34] For Hamilton, then, people will be loyal to the government if it is efficient, competent, and useful to them. Antifederalists noted that the logic of Hamilton's argument would point to the conclusion that a monarchical or aristocratic government would be perfectly legitimate if it were administratively effective. Hamilton attempts to deny this when he wrote in *Federalist* 68 that, "we cannot acquiesce in the political heresy of the poet who says: 'For forms of government let fools contest—That which is best administered is best.'"[35] Nevertheless, by emphasizing the quality of a government's administration as the main criterion for its ability to gain authority, Hamilton de-emphasized the questions of democratic legitimacy that were so important to the Antifederalists. As Sheldon Wolin notes, Hamilton argued for the legitimacy of the new state "not by [discussing] its ground in the aspirations and needs of the people, but in reference to abstract principles of organization."[36] In the view of the Antifederalists, though, a good administration cannot in and of itself foster loyalty in America. As Brutus succinctly put it, "let the administration of [the new government] be good or ill, it still will be a government, not according to the will of the people, but according to the will of a few."[37] Lacking the "confidence, respect and affection" of the people, the government will be either "nerveless and inefficient," on the one hand, or brutally repressive on the other.[38] Either way, it certainly will lack the authority to persuade people to sometimes sacrifice their private interests for the common good.

According to the Antifederalists, it was not they who had given short shrift to the principle of authority; rather, it was Federalists like Hamilton who had largely spurned authority in favor of the opposing principle of force. Hamilton asserted in *Federalist* 1 that the new government would not be the result of "accident and force."[39] But in Hamilton's justification of the new government, force in fact plays a primary role. In *Federalist* 15, Hamilton writes that the new government needs to use force not only against external enemies, but also sometimes against "the persons of the citizens—the only proper objects of government." Hamilton continues: "Government implies the power of making laws. It is essential to the idea of a law, that it be attended with a sanction; or, in other words, a penalty or punishment for disobedience."[40] The Antifederalists believed that Federalists such as Hamilton were fully aware that the new government would operate on the basis of force. As the Minority of the Convention of Pennsylvania put it,

> The framers of this constitution appear to have been aware . . . that no dependence could be placed on the people for their support; but on the contrary, that the government must be executed by force. They have therefore made a provision for this purpose in a permanent STANDING ARMY, and a MILITIA that may be subjected to as strict discipline and government.[41]

Antifederalists such as Brutus, Charles Turner, Mercy Warren, and Melancton Smith would agree that as a last resort, force needs to be used to compel the wicked to obey just laws. As Smith put it, the government should be "calculated to cherish the love of liberty . . . yet it [must have] sufficient force to restrain licentiousness."[42] However, the Antifederalists believed that a free government should be primarily based not on the external control of the sword, but rather on the internal control that is the result of education. In their view, by emphasizing force, Hamilton gives short shrift to education and the possibility of creating a virtuous citizenry. "Why has government been instituted at all?" asked Hamilton. "Because the passions of men will not conform to the dictates of reason and justice, without constraint."[43] In contrast to Hamilton, the Antifederalists hoped that the citizenry would be educated to the point where it could by and large control its *own* passions. Charles Turner wrote that, "It is EDUCATION which almost entirely forms the character, the freedom or slavery, the happiness or misery of the world." Turner believed that if the education of the citizenry is sufficiently advanced, then "the rigours of government" can be decreased, "in proportion to that increase of morality which may render the people more capable of being *a Law to themselves*."[44] This is a Tocquevillian idea, for Tocqueville believed that a people with internalized moral and religious authority can do without powerful political elites dominating their local affairs.

Moreover, the distinction made by the Antifederalists between rule based on force and rule based on persuasion is a distinction that also runs throughout Tocqueville's thought. Like the Antifederalists, Tocqueville fervently believed in the moral *and* practical superiority of governments that rest on genuine authority—that is, on persuasion—rather than on force.

As for the moral aspects of this issue, there are several passages in which Tocqueville refers to the moral grandeur associated with freely given obedience, as opposed to the moral degradation involved with submitting to coercion. For instance, Tocqueville writes, "When a man submits to force, that surrender debases him; but when he accepts the recognized right of a fellow mortal to give him orders, there is a sense in which he rises above the giver of the commands."[45] Similarly, in his discussion of the Indians he writes:

> [T]he Indian lives on the extreme edge of freedom. . . . Even his family had hardly any authority over him, and he has never bent his will to that of any of his fellows; *no one has taught him to regard voluntary obedience as an honorable subjection*, and law is unknown to him even as a word. He delights in this barbarous independence and would rather die than sacrifice any part of it.[46]

As a final example, Tocqueville wrote, "Religion inclines the human mind to stop by itself and to offer obedience, the free choice of a moral and independent being." In contrast, majority opinion "*compels* the human mind to stop, despite what it may want."[47]

Taken together, these passages suggest that freely given obedience is ennobling because it moves one beyond the passion for an unlimited freedom that is actually a passion for mere license. By voluntarily obeying political and religious authority, people demonstrate that they are now able to exercise self-mastery, and they are now pursuing the just and the good not because they must, but because they truly desire to do so. As Jack Lively has perceptively noted, Tocqueville believed that "without the possession of uncoerced choices of action men could not express themselves as moral agents. . . . [T]he value of liberty was . . . that it allowed the individual the possibility of moral action."[48] In my view, Tocqueville's view of liberty is largely a positive one; genuine liberty for him must involve the pursuit of the just and the good. However, Tocqueville believed that negative liberty is a necessary starting-point for this genuine liberty, for if the choice of the just and the good is to have any moral value, it must be an uncoerced choice. According to Tocqueville, "virtue" is the "*free choice of what is good*."[49] If people are to have their dignity as moral agents respected, they must be able to make decisions free of coercion. As Tocqueville put it, "Men must walk in freedom, responsible for their acts."[50] And yet, true freedom for Tocqueville is more than simply the absence of coercion; true freedom comes when one voluntarily pursues the good. Hence, like the Antifederalists, Tocqueville rejected rule-by-force because it destroys both negative *and* positive liberty.

In addition to this moral justification for rule based on persuasion rather than force, Tocqueville also had a practical justification. According to Tocqueville, "Despotism by itself can maintain nothing durable. . . . you will never find true power among men except in the free concurrence of their wills."[51] Hence, Tocqueville would have agreed with the Antifederalists that a genuinely powerful, energetic, and enduring government can only arise if it rests on the affection, respect, and freely given support of the people. According to Tocqueville, "In America the force behind the state is much less well regulated, less enlightened, and less wise, but it is a hundred times more powerful than in Europe. . . . what one [finds] is a picture of power, somewhat wild perhaps, but robust, and a life liable to mishaps but full of striving and animation."[52] In another passage, he writes that, "Democracy does not provide a people with the most skillful of governments, but it . . . spreads throughout the body social a restless activity, superabundant force, and energy never found elsewhere. . . ."[53] Like the Antifederalists, Tocqueville thus suggests, *contra* Hamilton, that a republic without brilliant administration can nevertheless be "a hundred times more powerful" and have more "energy" than a nation with superb administration. The reason that America was so powerful and energetic, in Tocqueville's view, is that the people felt that they were the true makers of the law. Following Rousseau, Tocqueville believed that in the modern era, governments would only have "great authority" if the people were convinced that they were submitting to laws genuinely of their own making. As Tocqueville put it,

> It is not always feasible to call on the whole people, either directly or indirectly, to take its part in lawmaking, but no one can deny that when that can be done the law derives great authority therefrom. This popular origin, though often damaging to the wisdom and quality of legislation, gives it peculiar strength. . . . In the United States, except for slaves, servants, and paupers fed by the township, no one is without a vote and, hence, an indirect share in lawmaking. . . . Therefore, however annoying a law may be, the American will submit to it, not only as the work of the majority but also as his own doing; he regards it as a contract to which he is one of the parties.[54]

Both Tocqueville and the Antifederalists agreed, then, that if the people do not feel like they are ultimately the true authors of a government's laws, then the government will be weakened, no matter how efficient and wise is the administration of the government.

The Antifederalists on Participatory Institutions

As we have seen in chapter 1, Tocqueville argued that the key task of leadership in democratic times is not "to do great things with men," but rather "to make men great."[55] To accomplish this task, leaders must build local participatory institutions that can work to develop the political and moral capacities of the citizenry. The Antifederalists had a very similar understanding of the crucial educative role of participatory institutions. One important example comes from A [Maryland] Farmer's discussion of the Constitution's failure to guarantee trial by jury in civil cases. Antifederalists often defended trial by jury as an important bulwark against governmental oppression. But A [Maryland] Farmer, anticipating Tocqueville, probed more deeply into the nature of the jury as a democratic institution.

Tocqueville argued that the jury should be considered not only for its "judicial" effects, but for its "political" effects as well.[56] That is, he was interested not just in the question of whether the jury efficiently renders just verdicts. Rather, he was also interested in the educative impact of the jury on the jurors. Tocqueville's discussion of the jury is a good example of his general mode of analysis. Tocqueville looked at all institutions—such as universal manhood suffrage, civic associations, manufacturing labor, and juries—not primarily with an eye toward assessing their practical utility. Rather, he was interested in how these institutions shaped the character of the people who participate in them. Tocqueville wrote, "I do not know whether a jury is useful to the litigants, but I am sure it is very good for those who have to decide the case. I regard it as one of the most effective means of popular education at society's disposal." In Tocqueville's view, the "practical intelligence and the political good sense of the Americans" was largely due to their participation in juries.[57] Tocqueville's claim here fits into his larger argument about the general relationship between political education and political participation: the best way to politically educate a people is to allow them to exercise political responsibility.

A [Maryland] Farmer makes exactly the same argument about juries. Responding to the charge that the people are too "ignorant" to be jurors, he writes that,

> There is some truth in these allegations—but whence comes it—The Commons are much degraded in the powers of the mind:—They were deprived of the use of understanding, when they were robbed of the power of employing it.—Men no longer cultivate, what is no longer useful,—should every opportunity be taken away, of exercising their reason, you will reduce them to that state of mental baseness, in which they appear in nine-tenths of this globe—distinguished from brutes, only by form and the articulation of sound—*Give them power and they will find understanding to use it.*... [58]

A [Maryland] Farmer here precisely anticipates Tocqueville's claim that, "No better means exists of making men contemptible than to show contempt for them."[59] Tocqueville and A [Maryland] Farmer also believed that the opposite was true: If leaders give the people power and responsibility, the people will tend to rise to the occasion.

Both Tocqueville and A [Maryland] Farmer insisted that a pessimistic view of human nature must be jettisoned in favor of the belief that people can be elevated if they are given a proper participatory education. Hence, when discussing the French people with Gobineau, Tocqueville declared:

> You proudly despise the human species, at least ours; you believe it not only fallen but also incapable of ever raising itself up. Its very constitution condemns it to servitude. . . . For myself, feeling that I have neither the right nor the taste to entertain such opinions on my race and on my country, I think that it is not necessary to despair of them. In my eyes, *human societies like individuals become something only through the practice of liberty.*[60]

A [Maryland] Farmer similarly rejected misanthropic theories of human nature, and insisted on the American people's capacity for self-rule. Sounding much like Tocqueville, he wrote:

> That the people are not at present disposed for, and are actually incapable of, governments of simplicity and equal rights, I can no longer doubt—But whose fault is it? We make them bad, by bad governments, and then abuse and despise them for being so. Our people are capable of being made any thing, that human nature was or is capable of, if we would only have a little patience and give them good and wholesome institutions. . . . [61]

As the example of the jury illustrates, the Antifederalists believed that the framers of the Constitution had failed to create "good and wholesome institutions" insofar as they largely abandoned the task of founding and maintaining institutions that would foster the political participation—and thus the political *education*—of the people.[62]

The Antifederalists agreed with Tocqueville that mores were central to the success of a republic, but they also emphasized, as Tocqueville often did, that institutions were of crucial importance insofar as they shape the mores of the people. For instance, Tocqueville wrote that "nations

do not grow old as men do. Each fresh generation is new material for
the lawgiver to mold." By building institutions that "make men care for
the fate of their countries," the lawmaker can help produce citizens who
will preserve liberty in democratic times.[63] The battle over the Constitution was, of course, a battle over *institutions*, and the key concern of
the Antifederalists was with the Tocquevillian question of whether or not
the newly proposed institutions would produce liberty-loving citizens. As
Melancton Smith put it,

> Government operates upon the spirit of the people, as well as
> the spirit of the people operates upon it—and if they are not
> conformable to each other, the one or the other will prevail.
> In a less time than 25 years, the government will receive its
> tone. What the spirit of the country may be at the end of
> that period, it is impossible to foretell: Our duty is to frame
> a government friendly to liberty and the rights of mankind,
> which will tend to cherish and cultivate a love of liberty among
> our citizens.[64]

The Antifederalists opposed the Constitution, as A Customer succinctly
put it, because they believed its institutional framework would create
self-interested individuals devoted only to "the pursuit of wealth," as
opposed to a public-minded citizenry devoted to "politicks and religion."[65]
In other words, the Constitution would produce the kind of apathetic
and materialistic subjects that both the Antifederalists and Tocqueville
hoped to avoid.

The Antifederalists were opposed to the notion of creating one enormous republic in part because a large state only allows a tiny percentage
of the people to actively share in political rule. In a system of thirteen
confederated republics, a much higher proportion of citizens can participate
at the local and state levels. Moreover, by making the legislative districts
very large, and by making the terms of office relatively long, the framers
had decreased the amount of people who would be able not just to be
ruled, but also *to rule in turn*, as Aristotle would put it. Arguing for a more
frequent rotation of office, Melancton Smith declared that, "the true policy
of constitutions will be to increase the information of the country, and
disseminate the knowledge of government as universally as possible. . . . As
the Constitution now is, you only give an opportunity to two men to be
acquainted with the public affairs."[66] In short, the Antifederalists feared
that under the new Constitution, only the few would gain the education
that comes from actively participating in government.

One could argue that the new Constitution allows *local* and *state* politics to continue to flourish in a way that provides innumerable opportunities for citizen participation; however, the Antifederalists believed, as Smith put it, that ratification will mean that the "state governments, without object or authority, will soon dwindle into insignificance, and be despised by the people themselves."[67] Local governments would also lose significance, because power under the new regime would be centralized in the nation's capital. The only people who could genuinely experience public liberty, then, would be a small number of national officials.

Tocqueville, the Antifederalists, and Internalized Authority

As we have seen in chapter 1, Tocqueville believed that the doctrine of self-interest properly understood has an important role to play in the education of American democracy; however, Tocqueville also believed that the doctrine should be complemented by the religious and republican traditions, in order to elevate the citizens (at least some of the time) beyond interest-based politics.

Like Tocqueville, the Antifederalists looked to religion for authoritative norms that could point people toward the common good. Tocqueville wrote that, "Anglo-American civilization" is the "product of two perfectly distinct elements which elsewhere have often been at war with one another but which in America it was somehow possible to incorporate into each other, forming a marvelous combination." These two elements are "the *spirit of religion* and the *spirit of freedom*."[68] The Antifederalists exemplify Tocqueville's claim that Americans have tried to combine the spirit of religion and the spirit of freedom. Far more than their opponents, the Antifederalists emphasized the necessity of religion for a successful republic. Many of them argued that the problems Americans faced were not primarily the result of institutional defects, but rather the result of moral corruption that religion could address. As Alfred put it, "Perhaps the real evils we labor under, do not arise from [our political institutions]—There may be many other causes, to which our misfortunes may be properly attributed—Read the American constitutions, and you will find our essential rights and privileges well guarded and secured. May not *our manners* be the source of our national evils?"[69] Similarly, Mercy Warren wrote that, "a violation of manners has destroyed more states than the infraction of laws."[70] Much like Tocqueville, the Antifederalists believed that manners—or what Tocqueville calls *moeurs*—are crucial in shaping the fate of nations. And also like Tocqueville, the Antifederalists believed that manners should be shaped largely by religion. As Charles Turner put it, "without the prevalence of *Christian piety, and morals,* the best republican Constitution can never save us from slavery and ruin."[71] As the preceding quote suggests, the Antifederalists tended to speak of morality and religion almost interchangeably. Much like Tocqueville, they tended to assume that in order to be moral, people had to be religious.

As noted earlier, Main has suggested that the Antifederalists sought "to continu[e] the struggle for . . . individual freedom from restraint."[72] This claim can be misleading, though, for the Antifederalists certainly did not seek freedom from *moral* restraint. Like Tocqueville, many Antifederalists distinguished between liberty and license, and many believed that true freedom is not simply doing whatever one desires. For instance, David attacked the irreligious people of Rhode Island for doing "whatever they please without compunction. . . . [T]hey have no principles of restraint but laws of their own making; and from such laws may Heaven defend us."[73] Similarly, Mercy Warren condemned impious people who want to be "released from the restraints on their appetites and passions: restraints dictated by reason and revelation; and which, under the influence of sober reflection, forbid the indulgence of all gratifications that are injurious to man."[74]

Another important expression of the Antifederalist view on freedom comes from "William Penn." According to William Penn, the best government is "that which takes from [man] the least share of . . . liberty." Thus far, it appears that William Penn is making a quintessentially liberal, or even libertarian, argument. But then he asks: "What is liberty? What is that supreme good which every one feels, and so very few can define?—I would call it *the unlimited power of doing good.*"[75] Thus, even though William Penn, like other liberals, views *liberty* as the end of government, his definition of liberty is not the classic liberal notion of negative liberty. Rather, William Penn suggests, as did Winthrop and Tocqueville, that true freedom is not doing whatever one wants, but rather it involves doing only the "just and good."[76]

For both Tocqueville and the Antifederalists, Christianity provides positive ideals that can guide liberty. In the view of both Tocqueville and the Antifederalists, equality was one of these ideals. Aristocrotis, for instance, asserts that Christianity "prohibits slavery," for "it commands to call no man upon earth master or lord."[77] In Aristocrotis' view, Christianity is thus a scourge to the type of tyrannical government that the Constitution would create. Tocqueville would similarly suggest that Christianity teaches equality, and Tocqueville also pointed to the political implications of this doctrine: "Christianity, which has declared all men equal in the sight of God, cannot hesitate to acknowledge all citizens equal before the law."[78]

As the example of equality suggests, the positive ideals that the Antifederalists found in Christianity tended to overlap with their republican ideals. In her *History of the Rise, Progress, and Termination of the American Revolution*, Mercy Warren attempts to refute the charge that the growth of republican ideas in Europe led to the rise of impiety in modern Europe. Warren and other Antifederalists also believed in the inverse: Far from being opposed to republican ideas, Christianity actually *supports* republicanism. She writes, "It may be observed in the character of . . . modern republics, that religion has been the grand palladium of their institutions. Through all the free states of Italy, democracy and religion have been considered in union."[79] After all, she suggests, the virtues and vices that are celebrated or condemned by republicanism are often the same virtues and vices celebrated or condemned by Christianity.

This is a point that was made centuries earlier by St. Augustine. In a letter to Marcellinus, Augustine argues against the notion that "the preaching and teaching of Christ are not at all suitable for the morals of a republic."[80] The Christian virtues, he suggests, are actually "a great benefit for the republic," for as he noted in a letter to Nectarius, Christian churches teach precisely the same values that Cicero believed Roman citizens should be taught. These values include, according to Augustine, "frugality and continence, . . . fidelity to the marriage bond, and chaste, honorable, and upright morals."[81] A good Christian, then, can make for a good citizen of a republic.

In a similar vein, Warren's commitment to Christianity and her commitment to republicanism often blur together, so that one does not know where one ends and the other begins. For instance, Warren feared that one day Americans would be "a degenerate, servile race of beings, corrupted by wealth, effeminated by luxury, impoverished by licentiousness, and become the *automatons* of intoxicated ambition."[82] In this passage, it seems that Warren is motivated by both the Christian *and* republican opposition to greed and self-indulgence. Moreover, when Warren laments, as many Antifederalists did, that America might become "too selfish and avaricious for a virtuous republic," she again invokes both Christian and republican ideas, for both of these traditions call for frugality rather than avarice, and self-sacrifice rather than selfishness.[83]

To conclude this section on the Antifederalists and religion, it must be noted that many Antifederalists were opposed to the provision of the Constitution that states that "no religious Test shall ever be required as a Qualification to any Office or public Trust under the United States."[84]

With their opposition to the ban on religious tests, one can see that the Antifederalists were sometimes willing to use state power to promote and maintain religious orthodoxy. Tocqueville, in contrast, insisted that church and state should remain separate. Tocqueville certainly agreed with the Antifederalists that religion was necessary in a democracy, but Tocqueville was convinced that "any alliance with any political power whatsoever is bound to be burdensome for religion."[85] In other words, the Antifederalists were far more willing than Tocqueville was to have governmental leaders *actively* support Christianity; as Storing notes, "many Antifederalists supported and would even have strengthened the mild religious establishments that existed in some states."[86] Tocqueville was, as I argued in chapter 1, a *liberal*-republican who insisted that political leaders should not directly promote religion; in contrast, the Antifederalists sometimes moved toward an illiberal conception of the relationship between religion and the state. In my view, the Antifederalist claim that religion is healthy for a democracy is a claim that remains worth taking seriously, and there is much to be learned from the Antifederalists on the subject of authority and leadership. However, their support of religious tests and of state-established religion reminds us that the Antifederalists by no means offer a perfect blueprint for American political life today.

The Antifederalists and the Education of a Free People

The Antifederalists, like Tocqueville, hoped for an active citizenry that could successfully engage in self-rule. But for this to be possible, authority was required to educate the citizenry. The Antifederalist emphasis on developing the capacities of the citizenry is evident partly in their concern that the Constitution had not called for the creation of educational institutions. Charles Turner hoped that one of the first acts of the first Congress would be

> To recommend to the several States in the Union, the institution of such means of education, as shall be adequate to the divine, patriotick purpose of training up the children and youth at large, in that solid learning, and in those pious and moral principles, which are the support, the life and SOUL of the republican government and liberty, of which a free Constitution is the body; for as the body without the spirit is dead, so a free form of government without the animating principles of piety and virtue, is dead also. . . .[87]

Similarly, Denatus wrote that "the first, or second article" of the constitution should have established academies "at every proper place throughout the United States for the education of youth in morality [and] the principles of the Christian religion without regard to any sect, but pure and unadulterated as left by its divine author and his apostles."[88]

Article I, Section 8 of the Constitution does suggest that the federal government should "promote the progress of science and useful arts" (by granting patents), and this could imply a concern with scientific education. However, the Antifederalists noted that the Constitution is conspicuously silent on the matter of *moral* education. Denatus writes that human beings

> are subject to many jarring propensities. Among these, vanity, ambition, and the love of riches, are not the least.—While reason and conscience can confine the passions, their action and re-action on each other, constitute human happiness. But when they overcome reason and conscience, they produce our misery. To guard against this misfortune, as much as human foresight could discover, ought to have been the chief business of the late foederal convention.[89]

But rather than make the moral education of the citizenry their "chief business," Madison warned in *Federalist* 10 that "we well know that neither moral nor religious motives can be relied on as an adequate control" over "the injustice and violence of individuals."[90] Instead of trying to control the dangerous passions through education, Publius argued that these passions could be effectively neutralized if given free rein in a large and diverse republic. In other words, Publius seeks to create an institutional structure that would function well even with primarily self-interested citizens. After all, people will always tend to be "ambitious, vindictive, and rapacious," as Hamilton puts it in *Federalist* 6.[91] Publius, then, largely abandoned the ancient hope of making men more virtuous; Publius instead accepts men as they are, with all their avarice and self-regarding behavior.

In fairness to Madison, it should be noted that he did not believe that a republic could survive if it *completely* lacked virtue. When debating ratification of the Virginia state Constitution, Madison said, "No theoretical checks, no form of government can render us secure. To suppose that any form of government will secure liberty or happiness without any virtue in the people, is a chimerical idea."[92] Specifically, Madison believed that the people needed sufficient virtue to select skillful leaders; he did not argue, though, that the citizenry needed to be deeply attached to the common good. His overarching aim, then, was to create a political machine that would not depend on a high degree of civic virtue in the people in order to function well.

In contrast to Publius, Tocqueville in no way placed his faith in clever constitutional designs. Tocqueville wrote, "I accord institutions only a secondary influence on the destiny of men."[93] For Tocqueville, it was mores, not laws, which were primary. Much like the Antifederalists, then, Tocqueville believed that something like virtue was necessary if a republic was to thrive, and he believed that through education, people's virtuous qualities could be brought out. In 1831 Tocqueville wrote of France:

> I still hope more than I fear. It seems to me that in the midst of our chaos I perceive one incontestable fact. This is that for forty years we have made immense progress in the practical understanding of the ideas of liberty. Nations, like private people, need to acquire an education before they know how to behave. That our education advances, I cannot doubt.[94]

Like the Antifederalists, Tocqueville believed that through the proper kind of political and moral education, people can be made virtuous enough so that they can live freely. True freedom demands that the individual engage in self-mastery, and true freedom manifests itself when individuals who have mastered their passions then join together as citizens to collectively shape their common world. Much like Rousseau, Tocqueville believed that freedom is the noblest and grandest of people's faculties, but it can be attained in the modern world only under certain strict conditions, and only with a certain kind of education. As Tocqueville put it: "nothing is more fertile in marvels than the art of being free, but nothing is harder than freedom's apprenticeship."[95]

Because the Antifederalists hoped for a polity in which a virtuous citizenry could exercise self-rule, one must reject Kenyon's claim that the Antifederalists were "men of little faith." The Antifederalists actually had a tremendous amount of faith in the ability of ordinary citizens to run their own affairs, as long as they were properly educated.[96] Kenyon asserts that, "the speeches and essays of the Antifederalists were peculiarly lacking in the great expressions of faith in the people which are to be found in the writings of Jefferson, and even occasionally in *The Federalist* itself."[97] However, the evidence suggests that the Antifederalists *did* often celebrate the capacities of the people. For instance, A Customer attacks those who have abandoned "the old fashioned ides of 1775, viz. that the common people were good judges in the affairs of government; and that their time was well spent when it was devoted to the study of politicks."[98] Moreover, Kenyon's own one volume collection of Antifederalist writings includes the splendid satire by Montezuma, who mocks the idea "of drawing a line between" those who are supposedly "*ordained* to govern, and such as were *made* to bear the weight of government without having any share in its administration." Rejecting the idea that ordinary people are "totally incapable of thinking or acting in governmental matters," the essay by Montezuma suggests that ordinary people must play an active role in their own government.[99] Aristocrotis, another skillful satirist, also attacks the notion that the people should "mind their own business, and leave the affairs of government to those whom nature hath [allegedly] destined to rule."[100]

Whereas the Federalists lowered their sights and tried to work with the passions and the interests, the Antifederalists still clung to a faith that with the proper political and religious education, ordinary people could sufficiently (if never completely) overcome their selfish interests and passions to the point where republican government would be possible. It was the Federalists who in a sense gave up this ancient republican faith, for it is they who tried to found government on the principle of self-interest rather than on people's higher capacities.

Storing has argued that even though the Antifederalists were concerned with virtue, they should ultimately be considered modern liberals because "they see the end of government as the security of individual liberty, not the promotion of virtue or the fostering of some organic common good." Because they view "virtue and the common good [as] instrumental to individual liberty," any "resemblance to preliberal thought is superficial."[101] My analysis suggests, though, that in their understanding of authority, the Antifederalists did draw on preliberal notions in a more than superficial way. Modern liberals tend to view authority primarily as a threat to individual liberty. However, this was not the usual Antifederalist view. Like Tocqueville, they valued internalized religious and moral authority because they discipline individual liberty and provide it with worthwhile ends. This is a decidedly preliberal understanding of authority that draws on both classical and religious themes.

This notion of authority that one finds in Tocqueville and the Antifederalists points both forward and backward. It points backward to the ancients, who believed, as Plato puts it in the *Republic*, that the task of authority is "to educate human beings and make them better."[102] But this notion of authority also looks forward, to political scientists such as Burns, who argue that authority is not domination, but rather a process that leads "people upward, to some higher values or purpose or form of self-fulfillment."[103]

We have now seen that the Antifederalists rejected the Constitution in large part because of its threat to both authority and leadership in

America. First, it threatened the continued existence of educative authority, or at the very least it did not do enough to strengthen this type of authority. As the example of the jury exemplified, the Antifederalists feared that the Constitution had failed to create participatory institutions that would develop the political capacities of the people. Moreover, by creating a single "consolidated" government with a distant capital, the constitutional framework would diminish the local and state governments that alone could provide a participatory political education for the many. Furthermore, the Antifederalists feared that the Constitution would diminish the authority of religious and republican ideas. By building a system that both relied upon and promoted the principle of self-interest, the framers were weakening the authoritative ideals of both Christianity and republicanism. The Constitution's failure to provide for schools, and its ban on religious tests for office were further signs that the framers had neglected the moral and religious authority that is necessary to sustain a free people. In addition to weakening educative authority, we have seen that the Antifederalists feared that the Constitution would fail to provide for democratic leaders who are close to the people. The Antifederalists believed that representatives of the new government would lack genuine authority insofar as they lacked "the confidence of the people." Too distant from the people to be trusted, the representatives would not be able to persuade or educate the people. The representatives would not truly have the support of the people, and as a result the government would lack genuine energy and vigor.

Because the Constitution would lead to the decline of authority, liberty—in both its positive and negative senses—would also disappear. Without educative authority, liberty would degenerate into license, as people would be ruled by their passions or by their selfish interests. People would come to lack a salutary sense of what freedom is for—they would lack, that is, a sense of the good. Hence, positive liberty—the freedom to develop one's capacities and to strive toward the good—would be threatened. And without leaders who are close to the people, freedom in its simple negative sense would also be wiped out, for if the leaders do not have the confidence of the people, then *force* would be used to ensure obedience.

Tocqueville's Attempted Fusion of Antifederalism and Federalism

Like Tocqueville, the Antifederalists' main concern was with the fate of liberty in the modern world. Moreover, we have seen that the Antifederalists and Tocqueville often understood the need for leadership and authority in democratic times in strikingly similar ways. However, it should be noted that there is also a significant component of Tocqueville's thought that closely resembles Federalist rather than Antifederalist ideas on leadership. For as we have seen in chapter 1, Tocqueville endorses the Federalist theory regarding the role of representation. Like the Federalists, Tocqueville believed that at the national level, it is best to have the government controlled by elites who are distant from the people. For both the Federalists and Tocqueville, the representatives should think of themselves not primarily as the people's delegates, but rather as independent-minded leaders who can filter out the dangerous passions of the people. The Antifederalists, in contrast, articulate a model of leadership according to which leaders should remain close to the people. We have seen that this does not necessarily mean that the Antifederalists wanted leaders to always simply enact the views of the majority into law. On the contrary, the Antifederalists envisioned a process in which leaders engage in dialogue with the people and thus sometimes persuade the people to change their minds about public policies. In the view of the Antifederalists, this educative process can only take place, though, if the representative is known by the people, and is close to the people's values and aspirations.

In addition to agreeing with the Federalists regarding representation, it should also be noted that Tocqueville praised the basic framework of government created by the Constitution. Whereas the Antifederalists attacked the idea of a "consolidated" government that would act directly upon citizens, Tocqueville writes approvingly that, "In America the union's subjects are not states but private citizens."[104] Indeed, while Tocqueville's critique of administrative centralization has been widely celebrated, his praise for what he called "governmental centralization" is sometimes neglected. In praising "governmental centralization," Tocqueville often sounded like Publius. For instance, in his discussion of the German empire, Tocqueville reminds one of Publius criticizing the Articles of Confederation:

> The German Empire . . . has never been able to take full advantage of its powers. . . . But why? Because the national power has never been centralized, because the state has never been able to enforce obedience to its general laws, because the separate parts of this great body have always had the right and the ability to refuse their cooperation to the representatives of the common authority even in matters of common interest; in other words, because it has never had any centralization of government.[105]

Tocqueville vehemently opposed administrative centralization, for he wanted communities to run their own local affairs. But Tocqueville also insisted that a nation needed a strong central government for "the enactment of general laws" and foreign policy.[106]

Wilson Carey McWilliams has demonstrated that in certain respects, Tocqueville "refined and restated the Antifederalist case."[107] However, if one considers Tocqueville's views on representation and on governmental centralization, one can see that there is also a quasi-Federalist strand of thought running through Tocqueville's writings on America.[108] Ultimately, then, Tocqueville's understanding of leadership and authority is fascinating in part because it attempts to fuse Antifederalism and Federalism.

Tocqueville's effort to synthesize Antifederalism and Federalism rests on an attempt to distinguish between local and national politics. Tocqueville argued that at the *local* level, the people should actively rule themselves through participatory institutions, and they should also be nurtured by moral and religious authority. Only then will freedom be actualized, and only then will people's moral, intellectual, and political capacities be fully developed. In these respects, Tocqueville agreed with the Antifederalists. But when it comes to *national* politics, with all of their complexity, Tocqueville believed that wise representatives were needed who would exercise their own independent judgment, for most people will lack the necessary expertise that national government requires. Hence, Tocqueville wrote to John Stuart Mill that, "It is much less essential for the partisans of democracy to find means of governing the nation, than to teach the nation to choose the men most capable of governing; and to exercise sufficient influence over the general nature of their government without interfering with their individual acts or means of execution."[109] In this respect, Tocqueville tended to agree with the Federalists, for it is they who wanted elected elites to manage national affairs. Whereas the Antifederalists wanted Congressional representatives to "be a true picture of the people," both the Federalists and Tocqueville believed that the legislature should consist of a select group of exceptional statesmen who are different from most people insofar as they have superior wisdom and virtue.[110] In *Federalist* 57, Madison writes that, "The aim of every political constitution is, or ought to be, first to obtain for rulers men who possess most wisdom to discern, and most virtue to pursue, the common good of the society...."[111] This passage suggests that the primary aim of the framers was to ensure that the best people should rule. In contrast, the Antifederalists were more interested in forming a Constitution that would produce a public-spirited citizenry that could largely rule itself. In short, Tocqueville agreed with the Antifederalists regarding the importance of a politically active citizenry at the local level, but he simultaneously agreed with the Federalists regarding the necessity of rule by elites at the national level.

At first glance, Tocqueville's combination of Antifederalism and Federalism may have considerable appeal. However, Tocqueville's attempt to fuse Antifederalism and Federalism may, in the end, be less than fully coherent. For the question must be asked: Over the long-term, can Antifederalist local politics really coexist with the Federalist vision of national politics? According to the Antifederalists, the answer is no, and they would accuse Tocqueville of simultaneously desiring to have two political regimes that are in fact incommensurable. The Antifederalists and Tocqueville shared largely the same nightmare—namely, that an apathetic, materialistic, and self-interested citizenry would be dominated by an all-encompassing centralized power. The Antifederalists would argue, though, that Tocqueville failed to see how the Constitution *itself* would help lead to their shared nightmare. Deeply impressed by *The Federalist*'s brilliant arguments, Tocqueville may have been blind to the ways in which the Constitution could change not just the institutions, but the *spirit* of the American regime. In the Antifederalist view, the Constitution would work to eliminate the local freedom that both they and Tocqueville desired. Whereas Tocqueville blamed the rise of individualism, apathy, and materialism on the worldwide movement toward equality of conditions, the Antifederalists warned that the Constitution itself would have these same corrupting effects. For as Martin Diamond notes, Madison's system "involved a fundamental reliance on ceaseless striving after immediate interest (perhaps now immediate gratification)."[112] This means that Madison's constitutional machinery may have largely succeeded in eliminating the danger of majority faction, but it may have also produced a citizenry that is too self-absorbed and individualistic to maintain the freedom which Tocqueville teaches can only come from participating in public life.

To put it another way, unlike Tocqueville, the Antifederalists were able to perceive that the Constitution would cause the "revolutionary spirit in America," as Hannah Arendt put it, "to wither away."[113] By "revolutionary spirit," Arendt refers to the spirit of participatory freedom, which both she and Tocqueville celebrated.[114] In Arendt's view, "the fateful failure of the Constitution . . . to incorporate the townships and the town-hall meetings, the original springs of all political activity in the country, amounted to a death sentence for them."[115] Prescient in so many other respects, Tocqueville may have failed to understand that the framers of the Constitution had set the nation on a course that would result in the decline of a vibrant political life at the local level. Indeed, the Antifederalists would certainly not be surprised by the recent claims of social scientists that America's civic life is in disarray. For instance, the

Antifederalists would not be surprised by the low amounts of political and civic participation noted by such scholars as Robert Putnam, because the Antifederalists were convinced that the Constitution was not designed to facilitate or encourage active citizenship.[116] Nor would the Antifederalists be surprised by the prevalence of individualism noted by Robert Bellah et al., because the Antifederalists believed that the Federalists *intended* to create a regime that was built largely on the pursuit of self-interest rather than devotion to the common good.[117]

Despite the disagreement between the Antifederalists and Tocqueville over the Constitution, Tocqueville's thought is still closer, in the end, to the Antifederalists than it is to the Federalists. In a beautiful summation of the Antifederalist ethos, Storing writes that, "The Antifederalists saw, although sometimes only dimly, the insufficiency of a community of mere interest. They saw that the American polity had to be a moral community if it was to be anything, and they saw that the seat of that community must be the hearts of the people."[118] Tocqueville also fundamentally rejected the idea of "a community of mere interest." He once lamented, "No longer do ideas, but interests only, form the links between men. . . ."[119] And, he complained of France in 1848 that, "common opinions, feelings, and ideas are more and more being replaced by particular interests, particular aims, and points of view carried over from private life and private interests."[120] Both Tocqueville and the Antifederalists believed that authority is necessary to provide the common ideals that make a community transcend the politics of interest. They both remind us that without these authoritative ideals, a nation may be prosperous, but it nonetheless risks "moral squalor and ruin," as Tocqueville said of France in 1848.[121] They both remind us, in short, that democracy cannot truly thrive without authority.

Chapter 3

⊷⟹⟸⊶

Lincoln and Tocqueville
on Democratic Leadership and
Self-Interest Properly Understood

In this chapter, Abraham Lincoln's ideas on democratic leadership are examined through the lens of Tocqueville's political theory. Scholars have sought to understand Lincoln's thought by carefully considering it in the light of a wide variety of political thinkers, including Aristotle,[1] Machiavelli,[2] Locke,[3] Winthrop,[4] Bentham,[5] and Weber.[6] Detailed discussions of Tocqueville, however, are surprisingly scarce in the literature on Lincoln. Of course, Tocqueville has not been *completely* ignored in recent scholarship on Lincoln. Stewart Winger notes that "Tocqueville and the Whigs [including Lincoln] both jabbed at a bellicose Young America."[7] In another recent book on Lincoln and religion, Joseph Fornieri connects Lincoln to Tocqueville by suggesting that Lincoln's "biblical republicanism" exemplified Tocqueville's claim that in America "the spirits of religion and of freedom" work together in harmony.[8] Winger and Fornieri can help us begin to see the relevance of Tocqueville for understanding Lincoln's approach to religion, morality, and politics, but they do not compare Lincoln's and Tocqueville's ideas on democratic leadership, and the connections that they do make between Lincoln and Tocqueville are not fully drawn out.[9]

According to Michael Rogin, Lincoln's "vision spoke to desires for liberation deeply embedded in the culture and in Lincoln himself. Lincoln embodied the wish to be free."[10] Lincoln was, indeed, a great lover of liberty, and he fully deserved the name the "Great Emancipator." However, Lincoln did not believe that Americans should be emancipated from *all* forms of authority. Rather, Lincoln believed—and demonstrated—that it is the task of the democratic leader to guide, educate, inspire, and restrain the citizenry. Lincoln thus would have largely agreed with the admonition of Tocqueville in *Democracy in America*: "The first duty imposed on those who now direct society is to educate democracy; to put, if possible, new life into its beliefs" and "to purify its mores."[11]

I will argue that in certain respects, the case of Lincoln helps to confirm the wisdom of Tocqueville's ideas on the role of leadership in a democracy. But in other respects, Lincoln's thought exposes the weaknesses and limitations of Tocqueville's understanding of democratic leadership. Both Tocqueville and Lincoln had a similar understanding of the American character, and they both believed that the task of leadership was to elevate and educate this character. In order to accomplish this task, they both believed that leaders should rely largely—but not exclusively—on what Tocqueville called the doctrine of self-interest properly understood. Lincoln differed from Tocqueville, however, insofar as Lincoln suggested that leaders in a democracy must remain close to the people's fundamental values and aspirations. Lincoln was such an effective democratic leader in large part because he simultaneously critiqued *and* embraced those aspects of the American character that worried Tocqueville.[12] Lincoln and Tocqueville agreed that leaders should try to elevate and educate the citizenry, but Tocqueville usually failed to recognize the element of mutuality that successful democratic leadership requires. I also argue that while Lincoln and Tocqueville both believed in the importance of authoritative moral foundations in a democracy, Lincoln's version of foundationalism has a dynamic and flexible quality that is lacking in Tocqueville's theory.

To make my argument, I focus primarily on Lincoln's speeches and writings in the years before the Civil War, when his main goal was to thwart the spread of slavery. Lincoln's moral leadership in the years between the Kansas-Nebraska Act of 1854, and his election to the presidency in 1860, has already been brilliantly discussed by Harry Jaffa, William Lee Miller, and others. However, when we examine Lincoln's leadership before his presidency in the light of Tocqueville, our understanding of both Lincoln and Tocqueville is further deepened.

Lincoln, Tocqueville, and the Role of Self-Interest Properly Understood

Lincoln and Tocqueville had a deep understanding of the American character that in many respects was quite similar. Above all, they both recognized that the American character was marked by a strong concern with self-interest. Lincoln accepted, as did Tocqueville, that self-interest would always play a large role in American politics. And like Tocqueville, Lincoln believed that leaders should try to educate the people so that interest would become "properly understood," as Tocqueville put it. However, in the end, both Lincoln and Tocqueville recognized the limits of self-interest as a principle for politics, and they hoped for a democratic citizenry that could at times transcend altogether a politics based on self-interest.

Ultimately, Tocqueville hoped that religious, moral, and political authority could elevate the citizenry above a politics based on something higher than "miserable day-to-day interests."[13] And yet, Tocqueville certainly acknowledged that material self-interest would always play a large role in the modern, egalitarian world. For instance, Tocqueville wrote that religious authority can hope to "purify, control, and restrain" the "taste for well-being which men acquire in times of equality," but it can never "conquer it entirely and abolish it."[14]

Lincoln similarly accepted that self-interest, in one form or another, would always play a large role in American politics. In arguing for a National Bank system rather than a Sub-Treasury system, as a young Whig Lincoln declared:

> We then, do not say . . . that Bank officers are more honest than Government officers. . . . What we do say, is, that the *interest* of the Sub-Treasurer is *against his duty*—while the *interest* of the Bank is *on the side of its duty*. . . . And who that knows anything of human nature, doubts that, in many instances, interest will prevail over duty, and that the Sub-Treasurer will prefer opulent knavery in a foreign land, to honest poverty at home?[15]

Lincoln here reveals his agreement with one of the basic insights of the framers of the Constitution—namely, that since people are not angels, it is futile to assume that religious or moral education can ever completely eliminate our selfish passions and interests. A wise legislator, then, will try to design a political system in which interest and duty coincide. Lincoln argued that with the Bank system, "Its *interest* . . . is on the side of its duty . . . and consequently, even the dishonest amongst its managers, have no temptation to be faithless to it."[16] This argument parallels that of *Federalist* 51, wherein Madison argues that under the Constitution, "the private interest of every individual [will] be a centinel over the public rights."[17] Both Madison and Lincoln believed that institutions can be designed in such a way that private interests are harnessed for the sake of the common good. As we shall see, Lincoln believed that ultimately, these types of institutional mechanisms were insufficient for the task of maintaining a just political regime, for in Lincoln's view, a just regime requires substantive ideals, and not just clever institutional mechanisms that check (or even fruitfully employ) the passions and interests. Nevertheless, Lincoln believed that while these institutional mechanisms are insufficient, they are nevertheless a necessary starting point, given the melancholy facts of human nature.

Another example of Lincoln's conviction that institutions can usefully channel self-interest can be found in his discussion of the patent. In his Lecture on Discoveries and Inventions, Lincoln praises the invention of the patent as a mechanism that "added the fuel of *interest* to the *fire* of genius, in the discovery and production of new and useful things."[18] In other words, by providing a financial incentive for individuals to make discoveries that can end up helping everyone, the patent system manages to harness individual self-interest for the sake of the common good.

Lincoln accepted, then, as did Tocqueville and the framers, that for better or for worse, interest would play a very large role in American politics. A final example of this is his opinion on the draft. In a document that was never issued, Lincoln wrote:

> At the beginning of the war, and ever since, a variety of motives pressing, some in one direction and some in the other, would be presented to the mind of each man physically fit for a soldier, upon the combined effect of which motives, he would, or would not, voluntarily enter the service. . . . We already have, and have had in the service, as appears, substantially all that can be obtained upon this voluntary weighing of motives. And yet we must somehow obtain more, or relinquish the original object of the contest . . . To meet this necessity the law for the draft has been enacted.[19]

In Lincoln's view, public appeals to duty and the common good cannot be relied upon to cause people to overcome their aversion to something that they do not feel is in their own interest. Because of this realistic understanding of human motives, Lincoln insisted that a draft was necessary if free government was to be maintained. Since Americans are generally self-interested, they must in extreme cases be forced to work for the common good, at least during a crisis when the fate of the republic hangs in the balance. Lincoln did highly value persuasion, as my discussion of the Temperance Address will reveal; but if men could not be persuaded to enter the army voluntarily because of their narrowly self-interested motives, then they must be got involuntarily.[20]

"We have been mistaken all our lives," Lincoln once said, "if we do not know whites as well as blacks look to their self-interest."[21] But this raises a problem: How can people be induced to act justly? Lincoln believed that elected officials can often be induced to act justly if institutions are designed in such a way that interest and official duty coincide. But what about the citizenry? How are *they* to be induced to act justly? As we have seen in the case of the draft, Lincoln believed that during a great crisis, people can legitimately be forced to act justly—that is, they should be compelled to sacrifice their private interest for the common good. But Lincoln knew that although this principle was valid in times of great crisis, in normal times a free polity cannot rely on this principle of force and still remain a free polity. But if force cannot be relied upon, what is to prevent a free people from trampling the rights of others if they perceive it would be in their self-interest to do so? How can a free people be made to restrain itself and act in accordance with justice? This was the same problem faced by Tocqueville: In a nation that lacks the ordering institutions of an aristocracy, what is to prevent ordered liberty from degenerating into license?

Part of Lincoln's answer is that democratic leaders must persuade the citizenry that it is in their own self-interest to do what is right. This approach is precisely one of the strategies recommended by Tocqueville. As we have seen, in *Democracy* Tocqueville argues that leaders in democratic times should attempt to educate the people morally in part by using the doctrine of self-interest properly understood. Tocqueville was well aware of Montesquieu's argument that virtue was crucial to the success of any republic. But it is futile, in Tocqueville's view, for leaders to demand lots of purely self-sacrificing behavior from modern peoples, for in the modern age, when ties between people and between generations have been cut, most people will focus their thoughts on themselves. In the modern, egalitarian world, "private interest will more than ever become the chief if not the only driving force behind all behavior." But despite this dominance of private interest, moral leaders should not despair of the possibility that people might act in accordance with justice and the common good. Although most people will act according to self-interest, "we have yet to see how each man will *interpret* his private interest."[22] Through "the doctrine of self-interest properly understood," Tocqueville hoped that Americans could be taught that serving others will be to their own benefit. In *Democracy*, then, Tocqueville concludes that, "Contemporary moralists . . . should give most of their attention" to the doctrine.[23]

Throughout his career, Abraham Lincoln did indeed give much (if not most) of his attention to this doctrine. Tocqueville writes that American moralists often "eagerly call attention" to "those points where private advantage does meet and coincide with" doing what is right.[24] One early example of how Lincoln tried to point out the coincidence of justice and self-interest comes in his Temperance Address. Near the end of this speech, Lincoln suggests that the temperance cause is not only a just cause, but also a cause that will not harm the interests of anyone, including those who make or sell alcohol! As Lincoln puts it, "By [the temperance revolution], none [will be] wounded in feeling, *none injured in interest*. Even the dram-maker, and dram seller, will have glided into other occupations so gradually, as never to have felt the shock of change."[25] Although Lincoln's specific claim about the effects of the temperance movement on those who work in the liquor industry seems implausible, the passage is nevertheless revealing of Lincoln's constant strategy of arguing that doing what is right is also in accordance with private interest, or at least will not harm private interest.

In his speech on the *Dred Scott* decision, Lincoln openly discussed this Tocquevillian strategy of appealing to self-interest properly understood. At the end of his speech he turns to the issue of colonization. He states that,

> Separation, if ever effected at all, must be effected by colonization. . . . The enterprise is a difficult one; but "when there is a will there is a way;" and what colonization needs most is a hearty will. *Will springs from the two elements of moral sense and self-interest. Let us be brought to believe it is morally right, and, at the same time, favorable to, or, at least, not against, our interest*, to transfer the African to his native clime, and we shall find a way to do it, however great the task may be.[26]

It is not my present purpose to discuss the problems raised by Lincoln's call for colonization.[27] Instead, I want to call attention to the underlying philosophy of statesmanship that one finds in this passage. For Lincoln here articulates his strategy as a leader: He will appeal to the "moral sense" of the American people, but he will also appeal to their "interest." When appealing to their interest, however, he will not simply appeal to their preconceived, narrow notions of interest; instead, as a genuine leader he will *educate* people so that they properly understand their fundamental interests.

In a privately written piece "On Sectionalism," Lincoln explained why the anti-slavery cause would fail if it appealed solely to the "moral sense" of Northern whites. Lincoln noted that while advocates of slavery expansion sometimes find votes in the North, "restrictionists" never find votes in the South. Lincoln wrote that this is because [in slavery extension] the people of the South have an immediate palpable and immensely great pecuniary interest; . . . This immense, palpable pecuniary interest, on the question of extending slavery, unites the Southern people, as one man. But it can not be demonstrated that the *North* will gain a dollar by restricting it. Moral principle is all, or nearly all, that unites us of the North. Pity 'tis, it is so, but this is a looser bond, than pecuniary interest. Right here is the plain cause of *their perfect* union and *our want* of it.[28]

In order to overcome the power of the South's united pecuniary interest in slavery, Lincoln decided to follow a strategy whereby the North would be united by its moral sense *and* a proper understanding of its self-interest. If the moral sense and the self-interest of Northerners were both stoked by the Republican leadership, the anti-slavery cause could perhaps win out against a South united solely by pecuniary interest.

Self-Interest, Slavery, and the South

Because of his belief in the power of material self-interest, Lincoln was pessimistic regarding the possibility that the South could be persuaded voluntarily to abandon slavery. As we shall see, Lincoln did believe that it was actually in the self-interest (properly understood) of every American—North and South—to reject slavery. However, he did not think that Southerners would likely be brought to recognize their long-term interest in ending slavery, since their short-term, pecuniary interest in maintaining slavery was so enormous. As Lincoln put it at New Haven,

> The slaveholder does not like to be considered a mean fellow . . . and hence he has to struggle within himself and sets about arguing himself into the belief that Slavery is right. . . . Whether the owners of this species of property do really see it as it is, it is not for me to say, but if they do, they see it as it is through 2,000,000,000 of dollars, and that is a pretty thick coating.[29]

Tocqueville wrote that, "In America it is not virtue which is great, it is temptation which is small, which amounts to the same thing."[30] Lincoln would have agreed with the logic of Tocqueville's point, but Lincoln might have added that in the South, there is nothing "small" about temptation. In the South, the temptation of two billion dollars had succeeded in corrupting the moral sense of the whites. Northerners should be loath to judge their Southern brethren too harshly, though, for Northerners would no doubt also be unable to resist the temptation of two billion dollars if faced with it. As Lincoln put it at Kalamazoo, "our Southern brethren do not differ from us. They are, like us, subject to passions. . . ."[31]

According to Lincoln, the human soul naturally contains both self-ish and just impulses. At Alton Lincoln said, "the Bible says somewhere that we are desperately selfish. I think we would have discovered that fact without the Bible. I do not claim that I am any less so than the average of men, but I do claim that I am not more selfish than Judge Douglas."[32] And at Peoria Lincoln declared that, "Slavery is founded in the selfishness of man's nature—opposition to it, is his love of justice."[33] Taken together, these statements suggest that *all* of us are at least in part selfish, and hence slavery—or, more generally, mastery, the urge to dominate others—is a temptation for anyone who is given the opportunity to exercise it. The great temptation of mastery was made clear in Lincoln's fragment on "pro-slavery theology:"

> [S]uppose the Rev. Dr. Ross has a slave named Sambo, and the question is "is it the Will of God that Sambo shall remain a slave, or be set free?" The Almighty gives no audable answer to the question. . . . No one thinks of asking Sambo's opinion on it. So, at last, it comes to this, that *Dr. Ross* is to decide the question. And while he considers it, he sits in the shade, with gloves on his hands, and subsists on the bread that Sambo is earning in the burning sun. If he decides that God Wills Sambo to continue a slave, he thereby retains his own comfortable position; but if he decides that God wills Sambo to be free, he thereby has to walk out of the shade, throw off his gloves, and delve for his own bread. Will Dr. Ross be actuated by that perfect impartiality, which has ever been considered most favorable to correct decisions?[34]

Clearly, Dr. Ross is not an especially evil person; indeed, it would take a saintly person to be perfectly impartial in such a situation. Given what Lincoln calls the selfishness of human nature, it is difficult voluntarily to renounce mastery once one has enjoyed its conveniences.

Once slavery is allowed to arise, then, it is very difficult to eradicate, given its temptations. Hence, Lincoln wanted to ban slavery in the territories before it had a chance to become established there. Lincoln was not persuaded by the argument that due to considerations of climate and geography, slavery would not spread to Northern territories irrespective of whether or not it was officially banned. Slavery has no "natural limits" in Lincoln's view, because it is rooted, at bottom, not in climate, geography, or the current state of technology, but rather in the selfishness of human nature itself.[35]

Of course, Lincoln was aware that at one point in American history slavery *was* voluntarily relinquished, at least in part of the country. In 1855 Lincoln wrote: "That spirit which desired the peaceful extinction of slavery, has itself become extinct, with the *occasion*, and the *men* of the Revolution. Under the impulse of that occasion, nearly half the states adopted systems of emancipation at once; and it is a significant fact, that not a single state has done the like since."[36] Lincoln here echoed his earlier argument in the Lyceum Address, in which he stated that under "the powerful influence" of the revolution, "the jealousy, envy, and avarice, incident to our nature, and so common to a state of peace, prosperity, and conscious strength, were, for the time, in a great measure smothered and rendered inactive. . . . [T]hus, from the force of circumstances, the basest principles of our nature, were . . . made to lie dormant."[37] According to Lincoln, then, the American Revolution was one of those rare historical moments when the selfish side of people was almost entirely subdued by the side of our nature that loves both liberty and justice. But as Lincoln said in the Lyceum Address, "this state of feeling *must fade, is fading, has faded*, with the circumstances that produced it."[38] Now that the patriotic fervor of the Revolution has passed, the avarice of our nature has reemerged, and it will be virtually impossible to persuade Southerners to renounce their highly valuable human property. In the Lyceum Address, Lincoln hoped that "[r]eason, cold, calculating, unimpassioned reason," might be able to inspire the same love of liberty that the Revolution once inspired.[39] But Lincoln must have known that cold, calculating reason could not convince Southerners to emancipate the slaves; on the contrary, through the use of instrumental, calculating reason Southerners would most likely conclude, as Dr. Ross no doubt did, that it is in their self-interest to remain masters over other human beings.[40]

Self-Interest, Slavery, and the North

Although Lincoln had few hopes that Southerners could be made to see that it was in their own long-term self-interest to end slavery, he had high hopes that Northerners could be motivated by self-interest to oppose slavery expansion. To be sure, Lincoln primarily used moral arguments to attack slavery. Lincoln's political pragmatism and constitutional philosophy prevented him from becoming a full-fledged abolitionist, but his speeches still contained many withering attacks on slavery as intrinsically immoral. He called slavery a "monstrous injustice," and he insisted over and over again that the Republican Party should never cease to declare slavery to be a great moral wrong, and to treat is as such.[41]

But along with his frequent morality-based attacks on slavery, Lincoln often emphasized that Northerners also had a definite *interest* in thwarting the spread of slavery. To those who would say that white Northerners should "care not" whether slavery is voted up or down in the distant territories, Lincoln made a number of arguments designed to convince his constituents that slavery extension in fact threatened their self-interest properly understood.

One of Lincoln's main interest-based arguments was an economic argument. According to Lincoln's economic thought, there was no fixed class of wageworkers in America. People of limited means can work for someone else for a year or two, save money, and then eventually go into business for themselves. "If any continue through life in the condition of the hired laborer," said Lincoln at Milwaukee, "it is not the fault of the system, but because of either a dependent nature which prefers it, or improvidence, folly, or singular misfortune."[42] As Richard Hofstadter pointed out, Lincoln's argument about social mobility would soon be rendered largely anachronistic by the closing of the frontier and the concentration of capital that accompanied industrialization.[43] But in the 1850s, Lincoln's argument still seemed plausible to an audience of Northern whites. Lincoln tried to convince his audience that this argument would continue to be plausible, but only if the territories were left available for free white labor. As Lincoln said in his seventh debate with Douglas:

> I think we have some interest [in the territories]. I think that as white men we have. Do we not wish for an outlet for our surplus population, if I may so express myself? . . . Now irrespective of the moral aspect of this question as to whether there is a right or wrong in enslaving a negro, I am still in favor of our new Territories being in such a condition that white men may find a home—may find some spot where they can better their condition—where they can settle upon new soil and better their condition in life.[44]

By emphasizing the importance of the territories as a kind of safety valve, Lincoln thus never really directly refuted the logic behind George Fitzhugh's claim that:

> Until the lands of America are appropriated by a few, population becomes dense, competition among laborers active, employment

uncertain, and wages low, the personal blessings of liberty for whites will continue to be a blessing. We have vast unsettled territories; population may cease to increase slowly, as in most countries, and many centuries may elapse before the question will be practically suggested, whether slavery to capital be preferable to slavery to human masters.[45]

Lincoln stated at Milwaukee that the "mud sill" theorists fail to recognize that there is no fixed class of wage-workers in America; however, he failed to rebut Fitzhugh's argument that the absence of a fixed working-class in the North was dependent on the existence of unsettled territories for free whites to settle.[46] Indeed, without the safety valve of free territories, Lincoln implied, a permanent class of wageworkers, utterly dependent on their employers, could arise in America. The struggle against slavery expansion, then, was often presented by Lincoln as a struggle to maintain economic mobility for whites.

Tocqueville had also recognized that slavery could be attacked by appealing to the economic self-interest of whites. "In the United States," he observed, "people abolish slavery for the sake not of the Negroes but of the white men." Tocqueville argued that in the North, work is considered to be "honorable," and upward mobility is a distinct possibility; as a result, Northern society is bustling, prosperous, and entrepreneurial. In the South, labor is held to be "degrading," and social classes are largely fixed. As a result, the South is made up of "idle men," and its society is mostly stagnant. If white people want a vibrant and prosperous society, Tocqueville suggests, then it is in their interest to abolish slavery.[47]

In addition to arguing that white Northerners needed free soil in order to guarantee the possibility of upward mobility, Lincoln also pointed out that white Northerners have an *electoral* interest in thwarting the spread of slavery to the territories. Lincoln noted that, "The slaves do not vote; they are only counted and so used, as to swell the influence of the white people's votes. . . . Thus each white man in South Carolina is more than the double of any man in Maine. . . . I insist, that whether I shall be a whole man, or only, the half of one, in comparison with others, is a question in which I am somewhat concerned."[48] Lincoln rarely used the term "Slave Power;" nevertheless, his argument here fits into the larger argument of the Republican Party that the slave-owning South was attempting to dominate the federal government in order to benefit their own narrow interests.[49]

In the previous two examples, Lincoln appeals to relatively crude forms of self-interest: the interest that white Northerners have in increasing their economic well-being and their political power. This was a sectional appeal, and a racial appeal. Indeed, Lincoln sometimes seems to imply that the territories should be free not just of black slaves, but of black people *tout court*.

But from this somewhat base starting point, Lincoln's anti-slavery speeches usually ascended to discussion of a more universal, loftier interest—namely, the interest that *all* Americans have in maintaining the principles of free government. Lincoln tried to teach Northern whites that in the final analysis, when one defends the freedom of black people, one is defending one's own freedom as well. As Lincoln put it at New Haven,

> To us [in the North] it appears natural to think that slaves are human beings; *men*, not property; that some of the things, at least, stated about men in the Declaration of Independence apply to them as well as to us. I say, we think, most of us, that this Charter of Freedom applies to the slave as well as to ourselves, that the class of arguments put forward to batter down that idea, are also calculated to break down the very idea of a free government, *even for white men*, and to undermine the very foundations of free society.[50]

Lincoln taught, then, that when white people oppose slavery, in addition to promoting justice they are also ultimately promoting their own most fundamental interest—their interest, that is, in freedom. This is what Lincoln meant when he wrote that Republicans "consider [slavery] not only morally wrong, but a 'deadly poison' in a government like ours, professedly based on the equality of men."[51]

But how exactly were defenders of slavery undermining the freedom of *all* people, including whites? This was by no means self-evident, since slavery and freedom had coexisted in the ancient world and in America since its founding. The key point for Lincoln was that human freedom is justified only by the natural fact of equality. Because we are all equal by nature, no one has a natural right to rule over another person without his or her consent. Once one denies that "all men are created equal," however, then one opens the door not only to chattel slavery, but also to the idea of despotic government in general, to the idea that it is right for a person of superior strength or virtue to rule over other people without their consent—if necessary, by force. By undermining the Declaration's principle of equality, then, defenders of slavery were undermining the very foundations of freedom and democratic self-rule. As Lincoln put it, "Is there no danger to liberty itself, in discarding the earliest practice, and first precept of our ancient faith? In our greedy chase to make profit of the negro, let us beware, lest we 'cancel and tear to pieces' even the white man's charter of freedom."[52]

Lincoln pointed out that in order to justify slavery, one must deny the truth of the Declaration's claim that all people are created equal and thus have the same natural rights.[53] But once one does this—once one begins to make exceptions to the Declaration's great claim regarding human equality—then one starts to descend down a path that may end with one's own exclusion from the Declaration's great claim. Lincoln expressed this idea when he wrote: "And then, the negro being doomed, and dammed, and forgotten, to everlasting bondage, is the white man quite certain that the tyrant demon will not turn upon him too?"[54]

According to Lincoln, Stephen Douglas's ideas were paving the way for the rise of this "tyrant demon." As Lincoln put it, Douglas "is the most dangerous enemy of liberty, because the most insidious one."[55] Granted, Douglas did not explicitly call slavery a positive good, as many Southerners were then doing. However, Douglas refused to label slavery a wrong, and he explicitly denied that the Declaration applied to African-Americans. By undermining the Declaration's claim about equality, Douglas promoted despotism. For if some people are naturally superior to other people, then why should government rest on consent at all?

According to Lincoln, then, Douglas was so dangerous not solely—or even primarily—because his doctrine might lead to the spread of slavery into the North. Rather, his doctrine of popular sovereignty was so insidious because it undermined the American ideal of equality and hence undermined the foundation of freedom in America. Of course, Lincoln probably did not believe that a "tyrant demon" would one day literally enslave whites. But he did believe that Douglas's doctrine would change the *spirit* of the regime. He feared that if Douglas convinced people to view slavery with indifference—or worse yet, view it as a positive good—then America's foundational principle would be lost. The nation's institutions and mores would become shot through with the spirit of domination and mastery, rather than the spirit of liberty. The government might then remain democratic in form, but its spirit would be despotic. Insofar as American whites have an interest in maintaining democracy, then, they have a decided interest in opposing slavery.

We have now seen that Lincoln appealed to self-interest properly understood in order to cultivate an American will that is opposed to slavery. His argument tended to ascend from sectional appeals based on economic and electoral interests, to a broader appeal based on Americans' interest in maintaining the principles of free government. In the final analysis, this appeal to Americans' interest in freedom is not really an appeal to "interest" at all, but rather an appeal to what Lincoln called "the *love of liberty* which God has planted in our bosoms."[56] In the end, then, Lincoln elevated his audience by moving from appeals to material self-interest to appeals rooted in the grand passion for freedom.

Lincoln and Tocqueville on the Limits of Interest-Based Politics

We have now seen that Lincoln made great efforts to refine and elevate Americans' conception of their self-interest. However, Lincoln also sometimes tried to get Americans to move beyond self-interest altogether. For when it came to the question of slavery, Lincoln knew that arguments based on self-interest alone were inadequate.

Lincoln believed that slavery is rooted in the "selfishness" of human nature. One can say, then, that slavery emanates from self-interest in its most radicalized form. In Lincoln's fragment on pro-slavery theology, we can see that Dr. Ross finds slavery to be useful and convenient—in short, slavery maximizes the self-interest of Dr. Ross. But if slavery itself is rooted in a radical form of self-interest, then it is ultimately a logical contradiction to argue against slavery by appealing to that very same principle of self-interest. If Lincoln's arguments were *solely* based on self-interest, then he would have been promoting a principle that itself ends in domination. Hence, Lincoln always included in his speeches the argument that slavery was *intrinsically* immoral, irrespective of how it affects the interests of whites.

Lincoln explicitly warned against a politics that has self-interest as its *only* guidepost.[57] At Peoria Lincoln said that he hated slavery "especially because it forces so many really good men amongst ourselves into . . . insisting that there is no right principle of action but *self-interest*."[58] Lincoln believed that a politics based solely on interest can only end in the pursuit of mastery and the war of all against all. Thus, in a fragment on slavery, Lincoln argued with a hypothetical slave-owner as follows: "But, say you, it is a question of *interest*; and, if you can make it your *interest*, you have the right to enslave another. Very well. And if he can make it his interest, he has the right to enslave you."[59]

By making arguments that moved beyond self-interest, Lincoln behaved differently than the typical Americans described by Tocqueville. According to Tocqueville, Americans tend to explain *all* of their "disinterested" behavior in terms of "an enlightened self-love." Tocqueville is somewhat critical of this tendency, for he writes:

I think that in this they often do themselves less than justice, for sometimes in the United States, as elsewhere, one sees people carried away by the disinterested, spontaneous impulses natural to man. But the Americans are hardly prepared to admit that they do give way to emotions of this sort. They prefer to give the credit to their philosophy [the doctrine of self-interest properly understood] rather than to themselves.[60]

In contrast, Lincoln often tried to give credit where credit is due. While Lincoln used interest-based arguments, he also insisted that at bottom, the anti-slavery cause is rooted in the moral impulses of the American people. At Peoria, he asserted that "[s]lavery is founded in the selfishness of man's nature," whereas "opposition to [slavery], is [founded in] his love of justice." In the same speech, Lincoln said that opponents of slavery "consider slavery a great moral wrong; and their feelings against it, are not evanescent, but eternal. It lies at the very foundation of their sense of justice. . . ."[61] Instead of always justifying every good deed in terms of self-interest properly understood, Lincoln often tried to acknowledge—and thus tried to further foster—the better angels of our nature.[62]

In chapter 1 of this book, we saw that despite his praise for the doctrine of self-interest properly understood in *Democracy*, Tocqueville also clearly hoped that self-interest could at times be left behind altogether. Indeed, when one examines Tocqueville's speeches and writings on French leaders, one can see that he clearly hoped for leadership that moves beyond appeals to self-interest. In an 1837 letter, Tocqueville wrote:

When I consider the sorry intrigues to which our society is delivered in our day, the despicable charlatans who exploit it, the almost universal pettiness that reigns over it and above all the astonishing absence of disinterestedness . . . I sometimes wonder if what I take for an accident might not be the general rule. Is what we see before us, then, the natural bearing and the eternal condition of humanity? Is the man of our day at his full height? Has there never been a political world . . . which was led by considerations other than miserable day-to-day interests?[63]

Tocqueville hoped for a kind of leadership that could help raise people to their "full height," and, like Lincoln, he thus clearly rejected a politics based *solely* on interest. Moreover, Tocqueville suggests that if people are educated in the difficult art of being free, then they may be able to actually transcend a politics based on mere interest, and thus achieve a measure of greatness.

According to Tocqueville, Americans might at first work for the common good out of a sense of self-interest properly understood; however, participation in politics eventually can instill a considerable degree of genuine civic virtue in the people.[64] The general thrust of Tocqueville's view on this matter was beautifully expressed by Lincoln in one of his "Fragments on Government:"

> *Most governments* have been based, practically, on the denial of equal rights of men . . . ; *ours* began by *affirming* those rights. *They* said, some men are too *ignorant*, and *vicious*, to share in government. Possibly so, said we; and, by your system, you would always keep them ignorant, and vicious. We proposed to give *all* a chance; and we expected the weak to grow stronger, the ignorant, wiser; and all better, and happier together.[65]

Tocqueville and Lincoln both believed that a people without any share in government will indeed remain ignorant and vicious. But through the practical experience of self-government, the citizenry will grow stronger, wiser, and better.

Lincoln's Simultaneous Embrace and Critique of the American Character

We have now seen that both Lincoln and Tocqueville agreed that modern politics would be largely based on self-interest, but they both also recognized the limitations of interest-based politics. A key part of Lincoln's genius is that he simultaneously embodied *and* critiqued many of the troubling aspects of the American character that concerned Tocqueville. For while Lincoln critiqued a politics based *solely* on self-interest, he also openly embraced the pursuit of self-interest in his own life. Herndon's remark about Lincoln's ambition ("a little engine that knew no rest") is often quoted; what is not so often noted is that Lincoln himself often publicly conceded that he was motivated at least in part by worldly ambition.[66] In his last campaign speech of 1858, he told his audience: "I claim no insensibility to political honors."[67] Similarly, he wrote in a draft of a speech: "I claim no extraordinary exemption from personal ambition. That I like preferment as well as the average of men may be admitted."[68] Lincoln's concession here is notable, for American politicians often disavow any self-interested motives. For instance, in 1782 Thomas Jefferson wrote that his heart was "thoroughly cured of political ambition," and in 1796 he wrote to John Adams, "I have no ambition to govern men. It is a painful and thankless office."[69]

By publicly conceding his own self-interested motives, Lincoln in a sense bridged the gap between himself and his followers. In his early Temperance Address, we see Lincoln's belief that leaders must remain close to the people if they are to be successful. In this speech, Lincoln argues that previous reform movements have failed because they were led by "Preachers, Lawyers, and hired agents. Between these and the mass of mankind, there is a want of *approachability*, if the term be admissible, partially at least, fatal to their success. They are supposed to have no sympathy of feeling or interest, with those very persons whom it is their object to convince and persuade."[70] By conceding in his later speeches that he was partly self-interested, Lincoln created a "sympathy of feeling or interest" with his audience. Lincoln believed that persuasion rather than force was the morally appropriate means for leaders to try to bring about change in a free society. Lincoln also believed that persuasion was superior to force from a *practical* perspective. As Lincoln put it,

> When the conduct of men is designed to be influenced, *persuasion*, kind, unassuming persuasion, should ever be adopted. . . . If you would win a man to your cause, *first* convince him that you are his sincere friend. Therein is a drop of honey that catches his heart, which, say what he will, is the great high road to his reason . . . On the contrary, assume to dictate to his judgment, or to command his action . . . and he will retreat within himself, [and] close all the avenues to his head and his heart. . . .

Once the person has retreated within himself, said Lincoln, even "Herculean force" will be unable to motivate the person to change.[71]

Like the Antifederalists, then, Lincoln believed that leaders could only persuade their fellow citizens if they were considered to be genuine "friends and companions" of the people.[72] Friendship is premised, in part, on a sense of mutuality. In order to inspire feelings of mutuality between himself and his followers, Lincoln not only emphasized that his level of financial and political success was perfectly attainable by his fellow citizens; he also suggested that his level of *virtue* was perfectly attainable by the common person.[73] If Lincoln had presented himself as far superior to the people in terms of virtue, then friendship between him and the people would be impossible. Hence, Lincoln conceded that he, too, had a selfish side.

Lincoln thus offered followers his own person as a model for how someone can strive to be virtuous while remaining all-too-human. Most people will not bother trying to emulate a saint, since saintliness seems so far out of reach; the ordinary person can, however, strive to emulate a virtuous yet flawed person. By admitting that he shared the full range of motives that his followers had, Lincoln made it possible for them to really *listen* to him, as an equal and thus potentially as a friend.

While Lincoln often embraced the pursuit of self-interest, he also criticized Douglas for espousing a public doctrine that encouraged Americans to focus on self-interest to the exclusion of all other principles. Lincoln never referred to Tocqueville, but one can say that Lincoln essentially argued that Douglas would exacerbate precisely those aspects of the American character that Tocqueville found worrisome. Tocqueville feared that in the modern age, "interests only" will "form the links between men."[74] Lincoln believed that Douglas's doctrine would accentuate this dangerous modern tendency, for Douglas's doctrine of "popular sovereignty" taught that "there is a perfect right according to interest to do just as you please."[75] If a local majority found that enslaving other people was in their interest, then no moral principle should be allowed to prevent them from doing so, in Douglas's view.

At Freeport, Douglas said: "I tell you, increase, and multiply, and expand, is the law of this nation's existence."[76] For Douglas, then, the fundamental law of America is not a moral law, but rather a law based on self-interest writ large. If Americans feel that it is necessary, or convenient, for them to have more land, then they shall have it, irrespective of moral considerations: "[W]henever it becomes necessary, in our growth and progress to acquire more territory, [then] I am in favor of it, without reference to the question of slavery. . . . [J]ust as fast as our interests and our destiny require additional territory in the north, in the south, or on the islands of the ocean, I am for it. . . ."[77]

Douglas looked forward to the United States "increasing in wealth, in population, in power, and in all the elements of greatness, until we shall be the admiration and terror of the world."[78] Lincoln, in contrast, thought that America should be admired not for its success in advancing its economic and territorial interests on the world stage, but rather for its success in demonstrating to the world that self-government is possible. For Lincoln, the fundamental law of America is that "all men are created equal." If, in their self-interested scramble for profit, territory, and power, Americans forsake this fundamental principle, then the nation would not be "worthy of the saving," no matter how mighty and wealthy the nation becomes.

Just as Douglas's public doctrine promoted the pursuit of self-interest above all else, so, Lincoln thought, Douglas's own career exemplified the pursuit of self-interest that is unmoored from any higher purpose. Lincoln once wrote of Douglas: "He never lets the logic of principle, displace the logic of success."[79] In Lincoln's view, ambition, "within reasonable bounds, does good rather than harm," as he told General Hooker.[80] But ambition must be limited by principle. Hence, while Lincoln conceded his own desire for high office, he hoped that his own personal success would be "So reached, that the oppressed of my species," will "shar[e] with me in the elevation."[81]

Just as Lincoln both embraced and critiqued the American tendency to focus on self-interest, he also both embraced and critiqued the materialism of the American people. Tocqueville noted that in America, the pursuit of "physical pleasures" was rampant, and "the love of comfort has become the dominant national taste."[82] Tocqueville worried that in this constant pursuit of "petty aims," the Americans will "lose sight of those more precious goods which constitute the greatness and the glory of mankind."[83] At times, Lincoln promoted the materialistic attitudes that Tocqueville noticed in America. For Lincoln himself epitomized the perennial American quest for upward economic mobility. Lincoln taught that if people worked hard, they, too, could attain the prosperity that he himself had attained, and his own success story served to popularize further the idea that in America, anyone can rise up from obscurity and poverty to a position of wealth and prominence. Lincoln thus encouraged, to a degree, the restless striving for economic gain that Tocqueville noticed in middle-class America. Lincoln also embraced Americans' penchant for materialism when he emphasized, at Milwaukee, that farmers should always try "to push the soil up to . . . its full capacity."[84] Moreover, Lincoln's hope for ever greater material progress can be seen in his oft-expressed fascination with inventions that can make labor both more profitable and more convenient. It seems clear, then, that in Lincoln's view, the American regime should be dedicated in large part to the pursuit of commodious living.

But while Lincoln may have embraced the generally materialistic outlook of his fellow citizens, he also subtly warned them against its dangers. The idea behind the Kansas-Nebraska Act, Lincoln argued, "assumes that there CAN be MORAL RIGHT in the enslaving of one man by another. I object to it as a dangerous dalliance for a free people—a sad evidence that, *feeling prosperity we forget right*—that liberty, as a principle, we have ceased to revere."[85] Lincoln here warns a materialistic people that economic pursuits must always be subordinated to a larger moral framework. Douglas, in contrast, focuses on materialism to the exclusion of any moral principle, for as Lincoln puts it, Douglas teaches that even "man, with body and soul, is a matter of dollars and cents."[86] Lincoln recognized that the American regime was built largely on self-interest and the pursuit of commodious living. And yet, Lincoln always exposed the limitations of this framework, and he sought to infuse into this framework a sense of higher moral purpose. Lincoln may not have sought to radically transform the American character, but he always sought to *improve* it.[87]

Improving the People without Quitting Fellowship with Them

Lincoln and Tocqueville had a similar understanding of the American character, and they both had similar views on the promise—and the limitations—of the doctrine of self-interest properly understood. However, Lincoln's conception of democratic leadership was different from Tocqueville's. Much like the Antifederalists, Lincoln recognized that leaders in a democracy must remain close to the people's values and aspirations, and must operate in a spirit of mutuality with them.[88] We have seen in chapter 1 that Tocqueville, in contrast, suggested that the best leaders would be distant from the people. Notably, whereas Lincoln specifically warned in the Temperance Address that lawyers who seem distant from the people cannot be effective moral leaders, Tocqueville embraced the fact that lawyers in America were a quasi-aristocratic group, "increasingly separated from the people, forming a class apart."[89] Tocqueville, then, admired leaders who have the moral courage to defiantly criticize the people from above, whereas Lincoln teaches that leaders must approach their fellow citizens as equals if they hope to persuade them.

In chapter 1, I suggested that moral courage *and* closeness to the people are both important virtues of democratic leadership. While Tocqueville ultimately failed to combine the virtues of moral courage and closeness to the people in his theory of leadership, Lincoln brilliantly managed to exemplify both virtues. To use the terms that Tocqueville used when discussing the American clergy, one might say that Lincoln tried to improve the citizenry without quitting fellowship with them.[90] Lincoln remained close to the people by accepting, for the most part, their self-interested, materialistic tendencies. He was also close to the people insofar as he listened very seriously to public opinion. Indeed, as a young legislator, Lincoln gave voice to a conception of representation that would have appalled Tocqueville. In Tocqueville's view, elected officials must not be "passive agents" who simply implement the will of their constituents; instead, the representatives should always rely on their own independent judgment.[91] But, during his very first campaign for office, Lincoln wrote, "While acting as [the people's] representative, I shall be governed by their will, on all subjects upon which I have the means of knowing what their will is."[92] The mature Lincoln ceased speaking in such stark terms about the deference that the democratic leader must give to the people's wishes. And yet, Lincoln never gave up the idea that in a democracy, public opinion must be treated with great respect by leaders. Lincoln asserted that in a democracy, "public sentiment is every thing. With public sentiment, nothing can fail; without it nothing can succeed."[93] Hence, on a purely practical level, the leader of a democracy cannot afford to ignore public opinion, for he or she must work with it to a significant degree if anything is to be gotten done. But more importantly, as Jaffa has discussed, Lincoln believed that in a democracy it is *morally* problematic for leaders to ignore public opinion, for in a democracy, government must be by the consent of the people, and for Lincoln, if the government does not reflect public opinion to a considerable degree, then it can hardly be said that the government has the consent of the people.[94]

The mature Lincoln, then, had considerable respect for the public opinion of his fellow citizens. And yet, it cannot be said that the mature Lincoln debased himself by passively bowing down to the public's every whim, as Tocqueville feared leaders in America would.[95] James McPherson estimates that "perhaps two-thirds of white Americans" disagreed with Lincoln's claim that the Declaration of Independence was intended to include people of all races.[96] Lincoln had the moral courage, though, to reject majority opinion on this crucial point. In his speech on the *Dred Scott* decision, Lincoln pointed out that, "It is grossly incorrect to say or assume, that the public estimate of the negro is more favorable now than it was at the origin of the government."[97] But Lincoln refused to accept the current "public estimate of the negro" as the proper standard for political decision-making. Instead, Lincoln tried to *educate* the public by pointing out that its current "public estimate of the negro" was inconsistent with America's own permanent ideals. Lincoln tried to mould public opinion by showing the people where they had fallen short of their own ideals, their own "better angels." In stark contrast, Stephen Douglas and other Democrats believed, as Winger has shown, that "[t]he statesman was to embody and *follow* the will of the people, not lead and educate it."[98]

Wendell Phillips was wrong when he wrote of Lincoln: "The President never professed to be a leader. The President is the agent of public opinion. He wants to know what you will allow and what you demand that he shall do."[99] Lincoln was sensitive to the desires of the public, for Lincoln believed that "a universal feeling cannot be safely disregarded" by the democratic leader.[100] However, Lincoln refused to adopt the views of the American public when they conflicted with America's own "ancient faith." Just as Tocqueville feared "the dogma of the sovereignty of the people," so Lincoln criticized Douglas's dogma of "popular sovereignty."[101] Both Lincoln and Tocqueville worried that the blind worship of majority will can lead to the violation of transcendent principles of justice. Unlike Douglas, Lincoln would have strongly endorsed Tocqueville's statement that it is "an impious and detestable maxim that in matters of government the majority of people has the right to do everything. . . ."[102] With these words, Tocqueville anticipated the essence of Lincoln's critique of Douglas's ideas. Both Lincoln and Tocqueville were convinced that "justice . . . forms the boundary to each people's right."[103] Lincoln thus argued that the people of the territories have no right to vote slavery up, for nothing could be more unjust, and nothing would be a greater violation of the Declaration's ideals. This is not to suggest that Lincoln rejected the principle of majority rule. On the contrary, he insisted that, "A majority held in restraint by constitutional checks and limitations, and always changing easily with deliberate changes of popular opinions and sentiments, is the only true sovereign of a free people."[104] Lincoln was deeply committed to majority rule, but he also believed—as Tocqueville did—that the "popular opinions and sentiments" of the majority needed to be educated. By educating Americans about their first principles, Lincoln not only saved the Union, but he helped ensure that it would be a Union "worthy of the saving." And, as I suggested at the outset, Lincoln thereby fulfilled, perhaps more than anyone else, Tocqueville's hope for leaders who can put "new life into [the] beliefs" of a democracy.

Lincoln, Tocqueville, and Foundationalism

Lincoln and Tocqueville both explored the question: How can a democratic people be made to restrain itself? We have seen that a large part of the answer for both thinkers is that leaders should employ the doctrine of self-interest properly understood in order to convince people that it is in their own self-interest to act justly. And yet, we have seen that Lincoln, like Tocqueville, did not believe that American democracy could rely solely on self-interest, for a regime based solely on self-interest can easily degenerate into an unjust regime that is rife with the pursuit of domination and mastery. Ultimately, then, Tocqueville and Lincoln both believed that democracy could only survive if the citizenry had not only a well-educated sense of self-interest, but also a well-educated *moral* sense. As Tocqueville puts it in Volume I of *Democracy*: "[H]ow could society escape destruction if, when political ties are relaxed, moral ties are not tightened?"[105]

Tocqueville believed that perhaps the best way to develop the moral sense of the citizenry was through religion. According to Tocqueville, religion in America does not give Americans "their taste for liberty," but "it singularly facilitates their use thereof."[106] In other words, religion provides people with a sense of what freedom is *for*; it restrains the citizenry from believing that "everything is allowed," and it also provides people with positive ideals to strive toward, such as "the equality, the unity, and the fraternity of men."[107]

In contrast to Tocqueville, Lincoln relied not primarily on religion in order to educate Americans' moral sense, but rather on the republican ideals that he discerned in the Declaration of Independence. Of course, Lincoln did often use religious language and imagery to great effect, such as in his Second Inaugural. However, the logic of his argument against slavery was rooted not primarily in Christian theology, but rather in what he called his "ancient faith"—that is, the ideals of the Declaration. Tocqueville asked: "[W]hat can be done with a people master of itself if it is not subject to God?"[108] For Lincoln, a people "master of itself" needed to be subject to the moral principles of the Declaration. Lincoln believed that all people have an innate moral sense. However, Lincoln did not believe that this moral sense would spontaneously prevail in politics; instead, it needed to be properly educated. Specifically, Americans needed to be taught about the moral foundations of their republic, and for Lincoln, these foundations are laid bare in the Declaration.

For Tocqueville, shared Christian beliefs could serve as the "ideas in common" that are necessary for any "body social" to endure.[109] In an 1858 speech at Chicago, Lincoln suggested, in contrast, that it was the shared belief that "all men are created equal" that serves as the "electric cord" binding together Americans who may not have any "connection . . . by blood" to one another or to the founding generation.[110] Lincoln's position here differs not just from Tocqueville's; it also differs from that of William Galston. For whereas Lincoln insists that American identity must rest on shared moral *beliefs*, Galston argues that it is ultimately more appropriate, given the nation's "cultural heterogeneity," to rest American identity on "shared public *purposes*," namely, the purposes laid out in the preamble to the Constitution.[111] Furthermore, in defending his theory of "liberal pluralism," Galston suggests that while it is appropriate for "the founders of a political regime" to "publicly proclaim what they take to be moral, metaphysical, or religious truths as the basis of that regime," the government should refrain from "insisting that all citizens assent to those truths." Galston thus writes with approval that, "In the United States, naturalizing citizens affirm their loyalty to the Constitution, not to the Declaration of Independence. . . ."[112] Strictly speaking, Lincoln would probably agree with Galston that American citizens should not be *forced* to believe in the moral truths of the Declaration. After all, Lincoln found it justifiable to use military force against Southerners only when they broke the rules laid out in the Constitution by attempting to secede, and not when they denied the truths of the Declaration in the years leading up to the Civil War. Nevertheless, although he might accept the technical validity of Galston's point, Lincoln went to great lengths to emphasize the dangers America faces if widespread belief in the Declaration's principles declines. In short, Lincoln differed from Galston insofar as Lincoln *did*, in a sense, insist that all citizens should assent to the truths of the Declaration.

Indeed, Lincoln conceived of his great contest with Douglas as a battle to ensure that the American people remained attached to their belief in the idea that "all men are created equal." At one point, Lincoln even raised the ancient argument that the citizenry must beware, lest the youth be corrupted by ideas that are opposed to the spirit of the regime. When discussing Douglas's indifference to slavery, and his cramped view of the Declaration's philosophy, Lincoln put it this way at Chicago: "I ask you in all soberness, if all these things, if indulged in, if ratified, if confirmed and endorsed, *if taught to our children, and repeated to them*, do not tend to rub out the sentiment of liberty in the country, and to transform this Government into a government of some other form."[113] Of course, Lincoln did not advocate putting Douglas to death or exiling him, as the Athenians might have. And yet, as Jaffa rightly points out, Lincoln would not have virulently defended the free speech rights of those whose words undermine the principles of the regime.[114] For Lincoln was what one might call a "foundationalist" thinker. Against those contemporary political theorists who celebrate permanent "contestation," or the absence of "closure," as one of the attributes of a genuine democracy, Lincoln insisted that democracy requires consensus on certain principles. The justification for democracy lies in certain transcendent truths, and if people cease to believe in these truths, democracy cannot survive. Hence, those who speak out against these truths deserve to be silenced, if not by the coercive power of the state, at least by the power of other people's words. Lincoln said at Cooper Union, "If slavery is right, all words, acts, laws, and constitutions against it, are themselves wrong, and should be silenced, and swept away."[115] As Jaffa suggests, this implies that the opposite is also the case: If slavery is not right, then all words in its favor should also be silenced, and swept away.[116] Jaffa notes that Lincoln never explicitly advocated sedition laws. Instead, Lincoln tried to silence

Douglas and other advocates of slavery by the power of his own superior argumentation. The purpose of leaders in a democracy is, in large part, to teach the citizenry about their founding principles, and this involves refuting ideas that are *opposed* to those principles.

Tocqueville was also a foundationalist, but Lincoln's foundationalism has a dynamic and flexible quality that ultimately makes it more appropriate for a modern democracy than Tocqueville's version. Tocqueville believed that American democracy was successful in part because of its Puritan "point of departure." According to Tocqueville, the Puritans' political institutions and practices were always "contested," but their openness to innovation in politics rested on a foundation of "fixed religious beliefs."[117] Tocqueville was pleased to find that in nineteenth century America, "everything in the moral field is certain and fixed, although the world of politics seems given over to argument and experiment."[118] Like their Puritan predecessors, nineteenth-century Americans accept moral principles "without discussion," and these fixed moral principles provide them with "habits of restraint" that prevent a politically innovative people from acting according to the belief that everything is possible and everything permitted.[119]

For certain contemporary theorists such as Mark Reinhardt, then, Tocqueville's thought is ultimately unsatisfactory, because while Tocqueville advocates contestation in the political realm, he does not believe that democracy should "extend all the way down to foundations," as Reinhardt puts it.[120] In other words, Reinhardt opposes Tocqueville's insistence that democracy requires for its foundation an incontestable moral consensus.

On this issue of foundationalism Lincoln advances a highly valuable theoretical position that lies somewhere between Tocqueville's endorsement of moral dogmatism, on the one hand, and Reinhardt's anti-foundationalism, on the other. Both Tocqueville's recommendation of moral dogmatism and Reinhardt's anti-foundationalism have their dangers. On the one hand, Tocqueville's advocacy of an unexamined moral consensus can potentially lead to a stifling kind of conformity. Tocqueville claims that the Americans and their Puritan predecessors had freedom to debate and experiment in the world of politics, but fixed norms in the moral world. However, it is difficult to draw such a firm line between the moral and political realms. For example, if a society has fixed ideas about the immorality of, say, abortion or homosexuality, then there will most likely be little freedom to debate these issues in the political realm. By arguing that "in the moral field" everything should be "certain and fixed," Tocqueville might actually stifle political debate.

On the other hand, Reinhardt's apparent defense of anti-foundationalism goes too far insofar as it could lead to the destruction of *any* moral consensus, including even a moral consensus regarding the basic desirability of self-government. Patrick Deneen has wryly pointed out that "the question of whether we will continue to be a democracy will not appear on the next presidential ballot." In other words, democracy in fact requires certain forms of closure, and "relentless probing can actually threaten those 'democratic faiths' such as the priorities of equality and liberty."[121] If Deneen is right—as I think he is—then Reinhardt's claim that democracy should go "all the way down" is potentially dangerous because it can lead to the undermining of those principles which are the very conditions for democracy.

Lincoln's position on foundationalism lies somewhere between Tocqueville's position and Reinhardt's, but it is closer to Tocqueville's; like Tocqueville, Lincoln believes that American democracy can only survive if it has a certain moral consensus. Specifically, Lincoln believed that all American citizens need to believe in the Declaration's claim that all men are created equal. And yet, Lincoln also implicitly suggested—or at least, the example of his moral leadership should suggest to us—that the precise meaning and the precise application of America's first principles should not be entirely incontestable. The case of Lincoln suggests that although all American citizens should, indeed, believe that all people are created equal, there is room for debate about the exact meaning of this principle, and for debate about how it should be applied in practice.

Did Jefferson mean to suggest only that people are naturally equal, or did he also mean that we should strive for a polity in which all people are socially and politically equal? Which practices are excluded by the Declaration's principle of equality? Is chattel slavery excluded? How about the denial of suffrage to women and blacks? Lincoln offered his own particular answers to some of these questions, but by arguing for his particular position he implicitly suggested that other answers are conceivable. Whereas Tocqueville maintained that Americans should blindly accept "fixed" moral principles "without discussion," Lincoln engaged in a vigorous open discussion regarding the meaning of the nation's foundational principles. In doing so, Lincoln suggested, contra Reinhardt, that democracy requires a certain degree of moral consensus; but he also implied, contra Tocqueville, that the exact contours of this moral consensus need not be completely "fixed."

The spirit of Lincoln's flexible foundationalism is largely captured in Alfred North Whitehead's remark that,

> The art of free society consists in the maintenance of the symbolic code; and secondly in fearlessness of revision, to secure that the code serves those purposes which satisfy an enlightened reason. Those societies which cannot combine reverence to

their symbols with freedom of revision, must ultimately decay either from anarchy, or from the slow atrophy of a life stifled by useless shadows.[122]

Lincoln had great reverence for the broad principles of the Declaration, and yet he also subtly *revised* those principles. Of course, Lincoln always claimed that he was simply trying to restore the principles of "our fathers," whereas Douglas had sharply diverged from those principles.[123] However, as we shall see, Lincoln's return to first principles involved his own particular interpretation of those principles, and this interpretation amounted to a subtle reformulation of the founders' ideas.

By subtly revising the framers' principles, Lincoln brings to mind not just Whitehead's remark, but also Alasdair MacIntyre's claim that a healthy tradition is not made up of a completely fixed body of ideas, but rather is marked by change and debate. As MacIntyre puts it,

> all reasoning takes place within the context of some traditional mode of thought, transcending through criticism and invention the limitations of what had hitherto been reasoned in that tradition. . . . Moreover when a tradition is in good order it is always partially constituted by an argument about the goods the pursuit of which gives to that tradition its particular point and purpose.[124]

By making his own particular argument about what the pursuit of liberty and equality really entails, Lincoln helped inject new life into the best of American traditions—namely, the tradition of self-government.

Lincoln on the Declaration

How, then, did Lincoln revise America's founding principles? First, as Jaffa has pointed out, Lincoln modified the meaning of Jefferson's claim that "all men are created equal." For Jefferson, the phrase "all men are created equal" was a description of the prepolitical state of nature, but for Lincoln this phrase represents an aspirational ideal toward which the American political community should move.[125] As Lincoln put it, the authors of the Declaration

> meant to set up a standard maxim for a free society, which should be familiar to all, and revered by all; constantly looked to, constantly labored for, and even though never perfectly attained,

constantly approximated, and therefore constantly spreading and deepening its influence, and augmenting the happiness and value of life to all people of all colors everywhere.[126]

By holding forth this grand vision of human equality and human progress, Lincoln exemplified Tocqueville's idea that democratic leaders should keep alive "distant goals for human endeavor."[127] For Tocqueville, the task of authority is not only to restrain base passions, but also to inspire grand and noble ones. Because he used authoritative ideals not only to check the citizenry, but also to inspire them to move further toward justice, Lincoln can be considered a great Tocquevillian leader.

In addition to changing the Declaration's statement of equality from a description of the state of nature to an aspirational ideal, Lincoln also subtly changed the Declaration insofar as he interpreted it as an explicitly *democratic* document. As we have seen, for Lincoln "all men are created equal" meant that no one has a natural right to rule over anyone else. As Lincoln put it, "no man is good enough to govern another man, *without that other's consent*. I say this is the leading principle—the sheet anchor of American republicanism."[128] This principle of consent means that slavery is a violation of natural law. But it also means, for Lincoln, that democracy is the best form of government, for only under a democracy can the people actively consent to the rules that they live under. Lincoln frequently drew this connection between his anti-slavery convictions and his democratic beliefs. "As I would not be a *slave*," wrote Lincoln, "so I would not be a *master*. This expresses my idea of democracy. Whatever differs from this, to the extent of the difference, is no democracy."[129] For Lincoln, then, the principle of consent found in the Declaration delegitimates chattel slavery at the micro-level. But at the macro-level, the principle of consent tends to delegitimate all governments that are not "of the people, by the people, and for the people."

Lincoln's interpretation of the Declaration, however, is debatable, for the Declaration does not state that democracy is the best government or the only legitimate one. The Declaration states that the people should institute whatever government they believe will secure their natural rights. But what if the people believe that an enlightened monarch would protect their rights to "life, liberty, and the pursuit of happiness"? Could they not rightly consent to be ruled by such a king? It is difficult to rule this out according to the plain text of the Declaration.[130] However, Lincoln himself rejected the idea that a monarch could legitimately rule over a free people. As we have seen, in his First Inaugural, he said: "A majority, held in restraint by constitutional checks, and limitations, and always changing easily, with deliberate changes of popular opinions and sentiments, is the only true sovereign of a free people."[131] For Lincoln, consent must be active and continuous. The Declaration states that a government derives its "just powers from the consent of the governed." This could mean that a people can legitimately consent to be ruled by a monarch during a founding moment, and then abandon the public realm. But for Lincoln, it is illegitimate for a free people to simply choose a ruler and then exit the public stage. Rather, a free people must continue to always shape public affairs through their representatives, and, more generally, through public opinion. As Lincoln put it, "Allow ALL the governed an equal voice in government, and that, and that only is self-government."[132]

Lincoln thus in a sense democratized the Declaration. As Thurow points out, at Gettysburg Lincoln implicitly linked the principle that "all men are created equal" with the idea of "government of the people, by the people, and for the people."[133] In contrast, the Declaration itself does not draw this same link between its natural rights philosophy and democratic government.

In addition to subtly changing the meaning of the Declaration, Lincoln also tried to subtly change the very *status* of the Declaration. During his Cooper Union speech, Lincoln used the term "our fathers" to refer to the signers of the Constitution.[134] And yet, Lincoln's thought as a whole reveals that for him the real fathers of the nation were those who issued the Declaration. As Garry Wills and Willmoore Kendall have both argued—but from very different political perspectives—Lincoln tried to change the meaning of America by emphasizing the Declaration's promise of *equality*, a word that does not even appear in the Constitution.[135] Lincoln explained the relative importance of the Declaration versus the Constitution in the following manner: Whereas the Declaration's principle that "all men are created equal" is the "apple of gold," the "*Union* and the *Constitution* are the *picture* of *silver*, subsequently framed around it. The picture was made, not to *conceal*, or *destroy* the apple; but to *adorn* and *preserve* it. The *picture* was made *for* the apple—*not* the apple for the picture."[136] Although Lincoln never openly criticized the Constitution, he once implied in a letter that the Constitution might not adequately "adorn and preserve" the Declaration's great principle. "I believe," wrote Lincoln, that

> the declaration that "all men are created equal" is the great fundamental principle upon which our free institutions rest; that negro slavery is violative of that principle; but that, *by our frame of government, that principle has not been made one of legal obligation*; that by our frame of government, the States which have slavery are to retain it, or surrender it at

their own pleasure; and that all others—individuals, free-states and national government—are constitutionally bound to leave them alone about it.[137]

The Constitution, then, seems to be a frame of government that would allow the American people to damage the apple of gold that the Constitution was designed to protect. Lincoln never accepted the notion that the Constitution was actually *pro*-slavery; after all, as Lincoln pointed out, it never even uses the word "slavery," and so Lincoln believed that Chief Justice Taney was wrong when he asserted that "the right of property in a slave is distinctly and expressly affirmed in the Constitution."[138] Nevertheless, Lincoln came to see the Constitution as inadequate, for it clearly permits chattel slavery, and this means that it would permit the negation of America's founding principle.

In order to rectify this inadequacy, Lincoln tried, one might say, to *incorporate* the Declaration and its principles into the Constitution. Lincoln did this, in part, through his use of language. At Chicago Lincoln said: "I should like to know if taking the old Declaration of Independence, which declares that all men are equal upon principle and making exceptions to it where will it stop. If one man says it does not mean a negro, why not another say it does not mean some other man? If that declaration is not the truth, *let us get the Statute book, in which we find it and tear it out!*"[139] Lincoln knew, though, that in actuality, the Declaration was not in *any* statute book! The Declaration's principle was not, as he admitted, a matter of "legal obligation." Through the use of the term "Statute book," though, Lincoln tried to rhetorically give the Declaration a legal status that it in fact officially lacked.

As the Civil War progressed, Lincoln came to advocate a constitutional amendment that would at last make the principle of the Declaration a matter of "legal obligation" on all states, insofar as slavery was concerned. Lincoln lobbied hard for the Thirteenth Amendment both publicly and in private meetings with Congressmen. As was his constant strategy, Lincoln argued in favor of the amendment on the grounds of interest (or what he often called "policy") as well as on the grounds of morality. In June of 1864 Lincoln said,

> When the people in revolt, with a hundred days of explicit notice, that they could, within those days, resume their allegiance, without the overthrow of their institution, and that they could not so resume it afterwards, elected to stand out, such amendment of the Constitution as now proposed, became a fitting, and necessary conclusion to the final success of the

Union cause. . . . Now, the unconditional Union men, North, and South, perceive its importance, and embrace it.[140]

In this passage, Lincoln seems to suggest that the Thirteenth Amendment is, like the Emancipation Proclamation, a war measure to be taken not primarily for reasons of morality, but rather because it is a "fitting, and necessary" means for saving the Union. Once Congress passed the Thirteenth Amendment, though, Lincoln seemed to drop the pretense that the Amendment was a war measure. In his response to a White House serenade after the passing of the Amendment, Lincoln now called the amendment "the fitting *if not indispensable* adjunct to the consummation of the great game we are playing." Lincoln here concedes that the Thirteenth Amendment was not indispensable to winning the war at all, but was rather justified on ethical grounds. The rather limited Emancipation Proclamation, Lincoln admitted, did not fully "meet the evil" of slavery, whereas "this amendment is a King's cure for all the evils." It was to be celebrated not as a war measure, but as a "great moral victory."[141] At last, the Declaration's transcendent moral principle had been more fully incorporated into the constitutional framework itself.

Lincoln on Freedom

Lincoln's reinterpretation of the nation's founding principles also involved subtly changing the meaning of freedom in America. "The world has never had a good definition of the word liberty," Lincoln said in 1864, "and the American people, just now, are much in want of one."[142] In 1859, Lincoln had suggested that "the principles of Jefferson" were as perfect as the "propositions of Euclid."[143] But in 1864, Lincoln now suggested that Jefferson's understanding of liberty may in fact have been somehow deficient.

But what was wrong, in Lincoln's view, with the Fathers' understanding of liberty? Herbert Storing's essay on "Slavery and the Moral Foundations of the Republic" suggests a possible answer, even though the essay does not explicitly address Lincoln's ideas on freedom. Storing argues that "the very principle of individual liberty for which the Founders worked so brilliantly and successfully contains within itself an uncomfortably large opening toward slavery."[144] Storing does not mean to suggest that the Founders actually believed that slavery could be morally right. On the contrary, Storing, like Lincoln, argues that "all men are created equal" was indeed intended to include *all* people, and Storing therefore rejects the arguments advanced by both Chief Justice Taney and Wendell

Phillips that the Founders believed in the justice of slavery. Storing's point is that while the Founders may have believed that slavery was unjust, their theory of liberal individualism itself fosters an understanding of freedom that can lead to the unbridled pursuit of mastery. The problem is that Jefferson's Lockean theory of natural rights relies on an amoral notion of self-interest. As Storing puts it, there is thus a

> tendency, under the principles of the Declaration of Independence itself, for justice to be reduced to self-preservation, for self-preservation to be defined as self-interest, and for self-interest to be defined as what is convenient and achievable. Thus the slave owner may resolve that it is necessary to keep his slaves in bondage for the compelling reason that if they were free they would kill him; but he may also decide, on the same basic principle . . . that he is entitled to keep his slaves in bondage if he finds it convenient to do so. . . . American Negro slavery, in this ironic and terrible sense, can be seen as a radicalization of the principle of individual liberty on which the American polity was founded.[145]

Lincoln sought an understanding of liberty that was rooted in something more than mere self-interest. This entailed not only a rejection of the slave-holder's notion of freedom, but also a transcendence of the liberal individualist, or "negative" notion of freedom that was held by most of the Founders.

We have seen that the Antifederalists and Tocqueville combined in their political theories both positive and negative liberty. In other words, they believed that ultimately, one is not truly free unless one chooses the just and the good, after mastering one's own passions. And yet, they simultaneously believed that the choice of the just and the good will lack moral value if it is not voluntary, and so they also believed in the importance of negative liberty, the liberty to act without external restraints. A similar combination of negative and positive liberty can be found in Lincoln's political theory.[146] Lincoln's belief in "positive" liberty can be seen in his interpretation of a passage from *Genesis*. At Peoria, Lincoln declared:

> [According to Stephen Douglas,] the principle of the Nebraska bill . . . originated when God made man and placed good and evil before him, allowing him to choose for himself, being responsible for the choice he should make. . . . [But] the facts of this proposition are not true as stated. God did not place good and evil before him, telling him to make his choice. On

the contrary, he did tell him there was one tree, of the fruit
of which, he should not eat, upon pain of certain death. I
should scarcely wish so strong a prohibition against slavery
in Nebraska.[147]

Lincoln here suggests that choosing evil is not really freedom, as Douglas
seems to think; rather, choosing evil results from a failure to attain the
self-mastery involved in genuine freedom. Lincoln here returns to Winthrop's idea that, "There is a *liberty* of corrupt nature, which is affected
by *men* and *beasts* to do what they list. . . . But there is a civil, a moral,
a federal *liberty*, which is the proper end and object of *authority*; it is a
liberty for that only which is *just* and *good*. . . ." For both Lincoln and
Winthrop, then, the person who chooses evil is a licentious person who
does not know what freedom is for.[148]

Although Lincoln upheld the importance of positive liberty, he also
often gave voice to a negative conception of liberty, particularly when he
contrasted "genuine popular sovereignty" with Douglas's spurious version.
In contrast to Douglas, who argued that enslaving others can fall under
"popular sovereignty," Lincoln insisted that "each individual is naturally
entitled to do as he pleases with himself and the fruit of his labor, so far
as it in no wise interferes with any other man's rights."[149] This notion
of freedom was repeated in his speech at Baltimore, where Lincoln said
that, "With some the word liberty may mean for each man to do as he
pleases with himself, and the product of his labor."[150]

Lincoln believed that this negative notion of freedom played an
important role in a democracy; however, he also clearly believed that this
notion of freedom had its limitations. After all, at Baltimore he suggested
that America had *never* had a fully adequate notion of freedom. Ultimately,
I think that Lincoln would agree with Howard B. White's claim that true
"freedom is not at all freedom to do what one pleases. . . . [I]f freedom
is identified with doing what one likes, freedom to dominate is as much
doing what one likes as is freedom from domination."[151] Rather than
identify freedom with doing what one likes, Lincoln's ultimate definition
of freedom seems to involve self-mastery and the pursuit of the just and
the good.

But if Lincoln believed in the primacy of positive liberty, as a committed democrat—as a believer in government not only for, but also *by*
the people—Lincoln was convinced that the American people needed to
choose the good for themselves. In other words, democracy *does* require
a certain degree of negative liberty, for democracy means that the people
must choose their own collective path. Lincoln would put all of his efforts
into speeches designed to *persuade* the citizenry to choose the good, but

ultimately, they had to make the choice on their own, or else democracy would degenerate into dictatorship.

Hence, Lincoln wanted the actual abolition of slavery to be accomplished not by executive fiat, but rather by the more democratic means of a constitutional amendment, or even by the state legislatures themselves. Lincoln did, of course, eventually issue an Emancipation Proclamation. But while that document states, in passing, that emancipation is "sincerely believed to be an act of justice," its actual justification is that it is a "fit and necessary war measure."[152] The Emancipation Proclamation thus only applied to areas that were in rebellion against the Union. Lincoln issued such a narrow Emancipation Proclamation not just because of his conservative constitutional views, and not just because he feared antagonizing the loyal border states, but also because he was a committed democrat. He could try to lead the citizenry toward the just and the good, but they needed to take the actual steps themselves. When pressed by Salmon P. Chase to expand the Proclamation to areas loyal to the Union, Lincoln gave expression to this democratic philosophy:

> The original proclamation has no constitutional or legal justification, except as a military measure. . . . If I take the step [of applying the proclamation to areas not in rebellion] must I not do so, without the argument of military necessity, and so, without any argument, except the one that I think the measure politically expedient, and morally right? Would I not thus give up all footing upon constitution or law? Would I not thus be in the boundless field of absolutism?[153]

Lincoln was, of course, frequently accused of being precisely an absolutist during the war, and the charge has continued since his death. And yet, in the restraint he showed on the question of emancipation—and in his willingness to hold an election during a cataclysmic crisis—Lincoln revealed his strong attachment to democratic principles.[154]

Conclusion

We have seen that Lincoln followed Tocqueville's teaching on leadership and authority in many respects. Lincoln and Tocqueville agreed that leaders are needed to inspire, restrain, educate, and elevate a democratic citizenry. They also agreed that the doctrine of self-interest properly understood should play a role—but ultimately only a *limited* role—in the education of democracy. However, whereas Tocqueville hoped for quasi-aristocratic leaders who could elevate the people from above, Lincoln put his faith in leaders who remained close to the people. Tocqueville celebrated the leader who defies majority opinion; Lincoln agreed that leaders need to sometimes criticize public opinion, but he believed that they at the same time need to remain close to the fundamental values of the people. According to Tocqueville, "in democracies the love of physical pleasures, the hope to better one's lot, competition, and the lure of success anticipated all goad men to activity in their chosen careers and forbid them to stray one moment from the track. The soul's chief effort goes in that direction."[155] Lincoln, to a significant degree, encouraged all of these traits that the aristocratic side of Tocqueville disdained. For Lincoln himself embodied the competitive spirit of bettering one's lot, and Lincoln often upheld the pursuit of the *useful* arts and sciences. At the same time as he embraced the general character of the American people, though, Lincoln warned Americans about the excesses and limitations of their character, for he was critical of those who focus on interest and utility to the exclusion of moral principle.

Moreover, both Lincoln and Tocqueville believed that authority was necessary to provide moral foundations in a democracy, and to thereby teach people what freedom is *for*. They would thus both have rejected the idea that democracy can survive without foundations, and they also would have rejected the idea that America should be a procedural republic that fails to uphold any particular substantive notion of the good. However, whereas Tocqueville believed that moral authority should come largely from religion, Lincoln placed primary emphasis on the republican ideals that he derived from the Declaration of Independence. We have also seen that Lincoln's understanding of moral foundations contains an element of flexibility and dynamism that Tocqueville's understanding lacks.

In the end, then, Lincoln's theory of leadership and authority improves upon Tocqueville's. Because of his flexible foundationalism, which allows for more contestation and debate than one finds in Tocqueville's thought, and because of his greater emphasis on mutuality between leaders and led, Lincoln's theory of leadership and authority is ultimately even more conducive to the full flowering of democracy than is Tocqueville's theory.

Chapter 4

⊰≡⊚≡⊱

Wilson and Tocqueville on Leadership and the "Character Foundations of American Democracy"

Many American politicians have peppered their speeches with quotations from Tocqueville, usually in a superficial manner.[1] In the case of Woodrow Wilson, though, we have a unique example of an American president who can genuinely be called a serious student of Tocqueville. In 1883, Wilson wrote in his private notebooks that *Democracy in America* contained "quite the best philosophy since Aristotle."[2] Moreover, Tocqueville was one of six "Great Leaders of Political Thought" whom Wilson lectured on in 1895 and 1896.[3] Wilson read and deeply admired both *Democracy in America* and *The Old Regime and the French Revolution*.[4] With Wilson, then, we have not only an affinity between his ideas and those of Tocqueville, but direct influence as well. While Wilson's admiration for Tocqueville has been briefly noted by other scholars, the intriguing connections between Wilson's ideas and those of Tocqueville have not been fully explored.[5]

I focus this chapter on Wilson not only because his debt to Tocqueville has been insufficiently examined, but also because the role of leadership in a democracy—the main subject of this book—was also Wilson's over-arching theoretical and practical concern.[6] The problem of leadership in democratic times was to have been one of the main subjects of Wilson's projected *magnum opus*, "The Philosophy of Politics." In his "Memo-randa" for this never finished work, Wilson wrote that, "The most helpful service to the world thus awaiting the fulfillment of its visions would be an elucidation, a real elucidation, of the laws of leadership."[7]

In this chapter, I seek to shed new light on Wilson's ideas on leadership by arguing that Wilson can usefully be construed as a Tocquevillian. I focus on Wilson's complex understanding of the relationship between leaders, institutions, and the character of a democratic citizenry. In the "Memoranda" for his "Philosophy of Politics," Wilson wrote, "See Tocqueville on the character foundations of American democracy."[8] In the same vein, Wilson declares in *Constitutional Government* that, "Self-government is not a mere form of institutions to be had when desired, if only proper pains be taken. It is a form of character."[9] Like Tocqueville, then, Wilson was convinced that the success of a democracy was dependent not primarily on written constitutional procedures, but rather on the character (that is, the habits and mores) of the citizenry. As Wilson puts it in the "Memoranda," "Institutions are subsequent to character. They do not create character, but are created and sustained by it." At the same time, though, Wilson believed that institutions are of the utmost importance insofar as they *shape* the character of a people. "After being successfully established," Wilson writes, "[institutions] both confirm and modify national character, forming in no small degree both national thought and national purpose—certainly national ideas."[10] For Wilson, institutions and character are thus engaged in a complex dialectic.

Wilson provides an example of the formative power of institutions in his discussion of France in *The State*:

> [A] people made democratic in thought by the operation of a speculative political philosophy has adopted constitution after constitution created in the exact image of that thought. But they had, to begin with, absolutely no democratic habit,—no democratic custom. Gradually that habit has grown, fostered amidst the developments of local self-direction; and the democratic thought has penetrated, wearing the body of practice, its only vehicle to such minds, to the rural populace. Constitutions and custom have thus advanced to meet one another. . . . Institutions too theoretical in their basis to live at first, have nevertheless furnished an *atmosphere* for the French mind and habit: that atmosphere has affected the life of France,—that life the atmosphere.[11]

Much like Tocqueville and Burke, Wilson often criticized the French Revolution for trying to impose abstract ideas onto political reality.[12] But in this passage, we find that Wilson believed that the imposition of democratic institutions onto the French people *did* eventually succeed at producing democratic habits and a democratic character. For Wilson, then, character is primary, but, over the long-term, institutions can gradually shape a people's character.

Tocqueville also believed that institutions and character interact in a dynamic way. On the one hand, Tocqueville famously argues that character (or *moeurs*) are more important than laws and institutions for the success of a democracy. For instance, he writes that whereas Mexico has the same basic laws as the United States, Mexico still "cannot get used to democratic government."[13] Democracy in America, then, rests on the character of the people. At the same time, though, Tocqueville suggests that character is shaped by institutions. For example, Tocqueville argued that local participatory institutions in America, such as the town-hall meeting and the jury system, are valuable largely because they help to mitigate the individualism that threatens to delineate the character of Americans.[14]

Much like Tocqueville, Wilson believed that one of the key tasks of leadership is to build—and maintain—institutions that can instill in the people a more democratic character. In *The State*, Wilson describes this crucial task of the statesman. Wilson argues that the ancients were wrong to believe that a city-state's institutions could be "made 'out of hand' by any one man." Nevertheless, Wilson writes that the ancient myth of "a single lawgiver" who gives a regime "its essential and characteristic form" is a myth that contains "the shadow of a truth"; these legends are not completely wrong when they "suggest the overshadowing influence of individual statesmen as the creative power in framing the greater combinations of politics. They bring the conception of conscious choice into the history of institutions. They look upon systems as *made*, rather than as developed."[15] Wilson thus rejects the idea of a single founder, but he nevertheless clearly believed in the necessity of great creative statesmen who give shape to institutions, and thus give shape to the character of a people.

In this chapter, then, I examine different areas of Wilson's thought in which one finds an overriding concern with the relationship between leaders, institutions, and the "character foundations of American democracy." Throughout, I draw out the similarities (and some differences) between Wilson's ideas and those of Tocqueville. First, I examine Wilson's ideas on institutional reform at Princeton University, where he served as a professor beginning in 1890, and as president of the university from 1902 to 1910. Second, I examine Wilson's ideas on producing a more deliberative democracy through a) restructuring Congress, and b) turning public schools into "social centers." Third, I explore how Wilson's ideas on administrative centralization reveal a concern with warding off what Wilson called (in

Tocquevillian fashion) "habits of servitude." Fourth, I argue that Wilson tried to apply Tocquevillian ideas to the problems of a modern industrial economy. Fifth, I explore how Wilson's concept of "interpretive" leadership relates to the Tocquevillian task of educating democracy.

The last three sections of this chapter draw out some of the implications of viewing Wilson as a Tocquevillian thinker and leader. Ronald Pestritto has recently argued that Wilson is a Hegelian insofar as he is allegedly a historicist and a statist who departs from the natural rights thinking of the founders.[16] I argue that Wilson is better understood as a Tocquevillian, and I suggest that Wilson's Tocquevillian concern for cultivating the character of a democratic citizenry renders his thought more valuable than Pestritto allows.

I also conclude that Louis Hartz's claim that Wilson was a quintessentially liberal thinker must be qualified.[17] Michael Sandel has argued that along with the liberal tradition in America, there is also a republican tradition that focuses on the "formative project"—that is, on the creation of citizens who are capable of self-rule. In my view, Wilson's emphasis on character indicates that while he may have been a "liberal" thinker, he is a liberal, like Tocqueville, with a strong "republican" strand.[18]

According to Rogers Smith, American political thought contains not only liberal and republican traditions, but also a racist tradition of "ascriptive hierarchy."[19] All three of these traditions, I suggest, can be discerned in Wilson. For as I show in the final section of the chapter, Wilson invoked the concept of character to justify the subjugation of African-Americans as well as Filipinos. I here seek to build on Stephen Skowronek's recent work on Wilson. Skowronek has demonstrated that Wilson's liberalism and his racism are not separate and unrelated intellectual strands—as, according to Skowronek, Smith's work might lead one to expect—but rather they are conceptually intertwined with one another.[20] In a similar vein, I demonstrate that Wilson's republicanism and his racism are also conceptually intertwined, insofar as both of these intellectual strands rely upon Wilson's Tocquevillian concept of character. My aim in this chapter, then, is not only to reveal Wilson's considerable debt to Tocqueville on the subject of leadership, but also to employ Wilson as a case study that can shed further light on the interimbrication of liberalism, republicanism, and racism within American political thought.

Institutional Reform and Character-Formation at Princeton

Wilson's ideas for institutional change at Princeton University reveal his Tocquevillian conviction that the institutions created by leaders can shape character in crucial ways. Wilson made no sharp distinction between his ideas on education and his ideas on politics, and an analysis of his proposals for institutional reform at Princeton can shed light on his broader political theory. Wilson declared that "education, in a country like ours, is a branch of statesmanship."[21] As president of the university, Wilson treated the task of reform at Princeton with the same seriousness with which a statesman might turn to the great task of re-founding a nation. For Wilson, much was at stake. He told the trustees of Princeton that "the radical reorganization of our life [is] imperative, if the main ends for which that life is meant are to be attained."[22] The fate of what Wilson called "our university democracy" hung in the balance.[23]

Wilson tried (ultimately without success) to destroy Princeton's eating clubs because he believed that they encouraged the pursuit of materialism, individualism, and narrow self-interest. In short, for Wilson, the clubs embodied much of what Tocqueville found to be dangerous in the American character. The elite social clubs, Wilson wrote, have "cut [the students up] into groups and cliques whose social ambitions give them separate and rival interests quite distinct from, plainly hostile to, the interests of the University as a whole."[24] Just as Tocqueville worried that modern individuals might focus exclusively on themselves and their small "circle of family and friends," Wilson feared that the club system fostered a focus on the self that led students to ignore the common good.[25] As Wilson put it, the eating clubs "are splitting classes into factions . . . The younger classes are at no point made conscious of the interests of the University: their whole thought is concentrated upon individual ambitions, upon means of preference, upon combinations to obtain selfish individual ends, and the welfare of the University . . . is ignored."[26]

Wilson hoped to eliminate these factions by eliminating the clubs that produce them, and replacing them with four residential colleges. Wilson explained that his quad plan "is a plan to substitute for the present segregation of the classes a reunion of the classes, and for the present division of the University into small social segments, which constantly tend to war with one another and to cut the University into factions, larger segments, or, rather, vital groups, which could not possibly develop like rivalries and cliques."[27] Whereas the club-system divides the students from the faculty, and the students from one another, the quad plan would unite all members of the community around common ends—namely, the development of each person through the shared quest for truth. Wilson told his board of trustees that, "Intellectual and spiritual development, in the broadest sense of those terms, are the chief and, indeed, the only legitimate aims of university life."[28] For Wilson, the main goal of university life is thus similar to the chief aim of society as a whole. As Wilson puts it in *The State*, society is "an association of individuals organized for mutual aid. Mutual aid to what? To self-development."[29] In his view, the clubs counteract this goal; rather than develop the higher faculties, the clubs merely appeal to what is lower in students.

Wilson believed that students at Princeton should be bound together by common ideals that transcend the self; however, the organization of college life into clubs forces the new student to think primarily about his own narrow self-interest. For if the student fails to gain entrance into a club, he will be friendless and without any "social standing" at all. The task of gaining admission into a social club completely "absorbs the attention and all the planning faculties" of the freshmen and sophomores, thereby turning their minds and hearts away from what is genuinely important.[30]

In addition to promoting the pursuit of narrow self-interest, Wilson also pointed out that the clubs foster materialism insofar as they appeal to what Tocqueville called "the love of comfort." Tocqueville feared that the Americans' pursuit of "physical delights" might lead them to "lose sight of those more precious good which constitute the greatness and the glory of mankind."[31] In Wilson's view, the clubs exacerbated this dangerous tendency. Wilson thus denounced the

> increase in the luxury of the upper-class club houses. The two oldest clubs now have houses of extraordinary elegance and luxury of appointment and five other clubs are maturing plans for replacing their present comfortable structures with buildings which will rival the others in beauty, spaciousness, and comfort. . . . [The life of the clubs], as it becomes more and more elaborate, will become more and more absorbing, and university interests will fall more and more into the background.[32]

Wilson believed that the university community should be a place in which people are led by high ideals, thereby helping to ensure that the nation is not "submerged in waves of materialism."[33] One of the key goals of college education is to disabuse young Americans of the idea "that the chief end of man is to make a living!"[34] The club system is, therefore, highly damaging insofar as it makes the students focus only on worldly success and their own social ambitions. In short, the club system defeats the college's goal of making its students "better citizens and better comrades and more honest and just men."[35] This is greatly damaging to America, for in a democratic nation, as Wilson repeatedly pointed out, "the welfare of the commonwealth springs out of the character and the informed purposes" of the citizenry.[36]

Wilson did not just argue that all members of the university community should be bound together by common ideals; Wilson also argued that they should live together amid an equality of conditions. Whereas under the club system there was great inequality between those who were included and those who were excluded from the clubs, under Wilson's quad plan, "the forms and conditions under which each man in residence lives may so far as possible be the forms and conditions which are common to all."[37]

In contrast, when Wilson discussed the nation as a whole, he rarely suggested that economic inequality was *per se* dangerous to democracy. Instead, he emphasized that in America the goal should be equality of opportunity rather than equality of results. In an 1899 address, for instance, Wilson said that, "We no longer" read the Declaration of Independence "literally," for "if we believe that all men are born free and equal, we know that the freedom and equality stops at their birth . . . [A]fter you have once put men upon this starting line of birth and set them on their course they do not remain equal, the one outruns the other . . . and at the goal there is disparity, though at the starting line there may have been equality."[38] In this passage, Wilson seems unconcerned about the effects of any such "disparity" on democracy in America. But in his thoughts on Princeton, we see Wilson concede that inequality of conditions can be damaging to a democratic community.[39]

Wilson's ideas on education are also of interest insofar as they show Wilson attempting to discover forms of authority that eschew authoritarianism. In a 1909 essay, Wilson wrote that,

> The characteristic of the boarding-school is that its pupils are in all things in tutelage, are under masters at every turn of their life. . . . It is this characteristic that made it impossible and undesirable to continue the life of the boarding-school into the college, where it is necessary that the pupil should begin to show his manhood and make his own career. No one who knows what wholesome and regulated freedom can do for young men ought ever to wish to hail them back to the days of childish discipline and restraint of which the college of our grandfathers was typical. But a new discipline is desirable, is absolutely necessary, if the college is to be recalled to its proper purpose, its bounden duty.[40]

Wilson here suggests that a college (and implicitly, every democratic community) needs a form of authority—a "new discipline"—which guides people without dominating them.

In Wilson's concept of the preceptor, we find Wilson's vision of a leader who is an authority without being authoritarian.[41] In an address to Princeton alumni in Cleveland, Wilson said that,

> the point [of the Preceptorial system] is that the relationship is not so exclusively that of pupil and teacher as it used to be; . . . the new thing we are introducing is the independent pursuit of certain studies by men old enough to study for themselves and accorded the privilege in their studies of having the counsel of scholars [the preceptors] older than themselves. It is not merely that they are being led, but that they are becoming what every student ought to be, namely, reading men.[42]

Wilson hoped that students would view the preceptors not as stern masters, but rather as "their guides, philosophers and friends." The preceptors do not simply impose their knowledge onto the undergraduates. Instead, the preceptors are conceived by Wilson as "fellow-students" who engage with their students in a common quest for wisdom. The goal is not one of "cramming" students' heads full of information, but rather the "process is intended to be one of reading, comparing, [and] reflecting" together.[43]

Wilson here warned against a too sharp distinction between teachers and students, and he rejected the idea that students should be passive and voiceless. As Wilson put it, "the fundamental object is to draw faculty and undergraduates together into a common body of students, old and young, among whom a real community of interest, pursuit and feeling will prevail."[44] As seekers of truth, then, *all* members of the college community are essentially citizen-students. In short, in his ideas on college, one can see Wilson moving toward a model of *democratic* leadership—that is, a model of leadership in which leaders empower, elevate, and educate democratic citizens.

When he became President of the United States, Wilson tried to act according to a somewhat analogous conception of political leadership. He maintained that as president he was merely the chief counselor of the nation, and not its master.[45] Wilson often emphasized that his task as a democratic leader was to engage in *dialogue* with his followers.[46] As Wilson put it at a campaign speech in 1912, "I regard a meeting like this as a sort of conference in which we can become aware of one another's points of view and of one another's opinions about those matters which concern all of us."[47] In a similar vein, he said at Buffalo: "I can't understand you unless you talk to me. . . . I believe in government as a great process of getting together, a great process of debate."[48] Indeed, Wilson suggested in his First Inaugural that he could not be a successful president without the advice of his fellow citizens. He concluded the Address as follows: "I summon all honest men, all patriotic, all forward-looking men, to my side. God helping me, I will not fail them, if they will but counsel and sustain me."[49] In Wilson's vision of democratic leadership, then, the leader must approach his or her fellow citizens as equals and in a spirit of mutuality.

Institutionalizing "Common Counsel"

In Wilson's view, a successful democracy requires a citizenry with the habit of "common counsel"—that is, the habit of deliberation. Common counsel was one of Wilson's favorite phrases, and, as we have seen, he always insisted on the importance of dialogue for democratic politics.[50] Wilson's concern with fostering deliberation can be discerned in his attack on Congress's practice of government by committee. In *Congressional Government*, Wilson favored what he called "cabinet" government over "committee" government largely because he believed that the former would lead to a more vigorous and open debate about public affairs. Wilson wrote that the House of Representatives "delegates not only its legislative but also its deliberative functions to its Standing Committees." As a result, there is no "enlightenment of public opinion," since the public cannot even hear the committee debates. In Wilson's view, "The informing function of Congress should be preferred even to its legislative function."[51] This is a Tocquevillian comment: just as Tocqueville de-emphasizes the jury as a judicial institution and focuses instead on the way in which it shapes the character of the citizenry, so, too, does Wilson argue that a legislative system should be assessed not simply in terms of its law-making capacities, but also in terms of its educative effects on the public.[52]

In Wilson's view, the Constitution's separation of powers produced a Congress that was a poor educator. Since power is so dispersed in the American system, the people do not bother to concentrate their attention on anything that any particular congressperson does or says. For the young Wilson, if Americans were to have a "cabinet" government, akin to the governments of parliamentary systems, then Americans would become better educated about politics. This is because the cabinet system concentrates both legislative and executive power—and thus concentrates the attention of the citizenry—on a few notable individuals; the words and deeds of these powerful cabinet members would then shape public opinion.[53]

Wilson's desire to foster a more deliberative democracy is also evident in the criticisms that he made (before 1911) against proposals for direct democracy.[54] For instance, in *Constitutional Government*, Wilson rejected the idea that "the 'initiative' and the 'referendum' . . . are a more thorough means of getting at public opinion than the processes of our representative assemblies." Wilson believed that an "isolated opinion" is not as valuable as the opinions that grow out of "common counsel." As Wilson put it, "Common counsel is not aggregate counsel. It is not a sum in addition, counting heads. . . . [Common counsel] can be made up only by the vital contacts of actual conference, only in face to face debate, only by word of mouth and the direct clash of mind with mind."[55] In contrast to the kind of "common counsel" and debate that can take place in properly designed representative institutions, the initiative and the referendum simply entail the counting up of silent and isolated individual opinions. When measured by the standards of deliberative democracy, then, Wilson thought that the institutions of representative democracy were superior to the institutions of direct democracy.[56]

In *Congressional Government* and other early writings, Wilson sometimes seems to suggest that while elites should engage in deliberation, the average citizen should simply be a spectator who is educated by what he or she watches on the political stage. Later, though, Wilson emphasized the importance of active deliberation among *all* citizens. In *The New Freedom*, Wilson lamented that there is a "lack of a body of public opinion in our cities." This is because the busy urbanite

> doesn't talk to anybody, but he plunges his head into a news-paper and presently experiences a reaction which he calls his opinion, but which is not an opinion at all, being merely the impression that a piece of news or an editorial has made upon him. He cannot be said to be participating in public opinion at all until he has laid his mind alongside the minds of his neighbors and discussed with them the incidents of the day and the tendencies of the time.[57]

Wilson hoped to restore in urban areas the deliberative democracy that Tocqueville described in the townships of America.[58] Wilson believed that this could be done in large part by turning school-houses into social centers during the evenings. Wilson hoped that the schools would be "places of discussion, as of old took place in the town meetings. . . ."[59] Through this social center movement, then, the democratic habit of "common counsel" would be ingrained into ordinary citizens as well as elites.[60]

Tocqueville's political theory also consistently stresses the importance of *deliberative* democracy. For instance, in *The Old Regime*, he writes: "In a community of free citizens every man is daily reminded of the need of meeting his fellow men, of hearing what they have to say, of exchanging ideas, and coming to an agreement as to the conduct of their common interests."[61] Tocqueville complained that in the aftermath of the French Revolution, a plebiscitary form of mass politics arose that was the opposite of a genuinely deliberative democracy. As Tocqueville put it, "the so-called 'sovereignty of the people' came to be based on the votes of an electorate that was neither given adequate information nor an opportunity of getting together and deciding on one policy rather than another."[62] Wilson was thus writing in a Tocquevillian spirit when he insisted that, "There must be discussion and debate in which all freely participate."[63]

It should be noted that my Tocquevillian interpretation of Wilson poses a challenge to the argument—made by Jeffrey Tulis, Jeffrey Sedgwick, and others—that Wilson's vision of leadership leads to demagoguery insofar as it works to erode reasoned deliberation about public affairs. In the influential view of Tulis, Wilson made a radical departure from the framers through his creation of the "rhetorical presidency"; this vision of leadership is deeply problematic, Tulis argues, because it can easily degenerate into the mere manipulation of popular opinion by the president.[64] Much like Tulis, Sedgwick argues that whereas the framers sought the "insulation of the president from popular opinion," Wilson, in contrast, sought an "emotional or passionate . . . bond between leader and led."[65] In Sedgwick's view, Wilson conceived of the president as a "plebiscitarian democratic leader." Wilson's vision of presidential leadership was thus directly at odds, according to Sedgwick, with the founders' desire to promote "reflective deliberation on public issues."[66] But as I have shown, many of Wilson's ideas were aimed precisely at fostering "reflective deliberation on public issues." As a young man, Wilson sought to increase deliberation in Congress by creating a cabinet form of government. Moreover, his criticisms of the referendum, recall, and initiative suggest that he was very much *opposed* to a plebiscitarian form of politics that minimizes public debate. And, his enthusiasm for the social center movement suggests that, like Tocqueville, Wilson hoped that Americans would frequently engage in dialogue with their fellow citizens regarding public matters. In short, Wilson's oft-expressed goal of promoting democratic deliberation ("common counsel") calls into question the claim that Wilson's ideas promote the demagogic manipulation of popular opinion.[67]

Administrative Centralization: Theory and Practice

As revealed by his thoughts on Princeton, Congress, and the social center movement, Wilson was concerned with the question of how leaders, institutions, and laws can help produce a democratic character. This concern with character also underlies his frequently expressed opposition to administrative centralization. As early as 1879, in an essay on "Self-Government in France," Wilson revealed his appreciation of Tocqueville's argument that administrative centralization can damage the character of a people, rendering them less fit for self-rule.[68] "One has only to read de Tocqueville's *Ancien Regime*," Wilson wrote, in order to perceive how "the central government [in France] assumed *guardianship* of all the interests of the people, of even their most private concerns."[69] Without local associations to give them practice in the art of being free, the French people were left with what Wilson calls, in a Tocquevillian turn of phrase, "habits of servitude."[70]

It was precisely "guardianship" that Wilson would again denounce thirty-three years later when he opposed Roosevelt's plans for regulating the economy through centralized administrative agencies. Wilson argued that Roosevelt's proposed agencies would set up "an avowed partnership between the government and the trusts."[71] Together, bureaucratic and corporate elites would then be "benevolent guardians . . . who have taken the troubles of government off our hands."[72] One is reminded here of Tocqueville's "new despotism," which "relieves [its subjects] from the trouble of thinking and the cares of living."[73] Just as Tocqueville warned against the soft despotism of a nanny-state, so, too, did Wilson warn against the "paralysis which has sooner or later fallen upon every people who have looked to their central government to patronize and nurture them."[74] Wilson suggested that even if Roosevelt's proposed agencies *did* succeed in thwarting the trusts, the price would be the independence and the "vital energies" of the American public. Wilson and other New Freedom Democrats thus hoped to combat the trusts not through regulatory agencies, but through "non-bureaucratic and non-centralized" means, as Sidney Milkis puts it.[75] More specifically, Wilson argued that laws should be passed that would regulate competition and hence prevent trusts from arising in the first place.

Although Wilson argued against administrative centralization in his 1912 campaign, as president he created a number of federal regulatory agencies, including the Federal Trade Commission and the Federal Farm Loan Board.[76] Wilson, the exponent of provincial liberties, ironically ended up playing a significant role in the rise of the modern bureaucratic state.

How can this apparent reversal be explained? First, it should be remembered that while Wilson is rightly known as a statesman who often appealed to principles, Wilson also insisted on the importance of "expediency" in politics.[77] In a discussion of Burke, he writes, "Speculative politics treats men and situations as they are supposed to be; practical politics treats them . . . as they are found to be at the moment of actual contact."[78]

As a theorist, then, Wilson was consistently opposed to administrative centralization; as a practical politician, though, Wilson concluded that in order to combat the abuses of big business, independent regulatory commissions were indispensable. As Philippa Strum notes, Louis Brandeis

> helped persuade Wilson that the FTC should be a regulatory rather than a purely investigatory body. This ran counter to Brandeis's usual disapproval of extensive governmental regulatory involvement. [Brandeis] was nonetheless convinced that no law could cover all possible violations of antitrust policy, and an agency with the power to expand upon basic legislative policy should be created.[79]

In an address as governor of New Jersey, Wilson said that, "The rapidly changing circumstances of the time, . . . both in the political and in the industrial world, render it necessary that a constant process of adjustment should go on."[80] Given the realities of twentieth-century life, Wilson eventually found that he had to "adjust" his views on administrative centralization in order to rein in corporate abuses of power.

It is possible that Wilson was also driven to "adjust" his views on administration due to electoral concerns. According to John Milton Cooper, in the spring of 1914, Wilson feared that if the Democratic Party did not acquiesce to the public's demand for some administrative regulation of the trusts, then the Party might take a beating during the upcoming elections.[81] With these concerns in mind, Wilson created the FTC. At the same time, he did not completely abandon his former idea of attacking trusts through statutes, for he signed into law the Clayton Anti-Trust Act.

Wilson, then, was willing to "adjust" his philosophical opposition to administrative centralization after considering the constraints and conditions of political reality, including public opinion. From a Tocquevillian perspective, it is actually not too difficult to make this adjustment. For even Tocqueville believed that there was too *little* administrative centralization in America. As Tocqueville put it in a draft of *Democracy*, "decentralization has been brought to a level that no European nation could endure without uneasiness and that produces harmful results even in America."[82] If Tocqueville believed that America had too little administrative centralization in the 1830s, surely he would have believed that America had too little in the early twentieth century, given the new challenges and complexities of the industrial era. Wilson's embrace of the FTC and other regulatory agencies, then, is not necessarily inconsistent with Tocquevillian thought, given Tocqueville's belief that *some* increase in administrative centralization was necessary in America.[83]

In 1886, Wilson had, in fact, argued for increasing, to a degree, the amount of administrative centralization in America in his famous essay, "The Study of Administration." Wilson there noted that administrative science was created by German and French thinkers who had in mind "highly centralized forms of government." The task now is to adapt administrative science "to a complex and multiform state, and [make it] fit highly decentralized forms of government. If we would employ [administrative science], we must Americanize it . . . in thought, principle, and aim. . . ."[84] Wilson hoped, then, that America could retain its local liberties even as it empowered a national corps of efficient administrators. As president, he never fully managed to square this circle. He ended up with a piecemeal program in which he attacked social and economic problems at times with centralized administrative agencies, and at times through statute. The Federal Reserve, however, in some ways did achieve the synthesis that Wilson sought; as Cooper notes, it combined "government control with private participation and central authority with regional banks."[85] It thus tried to bring efficiency to the national economy while remaining responsive to local concerns.

On the whole, while Wilson did oversee the creation of agencies that increased the amount of administrative centralization in the United States, he by no means sent swarms of *intendants* throughout America in order to regulate all local affairs.[86] Indeed, his lectures at Johns Hopkins on administration reveal that he grappled a great deal with the question of how best to balance administrative centralization with local liberty. As Wilson put it in his lecture notes, "the problem to solve" is how to attain "administrative cohesion without administrative tyranny."[87] This is consistent with Tocqueville's desire to have *some* administrative centralization, but not so much that local freedom is lost.

Wilson, Tocqueville, and Industrial Democracy

Wilson's eventual embrace of regulatory commissions indicated that he had largely abandoned his original goal of actually eliminating all vast concentrations of economic power. Wilson had celebrated the entrepreneurial "man on the make" in the 1912 campaign, but as president he seemed to realize that under modern conditions, most Americans were destined to be employees rather than independent business owners or farmers. When Wilson finally accepted the fact that many Americans were destined to be employees of large corporations, he came to adopt many of the positions of Theodore Roosevelt's Bull Moose Party. For instance, whereas Wilson had once rejected as unconstitutional a federal minimum wage and a federal ban on child labor, he eventually came to accept these as expedient measures, and he also came to support maximum hours legislation.

To be sure, Wilson's acceptance of a basically fixed class of employees meant that he had to accept that Americans would be largely dependent on corporations, and it was dependency that he had once warned against. Wilson recognized, though, that this dependency could be lessened—if not completely eliminated—through certain public policies. For instance, in a Congressional address of 1919, Wilson called for "the genuine democratization of industry, based upon a full recognition of the right of those who work, in whatever rank, to participate in some organic way in every decision which directly affects their welfare or the part they are to play in industry."[88] Wilson's suggestion went unheeded, but it stands as a remarkable presidential statement in support of the idea that workers should be full participants in the corporations that shape their lives in so many respects.

In calling for a more democratized workplace, one might say that Wilson applied Tocquevillian insights to an area where Tocqueville himself mostly failed to apply them. As Mark Reinhardt has pointed out, Tocqueville's critique of "tutelary power" can be employed to shed light not just on the modern state, but also on the modern corporation. Corporations, Reinhardt argues, "will not tolerate citizens," but instead "demand subjects."[89] They therefore work "to isolate individuals, to prevent the development of the practices of self-government and to destroy these practices where they exist. . . ."[90] Moreover, corporations make important decisions—such as whether to close factories—which have tremendous public consequences, and yet the public has no say in these decisions. Much like Reinhardt, Jack Lively also criticizes Tocqueville for his "complete disregard of industrial organisation, an area which seems at least as relevant to his main theme as political organisation."[91] Lively overstates his case a bit, for Tocqueville *was* concerned with industrialization, as more recent scholarship has stressed.[92] But despite the element of overstatement, Lively's basic point remains useful. For Lively correctly notes that Tocqueville did little to apply his ideas on citizen empowerment and citizen participation to the realm of work. As Lively notes, Tocqueville's

> primary purpose was to outline the means by which men could be presented in their daily lives with the possibility or even necessity of co-operating with others to achieve common purposes. It was only through such experience that a sense of personal and social responsibility could be retained, withdrawal from public life halted and subservience to a monolithic public opinion relaxed. He stressed that the experience should be

immediate and intimate. . . . Yet he virtually ignored the major area of men's daily life, their work, and it is in this area above all that in present society there is the widest gap between men's activities and their control over them.[93]

To a large degree, Wilson made the theoretical move that Tocqueville mostly neglected. In his *Recollections*, Tocqueville attacked the revolutionaries of 1848 for bringing social and economic questions into politics. The great fault of the socialists, in Tocqueville's view, is that they were "aiming lower than the government and attempting to reach society itself, on which government stands."[94] In contrast, Wilson explicitly suggested that the pursuit of democracy in modern times inevitably involves economic questions. As Wilson put it in *The New Freedom*, "We are in a temper to reconstruct economic society, as we were once in a temper to reconstruct political society, and political society may itself undergo a radical modification in the process."[95]

Wilson recognized that the prevailing corporate structure was in tension with the kind of public-minded and active citizenship that Tocqueville celebrated. As Wilson put it,

> You know what happens when you are the servant of a corporation. You have in no instance access to the men who are really determining the policy of the corporation. If the corporation is doing the things that it ought not to do, you really have no voice in the matter and must obey the orders, and you have oftentimes with deep mortification to co-operate in the doings of things which you know are against the public interest. Your individuality is swallowed up in the individuality and purpose of a great organization.[96]

Tocqueville feared a modern world in which passive and isolated subjects allowed the state to make all-important public decisions. Wilson pointed out in 1912 that it was not just the *state* that was making crucial decisions in place of the citizenry, but also corporate elites. Wilson said that, "All over the Union people are coming to feel that they have no control over the course of affairs."[97] This was partly because bosses controlled political machines, but it also resulted from the fact that corporate boards could not be held accountable to their workers or to the public at large.[98]

Wilson applied the Tocquevillian rejection of paternalism to new conditions, by warning against a new danger: namely, the paternalism of corporations. Tocqueville could not have fully anticipated this danger, for in the America of the 1830s, Tocqueville found that industrialists were anything but paternalistic. Unlike past aristocrats, who were "obliged by law," or at least "by custom," to try to ameliorate some of the misery of their social inferiors, Tocqueville found that the industrialist of the 1830s leaves workers to fend for themselves. As Tocqueville put it, "the industrial aristocracy of our day, when it has impoverished and brutalized the men it uses, abandons them in time of crisis to public charity to feed them."[99]

Of course, in the early twentieth century many industrialists were still brutalizing their workers, and Wilson sought to prevent some of the worst abuses. For instance, he fought for workers' compensation as "an automatic operation of law," and as president he eventually came to support such legislative measures as the eight-hour day.[100] Just as Lincoln insisted that "the man" should be put "*before* the dollar," so, too, did Wilson insist that corporations should not be allowed to elevate "property rights" above "human rights."[101] But even as Wilson tried to protect workers against the worst abuses of corporations, he also warned workers about a day when seemingly benevolent corporations will take better care of their workers so as to make them more dependent on their employers. To put it in the terms that Tocqueville uses in his chapter on the new despotism, Wilson warned against a system of corporate capitalism in which companies will "degrade men rather than torment them."[102] In *The New Freedom*, for instance, Wilson points out that some companies have instituted "systems of profit sharing, of compensation for injuries, and of bonuses, and even pensions; but every one of these plans has merely bound their workingmen more tightly to themselves. . . . They are merely privileges which employees enjoy only so long as they remain in the employment and observe the rules of the great industries for which they work."[103] Thus Wilson feared the rise of massive corporations not only because of the damage they might do to the economy, but also because of the way in which they would damage the American character. As William Leuchtenberg puts it, Wilson feared that "by offering [employees] security and contentment," the benevolent corporation will "subtly destroy men's wills."[104]

Interpretive Statesmanship and the Education of Democracy

We have seen that Wilson engaged in a number of policy shifts: he eventually endorsed the creation of certain regulatory agencies, and he also came to embrace a number of social welfare measures that he had once opposed, such as a federal ban on child labor. In these cases, Wilson acted on the basis of political expediency, in the double sense of the term. That is, he acted as he did because he came to believe that these measures would be effective in practice, even if they departed from his abstract principles. As Daniel Stid convincingly argues, Wilson underwent "a genuine rethinking" as president regarding how the ideals of the New Freedom could best be put into practice, a rethinking that led him to embrace many of the social justice proposals of the Bull Moosers.[105] Wilson also acted expediently in the sense that he knew that if he did not shift ground, he would be so out of step with important elements of public opinion that his political career would be finished. Wilson recognized that in a two-person race in 1916, he would have to appeal to many of the people who voted for the third party candidates Roosevelt or Debs in 1912. This electoral concern probably played a role in his adopting a somewhat more activist approach to solving the problems of the American political economy.

This latter form of "expediency" should not be seen simply as a craven form of pandering to the public in order to achieve electoral success. Rather, Wilson's acknowledgment of the power of public opinion aligns him, to a significant degree, with Lincoln's conception of leadership. Lincoln believed that the leader must remain close to the people, for in a democracy, as Lincoln said, "public sentiment is every thing. With public sentiment, nothing can fail; without it nothing can succeed."[106] Wilson agreed with Lincoln that public opinion needs to be taken very seriously for both practical and moral reasons. Practically speaking, it is obvious that no one can get elected without the support of public opinion. As Wilson put it, a candidate plainly "would not fish for votes . . . among the minority."[107] Morally speaking, the democratic leader must respect public opinion, or else self-government would be replaced by paternalistic rule. Hence, Wilson wrote that "it is a dignified proposition with us . . . that as is the majority, so ought the government to be."[108] Leaders who fail to respect public opinion are setting themselves up as "guardians" or "trustees" of the people, and as Wilson put it in the 1912 campaign, "freemen need no guardians."[109]

Wilson argued that the task of the democratic statesman was to "interpret" public opinion. Wilson once wrote in his journal: "I receive the opinions of my day, I do not *con*ceive them. . . . It is a task, not of origination, but of interpretation."[110] If Wilson had not shifted ground in order to keep pace with changing public opinion, then he would be acting not as the *interpreter* of public opinion, but rather as an arrogant guardian or trustee. When Wilson changed his mind about federal intervention into the economy, then, he cannot be rightly condemned for simply abandoning his principles. As Stid points out, Wilson's policy shifts "had integrity at a fundamental level," for Wilson had always praised the leader for whom "convictions and polices evolv[e] over the years in response to the prevailing sentiments of public opinion, the logic of compelling ideas, and the experience of and responsibility for governing. . . ."[111]

Wilson, then, like Lincoln, believed for both practical and moral reasons that he had to remain close to the basic beliefs and aspirations of the people. But what about "moral courage," the willingness to resist unwise popular demands? Did Wilson achieve the synthesis of closeness to the people and moral courage which defined Lincoln's leadership?

From today's vantage point, one wishes that Wilson had at times exercised *more* moral courage. For instance, on the question of race, Wilson did not oppose the demands of Southern Democrats that the federal government be segregated. Wilson wrote to a Protestant minister who protested the segregation policy that it "is distinctly to the advantage of the colored people themselves."[112] In fact, the decision seemed to be aimed at subordinating blacks and at providing patronage jobs for white Democratic party loyalists.[113]

As Daniel Tichenor has shown, Wilson also lacked moral courage on the issue of women's rights. At the 1916 meeting of the National American Woman Suffrage Association, Wilson conceded that the suffragists had justice on their side, but he argued that in a democracy, the statesman has to heed the constraints of public opinion. As Wilson put it, "It is all very well to be ahead and beckon, but after all, you have got to wait for the body to follow."[114] Wilson, however, refused even to gently beckon the electorate toward justice for women; while Charles Evan Hughes endorsed a women's suffrage amendment in the 1916 election, Wilson refused to do so. Pressured by activists, Wilson did eventually support an amendment in 1917. However, he justified the amendment solely as a war measure, "thereby missing," as Tichenor puts it, "an important opportunity to educate the public concerning its *democratic* meaning."[115]

The ideas expressed in Wilson's speech at the N.A.W.S.A. meeting are consistent with the Burkean side of Wilson's thought, as expressed in his book *The State*. Wilson there argued that reform had to be the result of a slow, "organic" process. This means that attempting to impose onto a polity progressive reforms that violate public opinion will have disastrous results. As Wilson put it, "change which roughly breaks with the common thought will lack the sympathy of that thought, will provoke its opposition, and will inevitably be crushed by that opposition. Society can be changed only by evolution."[116] Wilson argued that the leader must remain not only close to public opinion, but also to the traditional practices—or "habits"—of the people, even if some of those practices are undesirable:

> Human choice [cannot] proceed by leaps and bounds: it has been confined to adaptation . . . Institutions, like morals, like all other forms of life and conduct, have had to wait upon the slow, the almost imperceptible formations of habit. . . . [T]he most ardent

reformers have had to learn that too far to outrun the more sluggish masses was to render themselves powerless.[117]

At times, then, Wilson stressed that it is futile for leaders to depart too far from public opinion. In these moments, Wilson downplayed the need for moral courage on the part of leaders.

On the other hand, when he turned his attention to the League of Nations, Wilson *did* exercise a considerable degree of moral courage, for the nation as a whole was largely skeptical about entering such an unprecedented international agreement. Undaunted, Wilson engaged in a speaking tour designed to educate Americans about the moral and practical necessity of the League. When it came to the League, then, Wilson did not play the role of the statesman who simply interprets what is already widely believed. Instead, Wilson hoped to play the role of the reformer described in his essay, "Leaders of Men":

> Men of strenuous minds and high ideals come forward . . . as champions of a political or moral principle. . . . Their souls are pierced with a thousand keen arrows of obloquy. . . . They stand alone: and oftentimes are made bitter by their isolation. They are doing nothing less than defy public opinion, and shall they convert it by blows? Yes, presently the forces of the popular thought hesitate, waver. . . . Again a little while and they have yielded. Masses come over the side of the reform.[118]

As the example of the League shows, Wilson *did* sometimes insist that leaders should educate and mold public opinion. In fact, Wilson made it clear that the ideal interpretive statesman is not just a passive instrument of the people's will; instead, the interpretative statesman should also *shape* the people's will. Thus, in a speech that he gave many times in the 1890s, Wilson declared that "we live in a nation that waits to be led . . . if we can convince or move it. . . . How we *cheat* ourselves by living in subjection to public opinion when we *might make it*!"[119] Wilson sometimes claimed to simply be the spokesman of the people, but in fact he never abandoned the sentiment that he expressed as a youth in a letter to a friend; he wrote that as aspiring leaders, they should learn "all the arts of persuasion, but especially . . . oratory . . . that we might have facility in leading others into our ways of thinking and enlisting them in our purposes."[120] In short, while he may not have always achieved the synthesis in his own practice of leadership, Wilson's theory of leadership *does* aim at the synthesis that Lincoln sought, for Wilson suggested that while leaders should respect public opinion, they should also sometimes try to educate and thus *shape* public opinion.

Of course, on the issue of the League, Wilson's efforts to shape public opinion were by no means a complete success. According to Cooper, while most Americans in 1920 were not full-fledged isolationists, it is also the case that, "Wilson's program only enjoyed minority support."[121] Ultimately unsuccessful in his pedagogical efforts regarding the League, Wilson seemed to content himself, at the end of his life, with the idea that public opinion would one day come to embrace the path that he had pointed out. After he left office, Wilson told his daughter that, "I think it was best after all that the United States did not join the League of Nations," since that would have been "only a personal victory" for Wilson. "Now, when the American people join the League," Wilson said, "it will be because they are convinced it is the right thing to do, and then will be the *only right* time for them to do it." Wilson concluded to his daughter that, "Perhaps God knew better than I did after all."[122] As a democratic statesman, then, Wilson was convinced that it would have been not only practically impossible—but also morally wrong—to have imposed the League onto the nation. Like Lincoln, who would have preferred that the slaves be emancipated by democratic processes rather than by executive fiat, Wilson believed that in a democracy, the people should ultimately have the liberty to choose their own collective path. The democratic leader should strive to *persuade* and *educate*, but not *dominate*.

Wilson and the Education of Democracy

But if Wilson believed that one of the major tasks of leadership is education, what else did he hope to teach the public? Above all, Wilson hoped to teach Americans that leadership should be considered not primarily as a threat to democracy, but rather as necessary for its flourishing. (This is, of course, also the central theme of this book.) More specifically, Wilson tried to teach Americans to have greater respect for the importance of strong governmental leaders. As James Morone has argued in *The Democratic Wish*, Americans have had a "dread of government" ever since the colonial era. Due to their fear of strong government, Americans have long wished for a kind of pure democracy that can somehow dispense with "ministers who think." Morone concludes his book by suggesting that we need "a national reappraisal of ancient, powerful fears [of government.] The debate has not begun even on the conceptual level."[123] But in fact, more than a hundred years ago, Wilson tried to foster precisely such a debate. For in contrast to the long-standing libertarian tradition in American political thought, Wilson tried to teach Americans that governmental power and authority are necessary for the full flowering of American democracy. Wilson taught that while the "fear of *irresponsible* power" is "very proper and salutary," there is "no danger in power, if only it be not irresponsible. If it be divided . . . it is obscured; and if it be obscured, it is made irresponsible."[124]

Wilson recognized that Americans' fear of governmental power and authority had deep roots in American political culture. In "The Ideals of America," he wrote that in the aftermath of the Revolutionary War, "It was difficult to want any common government at all after fighting to be quit of restraint and overlordship altogether; and it went infinitely hard to be obliged to make it strong, with a right to command and a power to rule."[125] Wilson granted that the Constitution of 1787 was a great improvement over the Articles of Confederation, but he believed that the Constitution's separation of powers made it difficult for the nation to have "any single or consistent pattern of statesmanship."[126] The virtue of the Constitution is that it provides "stable safeguards against hasty or retrogressive action."[127] However, this "Newtonian" system of separated powers also ensured that the government will often be weak and inefficient when it attempts to grapple with public problems. Wilson thus believed that his task as an academic and as a statesman was to bring greater "concentration" and "integration" to American government.[128]

Daniel Stid has assiduously traced the various twists and turns in Wilson's thought regarding how American government could be made simultaneously more powerful and more accountable. In his early academic career, Wilson believed that this should be done by bringing to America a parliamentary, or cabinet, government. This would require a constitutional amendment allowing members of congress to serve in the president's cabinet. Later, Wilson became convinced that this type of constitutional change was unlikely to ever be enacted in America; meanwhile, the strong leadership exercised by Grover Cleveland had convinced Wilson that a gifted president could informally bring a quasi-parliamentary government to the United States without any amendment. In this scenario—a scenario which he laid out in *Constitutional Government*, and later enacted with considerable success in his first term of office—the president would work closely with his party in Congress and actively set the legislative agenda for the nation.

While Tocqueville greatly admired the framers' constitutional design, he may very well have welcomed Wilson's desire for stronger national leadership in America. For even as Tocqueville emphasized the educative benefits of decentralized administration, he also insisted on the necessity of what he calls *governmental* centralization. In a draft of his ideas on the subject, Tocqueville wrote:

What I call governmental centralization is the concentration of great social powers in a single hand or in a single place. The *power* to make the laws and the *force* to compel obedience to them. What I call administrative centralization is the concentration in the same hand or in the same place of a power to regulate ordinary affairs of the society, to dictate and to direct the everyday details of its existence. . . . The first however is far more necessary to the society than the other.[129]

Tocqueville's belief in the importance of a strong central government is also evident when he writes that, "Far from [fearing] the consolidation of sovereignty in the hands of the Union, I believe the federal government is getting visibly weaker."[130] Tocqueville clearly did not see this weakening of the central government as a positive trend. To take one example, he supported the National Bank as "the great monetary link of the Union," and he worried about its demise.[131] Wilson's desire for greater "concentration" and "integration" of national power thus may actually be consistent with Tocqueville's political theory.

In arguing for more dynamic governmental leadership, Wilson tried to reverse the long-standing idea that "power" and "liberty" are inevitably opposed. As Bernard Bailyn has demonstrated, the idea that power poses a constant threat to liberty was the underlying idea of the American Revolution.[132] The colonists believed that in a state of nature, there would be total liberty, but no security for anyone, and so a certain degree of power is necessary to keep order. However, since power tends to be of an encroaching nature, government is, at best, "a necessary evil," as Thomas Paine put it. In *Common Sense*, Paine writes: "Society is produced by our wants, and government by our wickedness; the former promotes our happiness *positively* by uniting our affections, the latter *negatively* by restraining our vices. . . . The first is a patron, the last a punisher."[133] In sharp contrast to Paine, Wilson declared: "I cannot imagine power as a thing negative, and not positive."[134]

Wilson here, in a sense, follows in the steps of Lincoln, who in a fragment wrote that, "if all men were just, there still would be *some*, though not *so much*, need of government." Lincoln thus agrees with Wilson that government does *not* stem solely from our vices, as Paine suggested. Lincoln writes that the restraint of "wrongs" is indeed *one* aspect of government, for government is needed to deter "crimes, misdemeanors, and non-performance of contracts." But beyond that, government is necessary for the positive tasks of creating and maintaining "public roads and highways, public schools, charities, . . . orphanages," and other public services. All of these tasks perhaps could be done without government, but not "so well," Lincoln wrote.[135] Government, then, is for Lincoln not just a restraining force, but a positive and creative force which promotes the common good.

Later, during the Civil War, Lincoln suggested that governmental power can also be a *liberating* force. As McPherson points out, it may be true that the Emancipation Proclamation did not immediately free any slaves, but it did instantly turn the advancing Union Army into "an army of liberation." Lincoln clearly came to believe, as McPherson points out, that "power was the protector of liberty, not its enemy—except to the liberty of those who wished to do as they pleased with the product of other men's labor."[136]

After Lincoln's death, his party during Reconstruction continued the effort to use governmental power as a way to protect the freedom of African-Americans in the South. Wilson, a Southerner by birth, was highly critical of Reconstruction, but he accepted the principle that government could be a liberating rather than a repressive force. As Wilson put it, "Freedom to-day is something more than being let alone. The program of a government of freedom must in these days be positive, not negative merely."[137] Specifically, Wilson believed that governmental power had to be wielded to restore economic freedom and improve working conditions. By passing laws that would battle monopolies, Wilson would ensure that "the man on the make" would once again have the liberty to rise up in the world.

For Wilson, then, strong leadership can enhance rather than diminish democracy. In addition to teaching that *leadership* is crucial for democracy, Wilson also taught that authority—specifically, *religious* authority—is necessary in a democratic regime. According to Wilson, democracy requires citizens who check their own tendencies toward greed and the pursuit of domination. This happens when citizens have internalized certain authoritative ideals. Like Tocqueville, Wilson believed that these ideals come, in part, from the religious heritage of Americans. In 1923, for instance, Wilson expressed his conviction that Christianity can help restrain the individualism and materialism of a capitalist society:

> By justice the lawyer generally means the prompt, fair, and open application of impartial rules; but we call ours a Christian civilization, and a Christian conception of justice must be much higher. It must include sympathy and helpfulness and a willingness to forego self-interest in order to promote the welfare, happiness, and contentment of others and of the community as a whole. This is what our age is blindly feeling after in its reaction against what it deems the too great selfishness of the capitalistic system.[138]

Like other Progressives, Wilson spoke too easily of America as a "Christian" nation; such language threatens to exclude non-Christians from full membership in the American polity. However, Wilson's views on the relationship between Christianity and politics are, in fact, not nearly as illiberal as some of his rhetoric would suggest. On the one hand, Wilson's language was sometimes exclusionary, such as when he declared that, "America was born a Christian nation. America was born to exemplify that devotion to the elements of righteousness which are derived from the relations of Holy Scripture."[139] But on the other hand, during a 1911 address at Carnegie Hall, Wilson emphasized that non-Christians could be full citizens. He said that, "Here is a great body of our Jewish fellow-citizens, from whom have sprung men of genius in every walk of our varied life, men who have become part of the very stuff of America, who have conceived its ideals with singular clearness and led its enterprise with spirit and sagacity."[140] By suggesting that American Jews have been able to "conceive" American "ideals," Wilson seems to move towards Lincoln's position that American citizenship is based not specifically on Christian beliefs, but rather on beliefs about liberty and equality that can be shared by all.

Moreover, in practice, Wilson did *not* try to blur the separation between church and state. Wilson believed that religion plays an important role in elevating the American character, but he maintained that it is not the role of the state to invade the realm of individual liberty by imposing religious teachings onto the people. Indeed, Wilson's Protestant interpretation of Christianity itself led him to emphasize the importance of individual liberty. In *The State*, Wilson suggests that individual rights in fact began with Christianity, which "gave each man a magistracy over himself by insisting upon his personal, individual responsibility to God. For right living, at any rate, each man was to have only his own conscience as a guide."[141] Wilson may have invoked religious ideals in his speeches and writings, then, but he did not believe that it is the task of the government to enforce "right living." Just as Tocqueville criticized the Puritans for "invad[ing] the sphere of conscience," so, too, did Wilson write with approval that, "Modern states have foregone most attempts to make citizens virtuous or frugal by law."[142] In Wilson's view, it is not primarily the state, but rather the home, the school, and the church which should "mold and control the rising generation."[143] As with Tocqueville, character-formation was to be left in large part (but not completely) to the institutions of civil society.

Wilson: Hegelian or Tocquevillian?

I have sought to demonstrate that, to a considerable degree, Wilson had a Tocquevillian understanding of the relationship between leaders, institutions, and the character of citizens. This interpretation of Wilson is at odds with the reading of Wilson offered by Pestritto in his important book, *Woodrow Wilson and the Roots of Modern Liberalism*. According to Pestritto, it is Hegel who was the primary philosophical influence on Wilson. In Pestritto's view, Wilson believed, as Hegel did, that "history would bring about the ideal end through the concrete development of the state."[144] Pestritto seeks to condemn Wilson—and recent liberal thought as a whole—for its departure from the "social compact theory" of the framers.[145] Pestritto views Wilson precisely in the same way that Harry Jaffa, in *A New Birth of Freedom*, views Calhoun: namely, as a Hegelian who abandons natural rights thinking in favor of a progressivism that denies that there is, as Jaffa puts it, an "unchanging ground of human experience."[146] Through his critique of Wilson, Pestritto tries to suggest that those who today aspire to use the federal government to address our social and economic problems are engaged in an essentially un-American enterprise rooted in Wilson's statist departure from the limited-government philosophy of the Founders.[147]

In contrast to Pestritto, I would emphasize that under Wilson a great deal of legislation was passed that improved the lives of ordinary citizens. As summarized by Eileen McDonagh,

> President Wilson's first Congress . . . passed the Federal Reserve Act, additional child labor legislation [which supplemented the Child Labor Act of 1912], the La Follette-Peters Eight-Hour Act, the Federal Trade Commission Act, the Clayton Anti-Trust Act, and the Seaman's Act (which freed sailors from bondage to their contracts). In 1916 the Sixty-Fourth Congress passed the Smith-Hughes Act, which established federal aid to state vocational education, the Adamson Eight Hour Day, the Keating-Owen Child Labor Act, the Rural Credits Act, and a new Federal Workmen's Compensation Act.[148]

If all of these public policy achievements are dismissed as the product of an essentially "Germanic" political theory that dangerously departs from the true principles of democratic self-government, then contemporary efforts to use government to address our common problems are also undermined. There is thus a great deal at stake in assessing whether or not Pestritto's interpretation of Wilson is fully convincing.

In my view, Wilson is more properly understood as Tocquevillian rather than Hegelian.[149] Although Pestritto's reading of Wilson as a Hegelian is often stimulating, it must be noted that the textual evidence for a direct influence on Wilson is far greater in the case of Tocqueville than it is for Hegel.[150] As we have seen, Wilson privately wrote that Tocqueville provides "quite the best philosophy since Aristotle," and Wilson often refers to Tocqueville in his speeches, writings, and lectures. This is simply not the case with Hegel. Indeed, in Wilson's vast published writings, there is only one notable reference to Hegel, in "The Study of Administration."[151] Moreover, in Wilson's private letters and notebooks—wherein Wilson might have felt at greater liberty to praise Hegel, if he so desired—there is only one significant mention of Hegel, in a love letter to his fiancée, Ellen Louise Axson.[152]

Ultimately, Wilson's thought is more Tocquevillian than Hegelian because Wilson believed, as Tocqueville did, that individual leaders can consciously help to shape the destiny of their polities. In an article that compares Tocqueville and Hegel, Catherine Zuckert notes that,

> Like Hegel, Tocqueville . . . sees modern politics as the product of an historical development which limits the political alternatives by bringing to light a new truth. . . . Unlike Hegel, however, Tocqueville sees that there is still uncertainty with regard to the outcome. Men who recognize the essential equality of all human beings may live in freedom, but the mere recognition of human equality will not suffice to produce that outcome. Indeed, Tocqueville thinks that Hegel's teaching with regard to the necessary course of history undermines the fundamental condition for the perpetuation of liberal democracy—the human being's belief in his ability to control his own fate.[153]

While Tocqueville thought that the progress of equality was a "providential fact," he also believed that it was up to human beings to determine whether equality led to servitude or freedom. As Zuckert notes, Tocqueville worried about the tendency of "democratic historians," who, influenced by Hegel, were "apt to deny the efficacy of statesmen or leadership altogether and conclude that events are the product of essentially uncontrollable forces."[154] According to Pestritto, Wilson believed, as Hegel did, "that human choice has but a small role to play in politics."[155] And yet, *pace* Pestritto, Wilson's own strenuous efforts to shape the institutions of Princeton and of the United States suggest that, like Tocqueville, Wilson *did* believe in the fundamental importance of individual thought, action, and choice.

Wilson also stressed the importance of individual choice—and thus rejected Hegelian fatalism—in an exchange of letters with his fiancée. Discussing their future plans, Ellen Axson wrote that, "I am sure that, however it turns out, it will all be *right*." Wilson responded: "That's rather an odd philosophy of yours, miss, that, whatever comes of this will be 'right': it is almost too near to saying that 'whatever is is right,' which is very far from being true." In his next letter to Axson, he explained further that "your little piece of philosophy . . . would justify one in letting things drift, in the assurance that they would drift to a happy result."[156] Like Tocqueville, then, Wilson insisted that rather than fatalistically "drift," human beings should carefully make the choices that will affect their destiny. Moreover, Wilson's criticism of the idea that "whatever is, is right," may very well have been intended as a criticism of Hegel's philosophy. Not all Hegel interpreters accept that the dictum, "whatever is, is right" accurately captures Hegel's teaching; nevertheless, it is a saying that has long been associated with Hegel, and it is striking that Wilson here explicitly criticizes it.[157]

In *The State*, Wilson again emphasizes that human agency *does* play a significant role in world affairs:

> [G]overnment was not all a mere spontaneous growth. *Deliberate choice has always played a part in its development.* It was not, on the one hand, given to man ready-made by God, nor was it, on the other hand, a human contrivance. In its origin it was spontaneous, natural, twin-born with man and the family. . . . *But, once having arisen, government was affected, and profoundly affected, by man's choice*; only that choice entered, not to originate, but to modify government.[158]

Wilson's conviction that leaders can choose to change the political landscape, albeit within certain constraints, is reminiscent of the following passage from Tocqueville, which Zuckert quotes: "A lawgiver is like a man steering his route over the sea. He, too, can control the ship that bears him, but he cannot change its structure, create winds, or prevent the ocean stirring beneath him."[159]

In addition to Zuckert, Dana Villa has also offered an illuminating comparison of Tocqueville and Hegel. According to Villa,

> Hegel's historical/cultural/psychological approach to the evolution of consciousness led him to stigmatize *independence* in *all* its forms. This is a mistake Tocqueville was able to avoid, even though he agreed with Hegel that anyone who thought they stood alone, with their destiny fully in hand, was delusional. Independence conceived as a basic mode of social being was, for Tocqueville, clearly a mistake. . . . Independence as an element of freedom, however, was not—as Tocqueville's emphasis on

local independence and the last book of *Democracy in America*
volume 2 makes plain.[160]

With Villa's distinction between Hegel and Tocqueville in mind, I would
again argue that Wilson is more Tocquevillian than Hegelian. For like both
Hegel *and* Tocqueville, Wilson rejected the notion of independence "as a
basic mode of social being." Hence, Wilson argued that "a man comes
to himself" only when he realizes that, "He is not isolated; he cannot
be. His life is made up of the relations he bears to others—is made or
marred by those relations, guided by them, judged by them, expressed in
them. . . . It is by these he gets his spiritual growth; it is by these we see
his character revealed, his purpose, and his gifts."[161] For Wilson, then, the
process of "coming to oneself," is decidedly *not* a process of cutting the
ties that bind one to others. At the same time, like Tocqueville—but unlike
Hegel—Wilson refrained from rejecting the notion of independence *tout
court*. Indeed, in *Constitutional Government*, Wilson extolled the concept
of independence in explicitly Tocquevillian terms: "De Tocqueville," he
writes,

> marveled at the "variety of information and excellence of dis-
> cretion" expected of the American citizen by the constitutional
> system under which he lives. . . . It throws upon him a great
> responsibility and expects of him *a constant and watchful
> independence*. There is no one to look out for his rights but
> himself. He is not a ward of the government, but his own
> guardian.[162]

Four years later, during his presidential campaign, Wilson argued that the
independence of the individual was now threatened by giant corporations.
Like Tocqueville, then, Wilson rejected the idea that the socially isolated
individual can be genuinely free; but, also like Tocqueville, Wilson sought
to combat "guardianship" out of a concern for the independence of the
individual.

⊷⊨◉⊨⊶

According to Pestritto, Wilson is a Hegelian historicist because in
place of "the founding's ahistorical notion of human nature," Wilson sub-
stituted the idea that "the human condition improves as history marches
forwards." For Pestritto, Wilson believed that the American people had
progressed to a stage where they no longer needed "the separation of
powers, and all of the other institutional remedies that the founders

employed against the danger of faction."[163] Pestritto's Wilson thus believed that the state should "be unfettered so that it can effect the will of the people."[164] But in my view, Wilson never actually abandoned the concept of a fixed human nature, nor did he completely discard the notion of limited government. In a 1907 Address Wilson declared that, "Not everything is changed: the biggest item of all remains unaltered,—*human nature itself*; and it is nothing to daunt a free people,—free to think and free to act, that the circumstances in which that old, *unalterable nature* now expresses itself are so complex and singular."[165] Wilson's argument, then, is that economic and technological conditions changed greatly since the founding, but human nature itself remains constant.

In part because he believed that human beings were by nature imperfect, Wilson was never as enthusiastic about direct democracy as was Theodore Roosevelt. According to Jean Yarbrough, Roosevelt believed that Americans had progressed ethically to a point where it was now safe to dispense with the system of checks and balances and put a pure democracy in its place.[166] Wilson, though, did not go nearly as far down the road toward endorsing the institutions of direct democracy as did Roosevelt. As discussed earlier, in his 1908 work *Constitutional Government*, Wilson sharply criticized the initiative and the referendum. In 1911, Wilson did reverse course insofar as he came to support (without much enthusiasm) the initiative, the referendum, and the recall of legislators. However, as Stid notes, Wilson came to endorse these measures primarily because he believed that it would be political suicide to do otherwise; if he had remained opposed to these reforms, he would never have gained the crucial support of "the Bryanite wing of the Democratic Party."[167] Moreover, it should be emphasized that Wilson *always* rejected the New Nationalists' desire to allow the recall of judges and judicial rulings. In short, as Bimes and Skowronek put it, Wilson as president "remained skeptical" about "the Progressives' fascination with structural reform."[168]

In Yarbrough's view, Theodore Roosevelt believed that "not even the Constitution" should stand in the way of "the popular will."[169] In contrast, Wilson never really abandoned the idea of limited government. Indeed, Yarbrough notes that Roosevelt attacked Wilson "precisely for his defense of limited government."[170] For Wilson insisted that there is no form of government higher than limited, or *constitutional*, government. "A 'constitutional' government," wrote Wilson, "is one in which there is a definite understanding as to the sphere and powers of government; one in which individual liberty is defined and guaranteed by specific safeguards, in which the authority and the functions of those who rule are *limited* and determined by unmistakable custom or explicit fundamental law."[171] In Wilson's view, if the people's representatives control the government, that government must still be limited by constitutional arrangements, or else the democratic majority will simply be "an arbitrary, self-willed master."[172] Wilson believed that a constitutional government must always lay out "the rights of the individual against the community," and these rights must always be protected by a "judiciary with substantial and independent powers, secure against all corrupting or perverting influences."[173] Hence, Wilson always opposed Roosevelt's suggestion that the American majority no longer needed to be checked by independent judges. Pestritto thus overstates the case when he suggests that Wilson wanted to jettison all restraints on government, due to the ethical progress made by Americans. As we have seen, this more accurately describes Roosevelt than it does Wilson. Wilson's belief that the permanence of human nature dictates the permanent need for certain political institutions is also evident in the following passage from *Congressional Government*: "I know that it has been proposed by enthusiastic, but not too practical, reformers to do away with parties by some legerdemain of governmental reconstruction, accompanied and supplemented by some rehabilitation, devoutly to be wished, of *the virtues least commonly controlling in fallen human nature*."[174] Wilson believed that our fixed human nature necessitates the continued existence of limits on government, as well as the continued existence of political parties.[175]

Wilson's Liberal-Republicanism

In addition to calling into question Pestritto's interpretation of Wilson, my reading of Wilson differs from the classic interpretation offered by Louis Hartz. For Hartz, Wilson was a Lockean liberal who "conceded the 'Americanism' of the Horatio Alger theme, arguing only that it was disappearing as a result of trusts and bosses."[176] Although he may have claimed to be striking out on a new, progressive path, Hartz believes that Wilson merely demonstrated "the pathetic enslavement of the Progressive tradition to the 'Americanism' that Whiggery had uncovered."[177] Hartz seems to suggest, then, that in 1912 Wilson simply wanted to restore the competitive and individualistic universe that reigned in America before the close of the frontier and the large-scale concentration of capital. However, while Wilson's 1912 campaign did emphasize economic opportunity in language that is sometimes reminiscent of the Horatio Alger myth, his Tocquevillian emphasis on character leads him to diverge from Hartz's liberal consensus. There is, in fact, a strong republican strand in Wilson's thought, for Wilson is concerned with how to "cultivat[e] in citizens the qualities of character that self-government requires," to use Sandel's terminology.[178]

Wilson's departure from Lockean liberalism is evident in his 1899 essay, "When a Man Comes to Himself." Wilson here rejects the common liberal idea that "political society" is "a necessary evil, an irritating but inevitable restriction upon the 'natural' sovereignty and entire self-government of the individual. That was the dream of the egotist."[179] In this essay, Wilson gives voice to the Aristotelian idea that political society is valuable not just because it leads to the material conveniences of life, but also because it can lead to the fulfillment of people's highest capacities. As Wilson put it, the so-called bonds of political society are actually

> indispensable aids and spurs to the attainment of the highest and most enjoyable things man is capable of. Political society, the life of men in states, is an abiding natural relationship. It is neither a mere convenience nor a mere necessity. It is not a mere voluntary association. . . . It is in real truth the eternal and natural expression and embodiment of a form of life higher than that of the individual—that common life of mutual helpfulness, stimulation, and contest which gives leave and opportunity to the individual life, makes it possible, makes it full and complete.[180]

True freedom, then, is not the absence of restraint, as liberals sometimes maintain, for true freedom is only possible *within* a political society that provides opportunities for self-development.

Wilson's conception of freedom is thus far richer than Hartz would suggest. In his essay "When a Man Comes to Himself," Wilson does *not* celebrate the autonomous individual who determines his or her own standards, as the title of the essay might lead one to expect. Instead, Wilson here insists that, "A man *is* the part he plays among his fellows."[181] In this and other essays, Wilson eschews the emphasis on private liberty that is typical of liberalism, and instead insists that "coming to oneself" is a process of realizing one's responsibilities to the community. As Wilson puts it, "When we say that a man has come to himself [we mean that he] has begun to realize that he is part of a whole, and to know *what* part, suitable for what service and achievement."[182] For Wilson, then, "atomistic social freedom," to use Hartz's term, cannot bring genuine happiness.[183] According to Wilson, "What every man seeks is satisfaction. He deceives himself so long as he imagines it to lie in self-indulgence, so long as he deems himself the center and object of effort. His mind is spent in vain upon itself."[184] Instead of speaking in the language of liberal individualism, Wilson here warns against the tendency to withdraw into the self that Tocqueville feared might predominate in America and in modernity as a whole.[185]

Hartz wants to include Wilson in his claim that, "Locke dominates American political thought, as no thinker anywhere dominates the political thought of a nation."[186] But Wilson explicitly rejects the kind of abstract social contract thinking that Locke engaged in. Following Aristotle, Wilson writes that, "Government came, so to say, before the individual and was coeval with his first human instincts. There was no place for contract. . . . Aristotle was simply stating a fact when he said, 'Man is by nature a political animal.'"[187] The list of "Great Leaders of Political Thought" that Wilson lectured on in 1895 and 1896 is here revealing. In addition to Tocqueville, Wilson chose to lecture on Aristotle, Machiavelli, Montesquieu, Burke, and Bagehot.[188] The absence of social contract thinkers such as Locke or Hobbes is striking. As this list indicates, Wilson most admired political theorists who view politics in rich historical, developmental, and cultural terms, as opposed to social contract theorists who view politics from an ahistorical point of view.[189] As Sheldon Wolin notes, social contract thinkers, with their abstract thought experiments, typically fail to engage in what Tocqueville (and, I would add, Wilson) believed to be crucially important: namely, "a genuine discussion of political culture, of the skills, experience, habits, and practices needed for society to be *politique*."[190]

For Pestritto, Wilson's rejection of the state of nature and social contract thinking is, so to speak, an unforgivable sin, for it means, in Pestritto's view, that Wilson fails to uphold the true principles of self-government. But if abandoning the state of nature and social contract thinking is a sin, it is one that Tocqueville also commits.[191] As Harvey Mansfield and Delba Winthrop note, Tocqueville "departs from an abstract, ahistorical state of nature . . . [Tocqueville] does not build his understanding of democracy on the liberal state of nature first conceived by Thomas Hobbes, Benedict Spinoza, and John Locke."[192] Summing up the position of Mansfield and Winthrop, Cheryl Welch writes: "Tocqueville, then, is a democratic liberal who unsettles the modern liberal project by ignoring its characteristic apparatus (the state of nature, the social contract, the right of consent, and sovereignty) and substituting an implicitly Aristotelian concern for judging and training souls."[193] By abjuring social contract thinking and the state of nature, Tocqueville (like Wilson) is thus able to focus on an analysis of the kind of character—or soul—that is most conducive to democratic self-government.

I have suggested in this chapter that Wilson has a "republican" concern with character. Does this mean that Wilson is a republican rather than a liberal? Although it is tempting to classify Wilson as a republican rather than a liberal, perhaps the best way to categorize him is to say that he *is* a liberal, but, like Tocqueville, he abandons liberalism's "characteristic apparatus," insofar as he abandons the idea of the state of nature and of the social contract.

Even though he dispenses with the state of nature, Wilson remains a liberal insofar as he still advocates the modern idea of rights. In this respect, he closely follows Tocqueville, who also ignores the theory of the state of nature, but still insists that modern states must respect individual rights, and seek to safeguard individuality. Tocqueville's advocacy of rights is perhaps made most forcefully in his claim that legislators in the democratic era must provide "clear and fixed limits to the field of social power." In Tocqueville's view, "Private people should be given certain rights and the undisputed enjoyment of such rights. The individual should be allowed to keep the little freedom, strength, and originality left to him."[194]

Wilson's advocacy of individual rights can be seen throughout his writings. For instance, he defends the modern idea of rights in *The State*, as he writes that there is a key "difference between the Democracy of Aristotle and the Democracy of de Tocqueville and Bentham. The citizens of the former lived for the State; the citizen of the latter lives for himself, and the State is for him. . . . The ancient State recognized no personal rights—all rights were State rights; the modern state recognizes no State rights which are independent of personal rights."[195] Moreover, we have seen that in *Constitutional Government,* Wilson insists that government must lay out "the rights of the individual against the community," and these rights must always be protected by an independent judiciary."[196] Like Tocqueville, then, Wilson is ultimately a liberal, because he endorses the focus on the individual, and on individual rights, which is characteristic of modern liberalism. But, also like Tocqueville, Wilson has an Aristotelian attachment to the idea that a democratic regime can only exist with citizens who have a democratic character; and, it is to the cultivation of this character that the statesman must turn his or attention. In short, both Wilson and Tocqueville are liberal-republican thinkers.

Character, Imperialism, and Conceptual Interpenetration

In the previous section, I discussed Wilson's fusion of liberalism and republicanism. But what of his notorious racism, and his defense of imperialism? With his racism and imperialism, the concept of character again plays a key role. For Wilson used this concept to argue that if a people lacks political maturity, then it is legitimate for a people with a more mature character to rule over them until the subjugated people has attained a proper education. Wilson invoked this argument to justify racial domination in the South. He writes that the discriminatory laws passed after the Civil War in the South were necessary, because African-Americans were like "a host of dusky children untimely put out of school"; they were "unpracticed in liberty, unschooled in self-control [and] excited by a freedom they did not understand."[197]

Wilson used similar language to justify American imperialism in the Philippines. In Wilson's view, the Filipinos had not yet developed a character that fits them for the burdens and responsibilities of self-government. As Wilson put it, the Filipinos were one of the "politically undeveloped races, which have not yet learned the rudiments of order and self-control."[198] Wilson, then, may have denounced the guardianship of corporations and party bosses in the 1912 election, but he found paternalism to be appropriate for the Philippine people: "They are children," he wrote, "and we are men in these deep matters of government and justice."[199]

Uday Mehta has argued that British liberals in the nineteenth century frequently used "the strategy of civilizational infantilism" to justify imperial rule over non-Western peoples. As Mehta demonstrates, John Stuart Mill and other British liberals argued that certain peoples had not yet progressed to the point where they possessed the "cultural and psychological . . . preconditions" for self-rule.[200] Wilson made this same type of argument about Puerto Rico and the Philippines; one day, Wilson claimed, the Puerto Ricans and Filipinos would be ready for the institutions of self-government, but for the present, they would have to be the wards of the Americans. As Wilson put it,

> it is our present and immediate task to extend self-government to Porto Rico and the Philippines, . . . so soon as they can be made fit. . . . [T]hese new tasks will undoubtedly teach us that some discipline—it may be prolonged and tedious—must precede self-government and prepare the way for it; that one kind of self-government is suitable for one sort of community, one stage of development, another for another; that there is no universal form or method either of preparation or of practice in the matter; that *character* and the moralizing effect of law are conditions precedent, obscure and difficult, but absolutely indispensable.[201]

Wilson argued, then, that the Filipinos and Puerto Ricans would be fit for self-government only after a (probably long) period of submission to an external authority.

In the case of both the Philippines and Puerto Rico, Wilson thus neglects Tocqueville's insight that the best way for a people to gain a democratic character is for them to actually participate in self-government.[202] As Tocqueville put it, "human societies like individuals become something only through the practice of liberty."[203] If people do not get to exercise political responsibility, they will never become responsible; without the practice of freedom, a people will never gain the habits of freedom. When it came to the American experience, Wilson did at times recognize this point, for he wrote:

> the theory of English and American law is that no man must look to have the government take care of him, but that every man must take care of himself, the government providing the means . . . but never itself taking the initiative. . . . Such an attitude presupposes both intelligence and independence of spirit on the part of the individual: *such a system elicits intelligence and creates independence of spirit.* . . . The stimulation of such requirements is all that he needs, in addition to his own impulses and desires, to give him the attitude and habit of a free man.[204]

Wilson here recognizes that paternalism can never produce a free-spirited character. If you want to elicit a character that is fit for self-rule, you need to allow for the *practice* of self-rule.

We can now see that Wilson's Tocquevillian concept of "the character foundations of democracy" is a concept that serves multiple purposes in Wilson's thought. On the one hand, Wilson's notion that democracy requires certain "character foundations" leads him to a civic republican project of trying to build institutions (such as "social centers" in urban areas, a "quad" system at Princeton, or a cabinet form of government in Congress) that will foster in citizens the virtues needed for self-government. On the other hand, Wilson also deploys the concept of character to exclude certain racial groups from full citizenship and from self-government.

Wilson's use of the concept of character for multiple purposes can be connected to Stephen Skowronek's analysis of Wilson. Skowronek has offered a strikingly original discussion of how Wilson's racist ideas relate to his liberal ideals.[205] According to Skowronek, Wilson's primary purpose throughout his academic career was to defend the post–Civil War South—with its system of white supremacy—against encroachment by the federal government. Skowronek points out that even *Congressional Government*, a book that is rarely thought to be concerned with race, contains key passages aimed at defending the racial hierarchy of the South against interference from the national government.[206] In Skowronek's view, Wilson's racist defense of the South cannot be separated from the liberal internationalism for which he would become world famous. Instead of seeing a racist strand in Wilson's thought that is distinct from the liberal strand, Skowronek demonstrates that there is "interpenetration" between Wilson's racism and his liberalism. For instance, when Wilson argued in 1917 for the right of self-determination for all peoples, he was employing the very same concept that he had earlier used to defend the South against the meddling of the federal government. As Skowronek puts it, "When Wilson envisioned 'every people free to determine its own polity, its own way of development, unhindered, unthreatened, unafraid, the little along with the great and powerful,' he was, in effect, turning the Southern voice into the voice of America on the world stage."[207]

How does the Tocquevillian interpretation of Wilson offered in this chapter relate to Skowronek's recent analysis of Wilson? A Tocquevillian reading of Wilson can be seen as consistent, in part, with Skowronek's ideas on Wilson. After all, if Skowronek's interpretation of Wilson is correct, then one reason Wilson may have been drawn to Tocqueville is that Tocqueville's celebration of localism and his critique of administrative centralization could be used (some would say distorted) to fit with Wilson's desire to defend white supremacy in the Southern states against possible interference by the national government. Moreover, as we have seen, Tocqueville's notion of "character" was used (again, some would say distorted) by Wilson to argue that African-Americans were unfit for full citizenship.

We have also seen, though, that Wilson was not interested in Tocqueville *solely* because the French theorist's ideas could be deployed to advance Wilson's racist purposes. On the contrary, Wilson also found in Tocqueville a source of inspiration for the project of creating a more deliberative democracy. Wilson thus had *multiple* purposes in the years before he became president. Whereas Skowronek focuses on Wilson's racist defense of the South as his overriding goal during his years as an academic, I would highlight that this was just one of Wilson's purposes during his academic years and during his 1912 campaign.[208] For Wilson also had in mind the republican goals of promoting deliberation and forging a democratic character among American citizens. To help attain these goals, Wilson found inspiration in Tocqueville's emphasis on character. Wilson found the concept of character to be useful, then, not only for his racist ends, but also for his republican ends. In other words, I would like to build on Skowronek by suggesting that there was "conceptual interpenetration" not only between Wilson's racism and Wilson's liberal idealism; in addition, one can also see "conceptual interpenetration" between Wilson's racism and his republicanism, for both his racism and his republicanism draw on the Tocquevillian notion of "the character foundations of American democracy." Just as Wilson used the concept of self-determination for both racist and liberal purposes, as Skowronek has shown, so, too, did Wilson use the Tocquevillian concept of character for very different purposes.

But if Wilson's use of character is linked to his racism, does that mean that the concept of character should be abandoned by scholars and statesmen? Not necessarily, for the republican concern for character is not inherently tied to a politics of racial exclusion. As Sandel notes,

> Some republican theorists have assumed that the capacity for civic virtue corresponds to fixed categories of birth or condition. Aristotle, for example, considered women, slaves, and resident aliens unworthy of citizenship because their nature or roles deprived them of the relevant excellences. . . . But the assumption that the capacity for virtue is incorrigible, tied to roles or identities fixed in advance, is not intrinsic to republican political theory, and not all republicans have embraced it. Some have argued that good citizens are made, not found, and have rested their hopes on the formative project of republican politics. This is especially true of the democratic versions of republican thought that arose with the Enlightenment. When the incorrigibility thesis gives way, so does the tendency of republican politics to sanction exclusion.[209]

While recognizing the troubling uses to which the Tocquevillian concept of character can be put, we need not abandon the concept altogether. Indeed, a discussion of character and of political culture remains a necessary one. For surely, efforts to enhance democracy today—whether in post-Communist states, the United States, or elsewhere—must involve attention to the character of the citizenry, and to the way in which institutions shape character. One can reject Wilson's racist and imperialist ideas, yet still find valuable his claim that democracy works best when its citizens have a character marked by "self-possession, self-mastery, the habit of order and peace and common counsel, and a reverence for law."[210] Ultimately, Wilson's ideas (and, of course, Tocqueville's) remain valuable in large part because they help us engage in the perennially important task of thinking through the complex relationship between leaders, institutions, and the character of a democratic people.

Chapter 5

⋆⇒◉⇐⋆

The Vocation of the
Democratic Moralist

Putnam, Tocqueville, and the
Education of Democracy Today

We have seen in this book that the Antifederalists, Abraham Lincoln, and Woodrow Wilson all suggested that a central task of leadership in America is to educate democracy. In making this argument, they each offer their own variation on a Tocquevillian theme. Like Tocqueville, these American thinkers suggest that leadership—and authority—should be understood not simply as dangerous to democracy, but rather as crucial for its fulfillment. In this final chapter, I seek to demonstrate that Tocqueville's ideas on leadership remain deeply important today. I make this argument primarily through a critical examination of Robert Putnam's influential ideas on American civil society.

Since the late 1980s, the role of civil society in American political life has been a major concern of social scientists, public intellectuals, and policy analysts.[1] The precise definition of "civil society" is often contested, but it is most commonly defined as the realm of associational life that is separate from both the state and the market. In the 1830s, Tocqueville concluded that American democracy was successful in part because of the extraordinary vitality of its civil society. In recent years, a great number of authors have followed in Tocqueville's footsteps by insisting on the importance of a healthy civil society for a healthy democracy. Perhaps the most widely known of these authors is Putnam. In *Bowling Alone*, Putnam argues that American civil society has eroded in recent decades. According to Putnam's data, Americans are not participating in civic, political, neighborhood, and family activities nearly as much as they did before the 1960s. Living largely isolated lives, Americans, according to Putnam, are not generating the amount of "social capital" that is necessary to sustain an efficient and vibrant democracy.

In *Bowling Alone*, Putnam calls Tocqueville "the patron saint of contemporary social capitalists," thereby invoking Tocqueville's authority for his own project.[2] A number of scholars, however, have asked the question: To what extent are Putnam's ideas genuinely consistent with Tocqueville's thought? Many of these scholars deny Putnam the status of a true "Tocquevillian," criticizing him for a skewed or truncated or simplistic view of Tocqueville's theoretical legacy.[3] Although I, too, ask whether Putnam is following in Tocqueville's footsteps, my focus in this chapter is quite different. My argument is that one of Putnam's primary rhetorical strategies in *Bowling Alone* is a remarkable example of "the doctrine of self-interest properly understood," a doctrine that Tocqueville found prevalent among "American moralists."[4] According to Tocqueville, instead of teaching Americans that they should involve themselves in their communities because this is the morally correct thing to do, American moralists teach their fellows that this involvement is actually in their own self-interest, properly understood. I argue that Putnam employs precisely this strategy in *Bowling Alone*; in other words, Putnam is a modern incarnation of the democratic "moralist" analyzed in *Democracy in America*. Putnam thus reveals his Tocquevillian pedigree not only in his conceptualization of civil society, but also in his enthusiastic use of "the doctrine of self-interest properly understood."[5]

However, can exhorting fellow Americans to act in their self-interest (properly understood) really repair the associational deficits and civic decline that Putnam identifies in his empirical work? As discussed in chapter 1, Tocqueville is actually ambivalent toward the "doctrine of self-interest properly understood." Because he held out some hope for the doctrine, Tocqueville would likely welcome Putnam's argument, and wish it success. Yet, because Tocqueville had not only hope but also fear when he considered the doctrine of self-interest properly understood, Tocqueville would likely retain some reservations about Putnam's approach, and he would ultimately have his doubts that Putnam's strategy could succeed in the task of restoring a healthy civic life to America. In this chapter, then, I use Tocqueville's writings to critically interpret Putnam's rhetorical strategy for revitalizing civil society. By considering him to be a modern version of the American moralist discussed by Tocqueville, new light can be shed on the merits, but also the limits, of Putnam's achievement. To help see the insufficiencies of Putnam's approach, I contrast Putnam's *Bowling Alone* with another work of scholarship that has reached a wide audience—namely, Robert Bellah et al.'s *Habits of the Heart*. Both Bellah et al. and Putnam are self-proclaimed neo-Tocquevillians, but there are important differences between them; understanding these differences can help illuminate the promise—but also the peril—of attempting to revive civil society by employing the language of self-interest properly understood.

While this chapter makes reference to George W. Bush as well as to Barack Obama, I am mainly concerned in this chapter not with the role of leaders in government, but rather with the leadership role of the public intellectual. As a public intellectual, Putnam has sought to teach a wide audience of readers that they must seek to rebuild community in America. Similar to the statesmen examined in earlier chapters, Putnam has thus sought "to educate democracy." By discussing the role of the public intellectual rather than the role of the statesman in this chapter, I may at first appear to be straying from my central theme of democratic leadership. However, in *Democracy*, Tocqueville himself seems to include "moralists" among those who must seek to "educate democracy."[6] For Tocqueville, then, the "moralist" is an important kind of democratic leader. Tocqueville never explicitly defines the term "moralist," but by this term he seems to refer to a specific type of philosopher—namely, a widely read philosopher who seeks to educate the citizenry on moral and political matters.[7] Hence, I think today's terms "public philosopher" and "public intellectual" both capture a good deal of what Tocqueville means by the term "moralist."[8] Tocqueville makes it clear that the proper goal of the democratic moralist and of the democratic statesman is often the same. For instance, in Volume II of *Democracy*, Tocqueville argues that both the moralist *and* the statesman should aim to instill "pride" rather than "humility" in the citizenry.[9] He also maintains that it is incumbent upon both "rulers" *and* "moralists" to try to inspire a democratic citizenry to pursue "distant goals."[10] By considering a public intellectual such as Putnam to be a kind of democratic leader, then, I remain within a Tocquevillian framework, because Tocqueville himself suggests that the statesman and the public intellectual (or "moralist," to use Tocqueville's term) have a shared purpose insofar as both should strive to make the citizenry more fit for self-government.[11]

Robert Putnam: A "Moralist" for Democratic Times?

During his journey to America, Tocqueville was struck by the degree to which Americans were active participants in politics. Indeed, Tocqueville goes so far as to compare the New England towns to ancient Athens.[12] According to Tocqueville, "It is hard to explain the place filled by political concerns in the life of an American. To take a hand in the government of society and talk about it is his most important business and, so to say, the only pleasure he knows."[13] Tocqueville found that Americans frequently participated in public life not only through the institutions of local government, but also through organizations that were not explicitly political. "Americans of all ages" Tocqueville wrote, "are forever forming associations . . . of a thousand different types—religious, moral, serious, futile, very general and very limited, immensely large and very minute."[14]

According to Putnam, the vibrant civic and political participation celebrated by Tocqueville has been disappearing from America since the 1960s. Putnam's empirical research leads him to conclude that, "Americans are *right* that the bonds of our communities have withered, and we are *right* to fear that this transformation has very real costs."[15] Putnam marshals data to demonstrate that our society has moved "toward individual and material values and away from communal values."[16] If we *do* belong to organizations, they tend to be national organizations that demand of us nothing more than a membership check. As for politics, most of us leave that to others; Putnam finds that compared to previous generations, Americans today are "reasonably well-informed spectators of public affairs, but many fewer of us actually partake in the game."[17] Putnam suggests, then, that the "individualism" that Tocqueville dreaded has thoroughly taken over the nation.[18] If Putnam is correct about the decline of civic and political engagement in America, then for Tocqueville this would mean that freedom is greatly endangered, for according to Tocqueville, freedom entails "full-blown and active participation in collective self-government," as Cheryl Welch puts it.[19]

But if individualism is a contemporary problem, how is it to be combated? We have seen that part of Tocqueville's answer is that democratic leaders should employ the "doctrine of self-interest properly understood" in order to convince Americans "that by serving his fellows man serves himself and that doing good is to his private advantage." According to Tocqueville, "Contemporary moralists . . . should give most of their attention to" this doctrine of self-interest properly understood, because it is "the best suited of all philosophical theories to the wants of men in our time" and is "their strongest remaining guarantee against themselves."[20]

From this perspective, Putnam can be seen as a democratic moralist *par excellence*. Rather than just describe the "collapse" of community, Putnam also hopes for a "revival," as the subtitle for the book *Bowling Alone* sums up. How, though, can the vibrant participatory life of the past be restored? One of Putnam's chief strategies for reviving political and civil participation is exactly the strategy discussed by Tocqueville in his chapter on self-interest properly understood. Putnam's key rhetorical device is to suggest that we should be active citizens *not* because it is a moral duty to help our community, and *not* because it will fulfill our nature as political animals, but rather because it is in our own self-inter-est to do so. Putnam uses social science methodology to demonstrate that participation in social and political life has a host of "salutary effects" for the individual: for instance, it increases an individual's longevity, psychological well-being, and career success. As Putnam puts it, "social capital makes us smarter, healthier, safer, [and] richer. . . ."[21] Putnam thus hopes to educate democracy by teaching his fellow citizens that they will reap direct benefits as individuals if they sacrifice their time and energy for the community.

Tocqueville would, no doubt, see Putnam's argument as quintessentially American, for Tocqueville notes that, "In the United States there is hardly any talk of the beauty of virtue. But they maintain that virtue is useful and prove it every day. American moralists do not pretend that one must sacrifice himself for his fellows because it is a fine thing to do so. But they boldly assert that such sacrifice is as necessary for the man who makes it as for the beneficiaries."[22] As a public intellectual (our modern term for "moralist"), Putnam's argument is precisely that civic virtue is "useful," irrespective of whether it is also "beautiful." In particular, Section IV of *Bowling Alone*, entitled "So What?," is an elaborate attempt to convince Americans that participation in social and political life is crucial to their individual well-being, irrespective of whether civic participation also happens to benefit the common good. Putnam sums up this over-arching theme in the final sentences of his book: "Institutional reform will not work—indeed, it will not happen—unless you and I, along with our fellow citizens, resolve to become reconnected with our friends and neighbors. . . . We should do this, ironically, *not because it will be good for America—though it will be—but because it will be good for us.*"[23]

Of course, Putnam does not rest his argument for social capital *solely* on its benefits to individuals; he also suggests that social capital has "externalities" that "benefit" the wider society. Putnam emphasizes that there is "hard evidence that our schools and neighborhoods don't work so well when community bonds slacken," and he maintains that social capital makes us "better able to govern a just and stable democracy."[24] And yet, even when he argues that social capital benefits the common good, Putnam still uses an economistic and utilitarian language.[25] He uses cost-benefit analysis, for instance, as he writes of the "dividends" that society and individuals can reap from an "investment" in social capital. In short, although Putnam believes that social capital is "simul-taneously a 'private good' and a 'public good,'" he does not suggest that commitment to others constitutes "*the* good" in any deep philosophical or religious sense of that term.[26] Putnam's book suggests that sacrificing some of our time and energy for others is *useful* (both to ourselves and to the larger society), but there is little suggestion that duty to others is a moral imperative.

Putnam claims that "social capital is closely related to what some have called 'civic virtue.'" He writes that, "The difference is that 'social capital' calls attention to the fact that civic virtue is most powerful when embedded in a dense network of reciprocal social relations."[27] But there is another difference as well: namely, "social capital" is a term that evokes utilitarian values, whereas the term "civic virtue" evokes a moral ideal according to which politics is a key aspect of the good life for human beings. Putnam writes that,

> By analogy with notions of physical capital and human capital—tools and training that enhance individual productivity—the core idea of social capital theory is that social networks have value. Just as a screwdriver (physical capital) or a college education (human capital) can increase productivity (both individual and collective), so too social contacts affect the productivity of individuals and groups.[28]

Putnam's language here—the language of "productivity," "value," and "capital"—is economistic and utilitarian. In the republican tradition, the term "civic virtue" is tied to the idea of *duty*. In contrast, the rhetoric of "social capital" is rooted in the languages of economics and utilitarianism, and these languages are rooted in the basic idea that individuals are best understood as rational actors who pursue their own self-interest. Even when Putnam discusses "social capital" as a "public good," then, he remains caught up in the language of self-interest, and not the religious or republican language of the common good. Tocqueville would be unsurprised by Putnam's argument, for Tocqueville finds that moralists in democratic times tend to abandon the old language of "sacrifice" in favor of the "less lofty" language of "self-interest."[29]

In *Bowling Alone*, Putnam does not explicitly acknowledge that he is trying to play the role of the democratic "moralist" described by Tocqueville, nor does he explicitly discuss the "doctrine of self-interest properly understood." In his earlier book *Making Democracy Work*, however, one does find explicit mention of this doctrine, and indeed, one finds in this earlier work a more drawn out (although still brief) discussion of how Putnam's ideas relate to the concerns of canonical political theorists such as Machiavelli, and contemporary political theorists such as William Galston.[30] According to Putnam, the goal of the study described in *Making Democracy Work* is to empirically test whether contemporary political theorists and intellectual historians who discern (and admire) a "republican tradition" are correct in their conviction that a democratic government cannot be successful unless it contains what Putnam calls a "civic community."[31] In this work, Putnam initially associates his term "civic community" with what republican theorists call "civic virtue." To help clarify the meaning of civic virtue, Putnam cites Quentin Skinner, who defines civic virtue as: "A steady recognition and pursuit of the public good *at the expense* of all purely individual and private ends."[32] By itself, this definition of civic virtue might lead one to conclude that Putnam thinks that the "civic community" involves the *sacrifice* of one's self-interest for the sake of the common good. Putnam goes on to argue, though, that citizenship in the civic community does not require one to "renounce" self-interest; it does not require us to be "altruists," as he puts it. Instead, Putnam argues that in "the civic community . . . citizens pursue what Tocqueville termed 'self-interest properly understood,' that is, self-interest defined in the context of broader public need, self-interest that is 'enlightened' rather than 'myopic,' self-interest that is alive to the interests of others."[33]

Putnam's subtle shift here—from the older language of sacrifice to the language of "self-interest properly understood"—reminds one of the distinction that Tocqueville made in his notebook entry on May 29, 1831. As we have seen, Tocqueville writes that one can distinguish between "the principle of the republics of antiquity," on the one hand, and "the principle" of the United States, on the other. The principle of the former called on citizens "to sacrifice private interests to the general good. In that sense one could say that they were virtuous." In contrast, the principle of the United States is "to make private interests harmonize with the general interest. A sort of refined and intelligent selfishness seems to be the pivot on which the whole machine turns. These people here do not trouble themselves to find out whether public virtue is good, but they do claim to prove that it is useful." For Tocqueville, then, the people of the United States "can pass as enlightened, but not as virtuous."[34] Putnam's movement away from the classical notion of "civic virtue," and toward social scientific concepts such as "social capital," is thus consistent with what Tocqueville saw as an American tendency to abandon the traditional language of sacrifice in favor of utilitarian arguments for active citizenship.

The Tocquevillian Case for Putnam's Rhetorical Strategy

Should we conclude, then, that Putnam's ideas are consistent with those of Tocqueville? Is Putnam following in Tocqueville's footsteps? Putnam and

Tocqueville both worry about the decline of a rich associational life, and they thus both fear individualism, which entails withdrawal from public life. Surely, Tocqueville would be troubled by Putnam's data regarding the decline in political and civic engagement. But would Tocqueville agree with Putnam's strategy of reviving community by appealing to the self-interest of individuals? As we have seen, there is certainly some evidence that suggests that Tocqueville *would* welcome Putnam's strategy of attempting to persuade Americans that it is in their own individual self-interest to work with others toward the common good. For Tocqueville suggests that "[c]ontemporary moralists" are well advised to "give most of their attention" to the doctrine of self-interest interest properly understood. If one focuses on this passage, then it seems that Tocqueville would consider Putnam to be a truly great democratic moralist, for *Bowling Alone* is filled with many clever attempts to demonstrate why doing good in the community is "good for us."

According to some of his critics, these attempts by Putnam to persuade us to become active citizens are doomed to failure. For instance, Scott McLean, David Schultz, and Manfred Steger ask: "Is it really possible to construct a public-spirited community on the privatistic motives of individuals?" They conclude that the answer is no, and that civic engagement actually stems not from "enlightened self-interest," but from "nonrational" motivations such as "identity, faith, and feelings of duty."[35] Schultz elaborates on this same point:

> A large part of Putnam's problem is rooted in his ontology of individualism. He begins with a theory of human nature as essentially one of isolated *homo economicus* and from that starting point hopes to construct a theory of the social. Such an aggregating task is impossible . . . It is illogical to begin with an individual rational maximizer and ask that person to join groups, participate, or develop a sense of sociality. . . . [36]

For these critics, then, Putnam's attempt to revive community by appealing to self-interest is a theoretical and practical absurdity. To defend himself against this charge, though, Putnam could point to the following passage from *Democracy*: "At first it is of necessity that men tend to the public interest, afterward by choice. What had been calculation becomes instinct. By dint of working for the good of his fellow citizens, he in the end acquires a habit and taste for serving them."[37] As a public intellectual, Putnam appears to be trying to use all of his reasoning powers to induce Americans to participate first by necessity, and afterward by choice. In other words, Putnam tries to persuade us that *if* we want to be "healthy, wealthy, and wise," then it is *necessary* for us to participate in the community; it is Putnam's fond hope that we will then develop the habit of participation, so that our future participation will become a matter of choice and taste.[38] As Putnam puts it in *Bowling Alone*, "associations and less formal networks of civic engagement instill in their members habits of cooperation and public-spiritedness. . . ." Recognizing the Tocquevillian provenance of this argument, Putnam then quotes *Democracy*: "feelings and ideas are renewed, the heart enlarged, and the understanding developed only by the reciprocal action of men one upon another."[39] Building on Tocqueville, then, Putnam appears to believe the following: We may start out as *homo economicus*, to use Schultz's term, but, if people can be persuaded to engage in civic and political activity out of self-interest, then, over time, their hearts and souls will move toward a more genuine form of civic virtue.[40]

The Tocquevillian Case against Putnam's Rhetorical Strategy

Clearly, then, one can find in Tocqueville's writings considerable justification for Putnam's rhetorical strategy, a strategy that exemplifies "the doctrine of self-interest properly understood." And yet, as discussed in chapter 1, Tocqueville was deeply ambivalent about the doctrine of self-interest properly understood, which means that he would also be ambivalent toward Putnam's rhetorical strategy.

Tocqueville's ambivalence toward the doctrine is evident even in the chapter in *Democracy* in which he appears to praise it. Tocqueville's enthusiasm for the doctrine is called into question by the following passage:

> The Americans . . . enjoy explaining almost every act of their lives on the principle of self-interest properly understood. It gives them pleasure to point out how an enlightened self-love continually leads them to help one another and disposes them freely to give part of their time and wealth for the good of the state. *I think that in this they often do themselves less than justice, for sometimes in the United States, as elsewhere, one sees people carried away by the disinterested, spontaneous impulses natural to man.*[41]

Tocqueville here suggests that the active citizenship of Americans is *not* always based on the doctrine of self-interest properly understood, and it is actually *unjust* to explain all of the Americans' public-spirited behavior by reducing it to self-interested motives. Interestingly, Putnam quotes much of this passage in *Bowling Alone*, but he leaves out the last sentence that I have quoted.[42] If he had included this sentence, then perhaps he would have been forced to consider the possible limitations of his own interest-based strategy for reviving civil society.

We have seen that Tocqueville's deep reservations about the doctrine of self-interest properly understood are expressed most powerfully in *The Old Regime and the French Revolution*, as he declares that, "The man who asks of freedom anything other than itself is born to be a slave."[43] Tocqueville's criticism of those who ask of freedom something other than itself could clearly be applied to Putnam, for Putnam urges us to love participatory freedom not for itself, but because of "'practical' considerations," as Tocqueville disdainfully puts it.[44] In *The Old Regime*, Tocqueville suggests that if freedom is to be preserved, then the citizenry must have "a genuine love of freedom," and not be attached to it for instrumental reasons. From this perspective, then, Putnam's attempts to persuade us that participatory freedom will bring us individual well-being might be inadequate, or even dangerous, for Tocqueville warns that, "those who prize freedom only for the material benefits it offers have never kept it long."[45] Upon this view, Putnam's emphasis on the practical benefits of participatory freedom is unlikely to lead to the maintenance of liberty over the long haul.

Putnam's Rhetorical Strategy: "Necessary" but "Incomplete"

We have observed that Tocquevillian arguments can be found to both justify and criticize Putnam's rhetorical strategy in *Bowling Alone*. This is because Tocqueville sometimes appears to endorse the doctrine of self-interest properly understood, and sometimes he criticizes it. As I suggested in chapter 1, Tocqueville ultimately finds the doctrine to be "necessary" but "incomplete" as a strategy for preserving freedom in the modern world. As discussed in chapter 3, Tocqueville's teaching on self-interest properly understood thus converges with Abraham Lincoln's views. As Jaffa notes, Lincoln believed that the framers' reliance on "self-interest" and "ambition" was "insufficient" for the task of sustaining popular government. "Lincoln would grant," writes Jaffa,

> that it is foolish to rely upon men's virtue when it is possible to prompt them by self-interest. But he would say that it is worse than foolish to think that self-interest can be the ultimate reliance of republican freedom. For men claiming republican

freedom—the right to self-government, a right whose very name is a synonym for virtue—cannot doubt that they must vindicate their claim by their virtue, when the supreme test comes.[46]

As we have seen, in an 1831 notebook entry Tocqueville also seemed to suspect that a "supreme test" might one day come, for Tocqueville wrote that "only the future will show" whether the "general good" can truly be sustained through a focus on "individual well-being." Tocqueville believed that for the moment, "intelligent selfishness" was a sufficient principle to keep "the machine" of American society in good working order. But one day, Tocqueville feared, "political passions . . . will be born" that might destroy the republic, unless they are countered, Tocqueville suggests, by genuine "public virtue."[47] Both Lincoln and Tocqueville, then, believed that it would be foolish for democratic leaders *not* to appeal to self-interest properly understood, but ultimately they both believed that a republic can only survive if the citizenry has a deep and genuine attachment to civic virtue.

Therefore, from the Tocquevillian perspective that I have advanced in this book, Putnam's work should be honored as a remarkable achievement insofar as it makes a great case for participatory freedom through appeals to self-interest. Putnam's argument, though, is incomplete, and must be complemented by the work of other, more traditional "moralists," such as Robert Bellah et al., who urge us to embrace a sense of commitment and obligation that transcends any calculations of self-interest.

Like *Bowling Alone*, *Habits of the Heart* is a serious work of scholarship that also reached a wide audience beyond the academy. Bellah et al. and Putnam both claim to be following in Tocqueville's footsteps, but the differences between them are stark. Bellah et al. argue that for much of American history, the biblical and civic republican traditions provided an authoritative moral framework for Americans. However, these traditions have largely disappeared, and they have been replaced (as Tocqueville feared they would be) by individualism. Building on Tocqueville, Bellah et al. suggest that Americans are now driven by two different forms of individualism: "utilitarian individualism," on the one hand, and "expressive individualism" on the other.[48] No longer guided by authoritative norms, Americans now tend to forge attachments only if it seems useful to do so, or if it feels like a pleasurable expression of the inner self. As Bellah et al. put it, "Utility replaces duty; self-expression unseats authority."[49] In such a world, obligations to friends, family, and to the public are necessarily fragile. For Bellah et al., then, the task for today is to somehow reappropriate the moral languages of civic republicanism and biblical religion; without such a reappropriation, it will remain highly difficult for Americans to recognize their dependence on one another, to recognize their obligations to each other, and to forge lasting commitments in either the public or private realms.

As part of their research, Bellah et al. spoke with many middle-class Americans. The first one we meet in the book, "Brian Palmer," was once devoted to career, but now focuses more on family life. Although Brian's new family-oriented life appears at first glance to be morally superior to his older way of being, Bellah et al. incisively point out that,

> his new goal—devotion to marriage and children—seems as arbitrary and unexamined as his earlier pursuit of material success. Both are justified as idiosyncratic preferences rather than as representing a larger sense of the purpose of life. Brian sees himself as consistently pursuing a utilitarian calculus—devotion to his own self-interest—except that there has been an almost inexplicable change in his personal preferences.

Bellah et al. note that Brian "keeps referring to 'values' and 'priorities' not justified by any wider framework of purpose or belief."[50] Speaking the language of individualism even as he claims to be more centered on family, Brian plainly "lacks a language to explain what seem to be the real commitments that define his life, and to that extent the commitments themselves are precarious."[51]

Bellah et al.'s critique of Americans such as Brian can be usefully applied to Putnam's work. Putnam, to his credit, extends the utilitarian calculus that is characteristic of individualism to society as a whole, for Putnam suggests that commitment to others has "salutary effects" for the community as well as the individual. However, even as he writes about the community as a whole, Putnam's terminology—the terminology of costs, dividends, and benefits—tends, as we have seen, to remain squarely within the parameters of utilitarian individualism. Putnam does not ultimately provide us with any other moral language as he urges us to take on commitments and obligations to others. Hence, we must ask of Putnam the same question that Bellah et al. raised about Americans like Brian Palmer: Are not the commitments to community that Putnam urges upon us highly precarious if they are not justified by something more than utility? What if another social scientist were to one day "prove" that the positive benefits of social capital were exaggerated by Putnam? Would people then not be acting rationally and justifiably if they chose to disengage from their commitments and obligations? This is to say that Putnam ultimately fails to provide us with what Bellah et al. call a "public philosophy" that moves beyond the language of utility and provides people with a "wider framework of purpose or belief."[52] Putnam's notion of "social capital" has struck a chord with many Americans who distantly remember—in a fragmented way—the authoritative languages of republicanism and biblical religion. In the end, though, Putnam does little in *Bowling Alone* to revive a language of commitment, obligation, and sacrifice. Without such a revival, however, the prospects for a revival of civil society must remain in question.

My claim here is that without the *language* of obligation the *practice* of nonindividualistic behavior cannot long endure. Alasdair MacIntyre reminds us, though, that the reverse is also true: a moral language cannot remain vital if the social practices that once gave the language its relevance disappear.[53] This means that in order to restore civil society we must seek to cultivate a *language* of obligation, but at the same time, we must seek to cultivate public spaces in which citizens can *practice* behavior aimed at the common good. In this way, there is hope that language and practice will eventually become mutually reinforcing.

Barack Obama is a notable example of a contemporary leader who does try to revive a language of obligation and commitment. On the one hand, in his speeches Obama often starts out by celebrating the "American Dream," and by doing so he encourages his audience-members to pursue their own self-interest as they seek to rise up in the world, just as Obama himself did.[54] When he speaks of the "American Dream," Obama acknowledges the powerful place of individualism in American political culture. Obama also teaches his audience, though, that "alongside our famous individualism, there's another ingredient in the American saga. . . . It is that fundamental belief: I am my brother's keeper. I am my sister's keeper . . . [55] Obama's full teaching is thus that it is only when one leaves behind a focus on self-interest that one's "true potential," as he puts it, can be fulfilled.[56] Hence, in his Knox College Commencement Address, Obama declared that, "Focusing your life solely on making a buck shows a certain poverty of ambition. It asks too little of yourself. You need to take up the challenges that we face as a nation and make them your own."[57] Ultimately, then, Obama is a democratic educator who acknowledges the power of self-interest, but who then seeks to elevate his audience by urging them to leave behind the apathy, passivity, and individualism that Tocqueville feared.

In some powerful moments from his First Inaugural Address, George W. Bush also criticized individualism. Bush gave voice to Tocquevillian themes when he called on Americans to be "citizens, not spectators; citizens, not subjects; responsible citizens, building communities of service and a nation of character."[58] Bush suggested, as Tocqueville did, that freedom should not simply be understood as unrestrained freedom of choice. Recognizing that citizens are bound to one another in networks of mutual obligation and shared responsibility, Tocqueville wrote that it is a serious mistake "to confound independence with liberty. No one is less independent than a citizen of a free state."[59] In much the same vein, Bush declared that, "We find the fullness of life not only in options, but in commitments. And we find that children and community are the commitments that set us free." In a manner that brings to mind Tocqueville's criticisms of excessive materialism and individualism, Bush called on Americans to transcend self-interest, and to seek "a common good beyond your comfort."[60] Similarly, in his Second Inaugural Address he asked "our youngest citizens" to "[m]ake the choice to serve in a cause larger than your wants, larger than yourself—and in your days you will add not just to the wealth of our country, but to its character."[61]

However, Bush's fine deployment of the language of commitment was not, on the whole, matched by efforts to build institutions that facilitate participation aimed at the common good. As a number of commentators have pointed out, after September 11, 2001, Bush did little to reinforce or build on the public-spirited yearnings of Americans by creating programs or polices that encouraged shared sacrifice and widespread civic participation.[62] As Robert Putnam put it in a 2002 article, while "the crisis [of September 11] revealed and replenished the wells of solidarity in American communities, those wells so far remain untapped." According to Putnam's data, the attacks led to an increase in civic-minded attitudes; however, the president and Congress offered very little in terms of concrete institutions and programs that could *channel* these positive attitudes.[63] In November of 2001, President Bush said: "Too many have the wrong idea of Americans as shallow, materialist consumers who care only about getting rich or getting ahead."[64] And yet, Bush himself had recently implied that *shopping* could actually be an act of patriotism, for it would show America's enemies that they could not succeed in weakening the economy.[65] Bush did eventually call on Americans to embrace "a new culture of responsibility" by serving "goals larger than self," as he put it in his 2002 State of the Union Address.[66] And in terms of concrete actions, he called on Congress to increase the size of Americorps, Senior Corps, and the Peace Corps. However, these proposals made no headway in Congress. And, as David Gergen noted, even with the proposed increases, these public service programs would still have reached "less than one half of one percent" of the 27 million young Americans aged 18 to 24. Gergen thus called for a "bold[er] program" that can create "a new sense of purpose in our national life."[67] Rather than offer this kind of bold program, Bush instead focused largely on tax cuts, even as war was being waged in Afghanistan and Iraq. It is to be hoped that future leaders will not only articulate a language of commitment, but will also rebuild—or boldly create—institutions that enable a politics of commitment and sacrifice. In this way, Americans will be both inspired *and* empowered to collectively address the public problems that they face as a nation.

In addition to Americorps, other plans to increase citizen participation should be given serious consideration. William Galston, an architect of the Americorps program, has argued in favor of making national service mandatory for all young Americans. Galston has advocated universal service in part because he believes it can help produce an "ethic of reciprocity," as opposed to the "duty-free understanding of citizenship" that threatens to prevail over American youth.[68] In *Deliberation Day*, Bruce Ackerman and James Fishkin suggest another way to foster participation. They write that, "We can, through an act of political imagination, create new institutions for redeeming the ancient promise of democratic citizenship." By instituting a national holiday for democratic deliberation, the authors hope, in part, to form citizens "who are comfortable interacting with one another in the special ways required to engage responsibly in the conduct of public business."[69] Through their institution-building proposals, both Galston and Ackerman and Fishkin are, in their own way, attempting to combat the "individualism" identified by Tocqueville, for their proposals would help counteract what Tocqueville called the modern tendency "to withdraw into the circle of family and friends."[70]

Because the proposals of Galston and of Ackerman and Fishkin would involve government programs, some may object that they cannot be included within Tocqueville's concept of civil society. For instance, Bruce Frohnen has argued that for Tocqueville, "the problem, to be blunt, is government. . . . [S]tate action, by taking away our reasons for joining together to take care of one another, isolates us and leaves us in the end with only our selfish, individual interests to pursue."[71] However, as Dana Villa demonstrates, Tocqueville's notion of civil society actually encompasses participatory institutions of *government*, such as town-hall meetings.[72] If we want to be true to Tocqueville's spirit today, then, we must seek to prevent the growth of a centralized state that rules through distant bureaucrats, but we need not reject governmental programs that genuinely help produce citizen participation.[73]

As we have seen, in *Democracy in America*, Tocqueville notes that it would be a mistake to conclude that Americans become active participants in their communities *solely* because of self-interest; as Tocqueville puts it, "in the United States, as elsewhere, one sees people carried away by the disinterested, spontaneous impulses natural to man." Today, a primary task of both public intellectuals and power-holders should be to nourish and encourage these noble impulses, by seeking to cultivate the language, and the institutions, which point us beyond the self, and toward the common good. In other words, if civil society is to be revived, we not only need the leadership of public intellectuals such as Putnam, who appeal to self-interest properly understood. We also need the leadership of public intellectuals such as Bellah et al., who can creatively invoke—and call on us to continue—traditions that transcend a politics based on self-interest.

Despite the limitations of *Bowling Alone*, Tocqueville would still likely view Putnam's book as a necessary one, for Tocqueville sometimes succumbed to the belief that leaders in democratic times must appeal "to personal interest, which provides the only stable point in the human heart."[74] And yet, at other moments, as Bellah et al. remind us, Tocqueville hoped that America's religious and civic republican traditions could lift the people beyond self-interest, and toward genuine virtue. Ultimately, from a Tocquevillian perspective, Bellah et al. and Putnam thus complement one another: Putnam gives voice to the Tocquevillian emphasis on the *necessity* of "self-interest properly understood," and Bellah et al. give voice to Tocqueville's conviction that the doctrine was *incomplete*, and must be supplemented by the religious and republican language of commitment and obligation. In the end, then, both Bellah et al. and Putnam should be praised as democratic moralists for our time; both can play an important role in what Tocqueville called the great task of educating democracy.

Conclusion: Leadership and Democratic Contestation

I have suggested that Tocqueville and Bellah et al. are likely correct that religion is valuable as an antidote to individualism. However, it should again be emphasized that in Tocqueville's view, *political* leaders should generally avoid trying to directly promote religion. This was the mistake the Puritans made, for according to Tocqueville, Puritan leaders brought "shame on the spirit of man" by trying to use the state to promote religion. For Tocqueville, then, political leaders should focus their energies not on trying to promote religion, but rather republicanism. According to Lincoln, American republicanism is open to all who profess a belief in freedom and equality. As Lincoln put it, Americans (of whatever nationality or religion) are "link[ed]" to one another insofar as they share a common "father"—namely, the moral principle that "all men are created equal."[75] Sandel similarly suggests that republicanism need not be "exclusive," or "tied to roles or identities fixed in advance."[76] And, indeed, as a result of great struggles, African-Americans, women, and other previously excluded groups have played key roles in the development of America's republican tradition. At its best, then, American republicanism has been able to find, as Sandel puts it, "democratic, pluralistic expression."[77]

American republicanism in its democratic, pluralistic mode has been constituted in large part by a debate about the meaning of its first principles. In *Democracy*, Tocqueville writes: "For society to exist and, even more, for society to prosper, it is essential that all the minds of the citizens should always be rallied and held together by some leading ideas; and that could never happen unless each of them sometimes came to draw his opinions from the same source and was ready to accept some beliefs ready made."[78] In America, it is the Declaration that provides us with "leading ideas," but the exact meaning of these ideas has been open to vigorous debate. Americans must all believe in the first principles of liberty and equality, but the precise meaning of these principles, and their precise application, must remain open to contestation. As Jean Bethke Elshtain and Christopher Beem put it, "we Americans are free insofar as we struggle together to decide who we are, what is important, what is desirable, and how we want to live together . . . Argumentation about what the common, civic, social good is, and a common sense of responsibility for what that good is, is constitutive of a viable democratic society."[79] One of the key tasks of the democratic leader, then, is to lead debate about the meaning and proper application of America's first principles. In *After Virtue*, we see that MacIntyre cannot abide American pluralism, with its "interminable" debate about moral questions.[80] And yet, insofar as this "interminable" debate has been a debate about the meaning of our first principles, this debate actually reveals the *strength* of American democracy, for "to be an American," as Mark Tushnet puts it, is to strive to realize our first principles, and this can only happen if we all engage in an "historically extended discussion" about the content and application of these principles.[81] Our debate will never be concluded, for we are a contentious people. But contentiousness is the essence of democracy; if we collectively struggle to interpret and apply shared ideals, while always recognizing that these ideals have authority over all of us, then there is still hope for democracy in America.

Notes

Introduction

1. Benjamin Barber, "Neither Leaders nor Followers: Citizenship under Strong Democracy," in *A Passion for Democracy* (Princeton, NJ: Princeton University Press, 1998), 95.

2. Jeffrey Tulis, *The Rhetorical Presidency* (Princeton, NJ: Princeton University Press, 1987), 12.

3. James MacGregor Burns, *Leadership* (New York: Harper & Row, 1978); Bruce Miroff, *Icons of Democracy: American Leaders as Heroes, Aristocrats, Dissenters, and Democrats* (New York: Basic Books, 1993); Marc Landy and Sidney Milkis, *Presidential Greatness* (Lawrence: University Press of Kansas, 2000). Landy and Milkis write, "As we explore presidential greats, we are compelled to ask whether they were democratically great. Were their great accomplishments compatible with the aspirations of a democratic people, or is the very term 'democratic leadership' an oxymoron" (3).

4. Miroff, *Icons of Democracy*, 1.

5. Kenneth P. Ruscio, *The Leadership Dilemma in Modern Democracy* (Cheltenham, UK: Edward Elgar, 2004), 3.

6. Ruscio puts the question as follows: "Can a democracy make room for an energetic, legitimate, and just leadership compatible with the principles of equality and liberty? Or are democracy and leadership simply irreconcilable?" (*The Leadership Dilemma*, 5). Although Ruscio and I share some similar concerns, Ruscio's book contains just one brief reference to Tocqueville. Ruscio seeks a theory of "liberal political leadership" that draws largely on John Rawls (xi), whereas the vision of leadership I articulate draws largely on Tocqueville, and can be termed a "liberal-republican" theory of leadership, as I discuss in chapter 1.

7. Samuel Huntington, "The United States," in *The Crisis of Democracy* (New York: New York University Press, 1975), 64.

8. Robert Paul Wolff, *In Defense of Anarchism* (New York: Harper & Row, 1970), 37.

9. Wolff, *In Defense of Anarchism*, 4.

10. Joseph Raz, *The Authority of Law* (New York: Oxford University Press, 1979), 11. The Lucas quotation is from John Lucas, *The Principles of Politics* (New York: Oxford University Press, 1985), 16.

11. Raz, *The Authority of Law*, 16.

12. Sebastian de Grazia, "What Authority is Not," *American Political Science Review* LIII (1959): 328.

13. John Schaar, "Liberty/Authority/Community in the Political Thought of John Winthrop," *Political Theory* XIX (1991): 504.

14. John Schaar, *Escape from Authority* (New York: Basic Books, 1961), 295 (emphasis added).

15. Robert Faulkner, *The Case for Greatness: Honorable Ambition and Its Critics* (New Haven, CT: Yale University Press, 2007), 13.

16. Faulkner, *The Case for Greatness*, 22, 177. In his discussion of Plato's Alcibiades, Faulkner does briefly consider the possibility that leaders can be moral educators when he mentions Socrates's claim that "the ruler" should "encourage human being at its best" (112). However, Faulkner does not dwell on this theme.

17. Alexis de Tocqueville, *Democracy in America*, trans. George Lawrence (New York: Harper & Row, 1966), 12.

18. In her book *On Revolution* (New York: Penguin, 1963), Hannah Arendt writes that, "Terminologically speaking, the effort to recapture the lost spirit of revolution must, to a certain extent, consist in the attempt at thinking together and combining meaningfully what our present vocabulary presents to us in terms of opposition and contradiction" (223). One can argue that Tocqueville and the American thinkers examined in this book took up this task, for they try to "think together" the concepts of leadership and democracy.

19. See Andrew Sabl, *Ruling Passions: Political Offices and Democratic Ethics* (Princeton, NJ: Princeton University Press, 2002), 249. See also Sabl, *Ruling Passions*, 92, 252–61 and Andrew Sabl, "Community Organizing as Tocquevillean Politics: The Art, Practices, and Ethos of Association," *American Journal of Political Science* XLVI (2002): 1–19.

20. Tocqueville, *Democracy*, 548.

21. Tocqueville, *Democracy*, 547–48.

22. Louis Hartz, *The Liberal Tradition in America* (New York: Harcourt Brace, 1955).

23. Dworetz's argument is aimed largely at what he calls the "curiously convergent interpretations of Locke" advanced by C.B. MacPherson and Leo Strauss; despite their differences, both of these scholars advanced, in Dworetz's view, an anachronistic misreading of Locke as a bourgeois individualist. See Steven Dworetz, *The Unvarnished Doctrine: Locke, Liberalism, and the American Revolution* (Durham, NC: Duke University Press, 1990), 12.

24. Dworetz, *The Unvarnished Doctrine*, 13.

25. John Locke, *Two Treaties of Government*, ed. Peter Laslett (New York: Cambridge University Press, 1960), 270.

26. Robert Bellah et al., *Habits of the Heart: Individualism and Commitment in American Life* (Berkeley: University of California Press, 1985), 143.

27. Wilson Carey McWilliams, *The Idea of Fraternity in America* (Berkeley: University of California Press, 1973), 109.

28. Michael Sandel, *Democracy's Discontent: America in Search of a Public Philosophy* (Cambridge, MA: Belknap Press of Harvard University Press, 1996).

29. McWilliams, *The Idea of Fraternity in America*, 98; Sandel, *Democracy's Discontent*, 6.

30. John P. Diggins and Mark E. Kann, introduction to *The Problem of Authority in America*, eds. Diggins and Kann (Philadelphia, PA: Temple University Press, 1981), 4.

31. Burns, *Leadership*, 25 (emphasis added).

Chapter 1. Toqueville on Leadership and the Education of Democracy

1. Tocqueville, *Democracy*, 12.

2. Plato, *Gorgias*, trans. W.C. Helmbold (New York: Macmillan, 1952), 79.

3. Harvey Mansfield and Delba Winthrop, "Tocqueville's New Political Science," in *The Cambridge Companion to Tocqueville*, ed. Cheryl Welch (New York: Cambridge University Press, 2006), 83.

4. As Burns puts it in *Leadership*, we must "distinguish leadership from brute power, leadership from propaganda, leadership from manipulation, leadership from pandering, leadership from coercion" (452). Inspired in part by Burns, Miroff argues in *Icons of Democracy* that, "Americans should beware of those who equate leadership with power, mastery, and efficiency" (358). Instead, Miroff urges us to celebrate leaders who "approach citizens through processes of mutuality and education," and who perceive citizens as "capable of greater ventures in self-government" (349). In a similar vein, Milkis and Landy suggest that, "Presidential words and deeds shape the quality and character of the citizenry. They can make the public more passive and self-regarding and submissive, or they can encourage it to be more energetic and public-spirited. . . . A democratic leader is one who takes the public to school." See Milkis and Landy, *Presidential Greatness*, 3–4.

5. Burns, *Leadership*, 4, 455, 452, 46, 462.

6. Burns, *Leadership*, 4.

7. Tocqueville, Speech in the Chamber of Deputies, January 27, 1848, in appendix III of *Democracy*, 754, 755.

8. Burns, *Leadership*, 4.

9. Tocqueville, letter to Arthur de Gobineau, September 16, 1858, in *Selected Letters on Politics and Society*, ed. Roger Boesche (Berkeley: University of California Press, 1985), 376.

10. Tocqueville, letter to Gobineau, January 24, 1857, in Selected Letters, 343.

11. Tocqueville, *Democracy*, 701.

12. Marvin Zetterbaum, "Alexis de Tocqueville," in *The History of Political Philosophy*, eds. Leo Strauss and Joseph Cropsey (Chicago: University of Chicago Press, 1987), 777.

13. Tocqueville, letter to Gobineau, January 24, 1857, in *Selected Letters*, 346–47.

14. Tocqueville, letter to Gustave de Beaumont, April 22, 1838, in *Selected Letters*, 130.

15. Tocqueville, *Democracy*, 525–28.

16. Tocqueville, *Democracy*, 506.

17. Tocqueville, *Democracy*, 240, 237. As Cheryl Welch notes, "Tocqueville's notion of liberty under democratic social conditions . . . suggests a certain kind of self-government even more than the claim to enjoy civil liberties." See Cheryl Welch, *De Tocqueville* (New York: Oxford University Press, 2001), 53.

18. Tocqueville, *Democracy*, 507.

19. Tocqueville, *Democracy*, 511.

20. Tocqueville, *Democracy*, 514.

21. Tocqueville, *Democracy*, 525.

22. Tocqueville, *Democracy*, 527.

23. Alexis de Tocqueville, *The Tocqueville Reader*, eds. Olivier Zunz and Alan S. Kahan (Oxford, UK: Blackwell, 2002), 51.

24. Tocqueville, *The Tocqueville Reader*, 51.

25. Tocqueville, *The Tocqueville Reader*, 51 (emphasis added).

26. Tocqueville, *The Tocqueville Reader*, 51.

27. Tocqueville, *Democracy*, 528.

28. Alexis de Tocqueville, *The Old Regime and the French Revolution*, trans. Stuart Gilbert (New York: Anchor, 1955), 169.

29. Tocqueville, *Democracy*, 528.

30. Tocqueville, *The Old Regime*, 169.

31. Tocqueville, *Democracy*, 705.

32. For useful discussions of how Tocqueville consistently wanted to base politics on principle rather than interest, see Roger Boesche, *The Strange Liberalism of Alexis de Tocqueville* (Ithaca, NY: Cornell University Press, 1987), 194–200 and Aurelian Craiutu, "Tocqueville's Paradoxical Moderation," *The Review of Politics* LXVII (2005): 609–15.

33. Tocqueville, letter to Eugene Stoffels, January 12, 1833, in *Selected Letters*, 81.

34. Melvin Richter, "The Uses of Theory: Tocqueville's Adaptation of Montesquieu," in *Essays in Theory and History: An Approach to the Social Sciences*, ed. Melvin Richter (Cambridge, MA: Harvard University Press, 1970), 97.

35. Tocqueville, *The Old Regime*, xii–xiv.

36. Tocqueville, *Democracy*, 527.

37. Tocqueville, *The Old Regime*, 169 (emphasis added).

38. Tocqueville, *Democracy*, 47.

39. Tocqueville, *Democracy*, 444–45.

40. Tocqueville, *The Tocqueville Reader*, 51.

41. Sandel, *Democracy's Discontent*, 5.

42. Tocqueville, *Democracy*, 243.

43. Dana Villa, "Hegel, Tocqueville, and 'Individualism,'" *The Review of Politics* LXVII (2005): 667.

44. Tocqueville, *Democracy*, 243.

45. Tocqueville found that in America, religion reinforced civic republican values. As Boesche notes, Tocqueville believed that religion "could extract individuals from an obsession with private affairs and teach them public duties." See Boesche, *Strange Liberalism*, 142. In contrast to my interpretation and that of Boesche, Villa argues that Tocqueville did *not* see religion as being of great importance in the battle against individualism. See Dana Villa, "Tocqueville and Civil Society," in *The Cambridge Companion to Tocqueville*, 237–38.

46. Boesche, *Strange Liberalism*, 195.

47. Harvey Mansfield and Delba Winthrop, editors' introduction to *Democracy in America*, by Alexis de Tocqueville (Chicago: University of Chicago Press, 2000), xxxviii–xxxix.

48. Mansfield and Winthrop, editors' introduction to *Democracy in America*, xxxviii–xxxix.

49. Plato, *The Republic*, trans. Allan Bloom (New York: Basic Books, 1968), 236.

50. Winthrop quoted in Tocqueville, *Democracy*, 46.

51. Tocqueville, *Democracy*, 318. For an excellent discussion of Tocqueville's belief in the importance of self-mastery as it relates to liberty, see Boesche, *Strange Liberalism*, 157–76.

52. Aristotle, *The Politics*, trans. Ernest Barker (New York: Oxford University Press, 1958), 234.

53. Tocqueville quoted in George Wilson Pierson, *Tocqueville in America* (New York: Oxford University Press, 1938), 119.

54. Tocqueville, *Democracy*, 292.

55. Tocqueville, letter to Louis de Kergolay, June 29, 1831, in *Selected Letters*, 53.

56. Tocqueville, letter to Kergolay, 52.

57. Tocqueville, *Democracy*, 448.

58. Alexis de Tocqueville, *"The European Revolution" and Correspondence with Gobineau*, ed. John Lukacs (Gloucester, MA: Peter Smith, 1968), 191.

59. Tocqueville, *Democracy*, 543.

60. Schaar, *Escape from Authority*, 295, 302.

61. Schaar, *Escape from Authority*, 295.

62. Tocqueville, *Democracy*, 434.

63. Tocqueville, *Democracy*, 252.

64. Tocqueville, *Democracy*, 433–34.

65. Tocqueville, *Democracy*, 436.

66. Tocqueville, *Democracy*, 432.

67. Tocqueville, *Democracy*, 432.

68. Hanna Pitkin, *The Attack of the Blob: Hannah Arendt's Concept of the Social* (Chicago: University of Chicago Press, 2000), 127. Pitkin's book offers an illuminating discussion of Tocqueville's influence on Hannah Arendt.

69. Abraham Lincoln, "Address at Gettysburg," November 19, 1863, in *Speeches and Writings 1859–1865* (New York: Library of America, 1989), 536.

70. William Galston, *Public Matters: Essays on Politics, Policy and Religion* (Lanham, MD: Rowman & Littlefield, 2005), 3. As Boesche notes, Tocqueville also acknowledged that religion has the potential to make people turn inward,

away from the duties of citizens. On the whole, though, Tocqueville thought that religion was not just compatible with, but necessary for, the survival of political freedom in the modern world, as Boesche discusses. See Boesche, *Strange Liberalism*, 187–89.

71. The Saguaro Seminar, "Social Capital Community Benchmark Survey Executive Summary," Kennedy School of Government, Harvard University, http://www.hks.harvard.edu/saguaro/communitysurvey/results2.html.

72. James Morone, *Hellfire Nation* (New Haven, CT: Yale University Press, 2003), 3, 5.

73. Tocqueville, *Democracy*, 42.

74. Specifically, Tocqueville criticizes the Puritans' draconian laws regulating such matters as adultery, fornication, "[i]dleness and drunkenness," "simple lying," "the use of tobacco," and "the worldly luxury of long hair." See Tocqueville, *Democracy*, 42–43.

75. Alan Wolfe, *One Nation After All* (New York: Viking, 1998), 49, 55. Wolfe notes that the issue of homosexuality presents an important exception to his conclusion that religious Americans are generally tolerant, since his research suggests that many Americans still disapprove of gays and lesbians (72–81).

76. Tocqueville, *Democracy*, 243.

77. For a fine defense of national service, see William Galston, "Some Arguments for Universal Service," in *Public Matters*, 68–74. That the idea of national service is growing in popularity is indicated by a *Time* magazine cover story, "The Case for National Service." See *Time*, September 10, 2007.

78. Tocqueville, *Democracy*, 543.

79. Tocqueville, *Democracy*, 545.

80. Tocqueville, *Democracy*, 545.

81. Tocqueville, *Democracy*, 297.

82. Tocqueville, *Democracy*, 546.

83. As Andrew Sabl notes, "in Tocqueville's favored democratic scheme, governing officers play no direct role in promoting religion." See Sabl, *Ruling Passions*, 92. For further discussion of this point, see also Patrick Deneen, *Democratic Faith* (Princeton, NJ: Princeton University Press, 2005), 231–34.

84. Tocqueville, *Democracy*, 544, 548.

85. Tocqueville, *Democracy*, 69.

86. Tocqueville quoted in James Schleifer, *The Making of Tocqueville's Democracy in America* (Indianapolis, IN: Liberty Fund, 2000), 194.

87. Tocqueville, *Democracy*, 235–36.

88. Tocqueville, *Democracy*, 236.

89. Tocqueville, *Democracy*, 512.

90. Tocqueville, *Democracy*, 512.

91. Richard Krouse, "Classical Images of Democracy in America: Madison and Tocqueville," in *Democratic Theory and Practice*, ed. Graeme Duncan (New York: Cambridge University Press, 1983), 74.

92. Tocqueville, *Democracy*, 515. Rousseau similarly writes that when an individual enters a properly constituted civil society, "*his faculties are so exercised and developed, his mind is so enlarged, his sentiments so ennobled, and his*

whole spirit so elevated that, if the abuse of his new condition did not in many cases lower him to something worse than what he had left, he should constantly bless the happy hour that lifted him for ever from the state of nature and from a stupid, limited animal made a creature of intelligence and a man" (emphasis added). See Jean-Jacques Rousseau, *The Social Contract*, trans. Maurice Cranston (New York: Penguin Books, 1968), 65.

93. Tocqueville, *Democracy*, 694.

94. Tocqueville, *Democracy*, 701.

95. Deneen, *Democratic Faith*, 4–12, 221–24.

96. Deneen, *Democratic Faith*, 97.

97. While Deneen does not mention Tocqueville's remark to Gobineau that all people are "equally capable of perfecting themselves," Deneen does briefly discuss the Tocqueville-Gobineau correspondence in the endnotes to his book. See Deneen, *Democratic Faith*, 342–43 n. 6; 343–44 n. 10.

98. Tocqueville quoted in Pierson, *Tocqueville in America*, 382.

99. Tocqueville, *Democracy*, 692.

100. Tocqueville quoted in Schleifer, *The Making of Tocqueville's Democracy in America*, 217.

101. Tocqueville quoted in Pierson, *Tocqueville in America*, 634.

102. Tocqueville, *Democracy*, 548.

103. Tocqueville, *Democracy*, 530.

104. Tocqueville, *Democracy*, 175. For another discussion of this passage, see Jeffrey Leigh Sedgwick, "Executive Leadership and Administration: Founding versus Progressive Views," *Administration and Society* XVII (1986): 420. I am indebted to this article for helping to stimulate my thoughts on the significance of Tocqueville's discussion of parties.

105. Tocqueville, *Democracy*, 645.

106. Wilson Carey McWilliams helpfully suggests that Tocqueville's analysis of great and small parties "points toward a desirable synthesis, a party both lion and fox that acknowledges self-interest but relates it to broader political principles." In other words, Tocqueville does desire parties with at least a strong *element* of greatness. See Wilson Carey McWilliams, "Tocqueville and Responsible Parties," in *Challenges to Party Government*, eds. John Kenneth White and Jerome Mileur (Carbondale: Southern Illinois University Press, 1992), 192.

107. Tocqueville, *Democracy*, 645.

108. Tocqueville, *Democracy*, 632.

109. Tocqueville, *Democracy*, 632.

110. Tocqueville, *Democracy*, 645.

111. Tocqueville wrote in *Democracy*: "I have no hesitation in saying that in the control of society's foreign affairs democratic governments do appear decidedly inferior to others. . . . [I]n a nation whose education has been completed, democratic liberty applied to the state's internal affairs brings blessings greater than the ills resulting from a democratic government's mistakes. But that is not always true of relations between nation and nation" (228).

112. Tocqueville, *Democracy*, 201. Madison wrote in *Federalist* 10 that the mechanism of representation will "refine and enlarge the public views, by passing

them through the medium of a chosen body of citizens, whose wisdom may best discern the true interest of their country. . . ." See Alexander Hamilton, James Madison, and John Jay, *The Federalist Papers* (New York: Bantam, 2002), 55.

113. Tocqueville quoted in Pierson, *Tocqueville in America*, 608. In a similar vein, Tocqueville also praised John Stuart Mill for drawing "so clear and fine a distinction between *delegation* and *representation.*" See Tocqueville, letter to Mill, December 5, 1835, in Alexis de Tocqueville, *Memoirs, Letters, and Remains of Alexis de Tocqueville* (London: Macmillan, 1861), vol. II, 19.

114. Tocqueville, *Democracy*, 138.

115. Tocqueville quoted in Pierson, *Tocqueville in America*, 674. Specifically, Tocqueville believed that Washington bravely resisted the public's desire to join France in its war against England. See Tocqueville, *Democracy*, 229.

116. Tocqueville, *Democracy*, 200.

117. Tocqueville, *Democracy*, 198. It should be noted that Tocqueville did not believe that the lower classes were intellectually inferior by nature. Rather, he argued that to become a great statesman one needs a great deal of education, and the laboring masses simply do not have the leisure time to "educate and develop their intelligence" (197).

118. For Tocqueville's criticisms of Jackson, see Tocqueville, *Democracy*, 278, 392–95.

119. For Miroff, "mutuality" is one of the keys to democratic leadership in general, and to Lincoln's brand of democratic leadership in particular. See Miroff, *Icons of Democracy*, 123. For Burns on leadership and mutuality, see Burns, *Leadership*, 4.

120. Tocqueville, *Democracy*, 258. I borrow the term "moral courage" from Jean Yarbrough's discussion of Thomas Jefferson. Yarbrough argues that when Jefferson discusses the virtues necessary for the republican statesman, Jefferson is "conspicuously silent about [the virtue of] moral courage. . . . Jefferson's faith in the capacity of the people to govern themselves prevents him from recognizing that there will always be occasions when the statesman must resist popular opinion." See Jean Yarbrough, *American Virtues: Thomas Jefferson on the Character of a Free People* (Lawrence: University Press of Kansas, 1998), 144.

121. See Alexis de Tocqueville, *Recollections: The French Revolution of 1848*, ed. J.P. Mayer (New Brunswick, NJ: Transaction Books, 1987), 88 (emphasis added).

122. Burns, *Leadership*, 19, 18 (emphasis in original).

123. Tocqueville, *Democracy*, 264.

124. Tocqueville, *Democracy*, 267.

125. Tocqueville, *Democracy*, 449 (emphasis added).

126. Tocqueville, *Democracy*, 258.

127. Sandel, *Democracy's Discontent*, 10.

128. On the notion of the "procedural republic," see Michael Sandel, "The Procedural Republic and the Unencumbered Self," *Political Theory* XII (1984): 81–96 and Sandel, *Democracy's Discontent.*

129. Tocqueville, *Democracy*, 434.

130. Tocqueville, *Democracy*, 42.

131. Tocqueville, *Democracy*, 701.

132. Tocqueville quoted in Schleifer, *The Making of Tocqueville's Democracy in America*, 313.

Chapter 2. The Antifederalists and Tocqueville on Democratic Leadership and Democratic Authority

1. Cecilia Kenyon, introduction to *The Antifederalists*, ed. Cecilia Kenyon (Indianapolis, IN: Bobbs-Merrill Company, 1966), cxii.

2. Jackson Turner Main, *The Antifederalists* (Chapel Hill: University of North Carolina Press, 1961), xiv.

3. Main, *The Antifederalists*, xiii–xiv. Saul Cornell also stresses the heterogeneity of the Antifederalists, noting that they consisted of "rich planters in the South, middling politicians in New York and Pennsylvania, and backcountry farmers from several different regions." See Saul Cornell, *The Other Founders: Anti-Federalism and the Dissenting Tradition in America, 1788–1828* (Chapel Hill: North Carolina University Press, 1999), 22.

4. Main, *The Antifederalists*, xiv.

5. Herbert J. Storing, ed., *The Complete Anti-Federalist* (Chicago: University of Chicago Press, 1981), vol. 6, 228. Hereafter cited as *CAF*.

6. Kenyon, introduction to *The Antifederalists*, cxii.

7. *CAF*, vol. 4, 285.

8. Niccolo Machiavelli, *The Prince and the Discourses*, trans. C. Detmold (New York: Random House, 1950), 399.

9. *CAF*, vol. 6, 237.

10. *CAF*, vol. 3, 106.

11. On the importance of "energy" in government, see *Federalist* 70 in Hamilton et al., *The Federalist*, 426–34.

12. Tocqueville, letter to Claude-Francois de Corcelle, September 17, 1853, in *Selected Letters*, 294 (emphasis added).

13. *CAF*, vol. 2, 264 (emphasis added).

14. *CAF*, vol. 2, 384.

15. Yves Simon, *Freedom and Community* (Bronx, NY: Fordham University Press, 1968), 121.

16. *CAF*, vol. 6, 199.

17. *CAF*, vol. 6, 153.

18. Rousseau asserts that, "Sovereignty cannot be represented," because "its essence is the general will, and will cannot be represented. . . ." See Rousseau, *The Social Contract*, 141.

19. *CAF*, vol. 3, 182.

20. *CAF*, vol. 6, 157.

21. *CAF*, vol. 6, 158.

22. *CAF*, vol. 6, 163.

23. *CAF*, vol. 2, 384.

24. Ralph Ketcham, introduction to *The Antifederalist Papers and the Constitutional Convention Debates*, ed. Ralph Ketcham (New York: Mentor, 1986), 19.

25. Cecilia Kenyon, "Men of Little Faith: The Antifederalists on the Nature of Representative Government," *William and Mary Quarterly* XII (1955): 39.

26. *CAF*, vol. 2, 385.

27. *CAF*, vol. 2, 265.

28. Hamilton et al., *Federalist 15*, in *The Federalist Papers*, 83; *Federalist* 11, in *The Federalist Papers*, 61, 65.

29. Sedgwick, "Executive Leadership and Administration," 415.

30. *CAF*, vol. 3, 111.

31. *CAF*, vol. 2, 384.

32. My argument here draws on Wilson Carey McWilliams' interpretation of the Antifederalists. He writes that in the view of the Antifederalists, only small districts "can give the representatives the authority (confidence) to *sacrifice* private interest. . . . In a large district, we may trust our representative to defend the district's interests; we are unlikely to trust his decision to sacrifice them." See Wilson Carey McWilliams, "Democracy and the Citizen: Community, Dignity, and the Crisis of Contemporary Politics in America," in *How Democratic Is the Constitution?* (Washington, DC: American Enterprise Institute for Public Policy Research, 1980), 93.

33. *CAF*, vol. 6, 174.

34. Hamilton et al., *The Federalist Papers*, 156.

35. Hamilton et al., *The Federalist Papers*, 416.

36. Sheldon Wolin, *The Presence of the Past* (Baltimore, MD: Johns Hopkins University Press, 1989), 95.

37. *CAF*, vol. 2, 383.

38. *CAF*, vol. 2, 370, 371.

39. Hamilton et al., *The Federalist Papers*, 3.

40. Hamilton et al., *The Federalist Papers*, 85.

41. *CAF*, vol. 3, 164.

42. *CAF*, vol. 6, 160.

43. Hamilton et al., *Federalist 15*, in *The Federalist Papers*, 86.

44. *CAF*, vol. 4, 221.

45. Tocqueville, *Democracy*, 238.

46. Tocqueville, *Democracy*, 318–19 (emphasis added).

47. Tocqueville quoted in Schleifer, *The Making of Democracy in America*, 262 (emphasis added).

48. Lively, *The Social and Political Thought of Alexis de Tocqueville*, 13.

49. Tocqueville quoted in Lively, *The Social and Political Thought of Alexis de Tocqueville*, 13. The quotation is from Alexis de Tocqueville, *Journeys to England and Ireland* (London: Faber & Faber, 1958), 117.

50. Tocqueville, *Democracy*, 92.

51. Tocqueville, *Democracy*, 94.

52. Tocqueville, *Democracy*, 92–93.

53. Tocqueville, *Democracy*, 244.

54. Tocqueville, *Democracy*, 240–41.

55. Tocqueville, *Democracy*, 701.

56. Tocqueville, *Democracy*, 270.

57. Tocqueville, *Democracy*, 275.

58. *CAF*, vol. 5, 39.

59. Tocqueville quoted in Pierson, *Tocqueville in America*, 661 (emphasis added). After writing this chapter, I found that another scholar has also linked this quotation to the ideas of A [Maryland] Farmer. See Jacqueline Edelberg, "Justice Here? Alexis De Tocqueville and the Role of the Jury in the American Judicial Process and Republican Democracy," *The Tocqueville Review/La Revue Tocqueville* XVII (1996): 71.

60. Tocqueville, letter to Gobineau, January 24, 1857, in *Selected Letters*, 347 (emphasis added).

61. *CAF*, vol. 5, 30.

62. The Antifederalists feared that the institution of the jury would decline under the Constitution, because while Article III of the Constitution declared that "the trial of all crimes . . . shall be by jury," it did not guarantee trial by jury in civil cases.

63. Tocqueville, *Democracy*, 94–95.

64. *CAF*, vol. 6, 160–61.

65. *CAF*, vol. 4, 202.

66. *CAF*, vol. 6, 165.

67. *CAF*, vol. 6, 167.

68. Tocqueville, *Democracy*, 46–47.

69. *CAF*, vol. 3, 142.

70. *CAF*, vol. 6, 238.

71. *CAF*, vol. 4, 221.

72. Main, *The Antifederalists*, xiv.

73. *CAF*, vol. 4, 248.

74. *CAF*, vol. 6, 238.

75. *CAF*, vol. 3, 169.

76. Christopher Duncan also helpfully connects the Antifederalists to the Puritans, noting that many "Anti-Federalists . . . believed in John Winthrop's 'federal freedom,' the freedom to do that which is right. This is clearly something very different from the freedom to do everything except that which is wrong, which a liberal or libertarian embraces." See Christopher Duncan, *The Anti-Federalists and Early American Political Thought* (DeKalb: Northern Illinois University Press, 1995), 156.

77. *CAF*, vol. 3, 206.

78. Tocqueville, *Democracy*, 16.

79. *CAF*, vol. 6, 234.

80. Augustine, letter to Marcellinus, in Augustine, *Political Writings*, trans. Michael Tkacz and Douglas Kries (Indianapolis, IN: Hackett, 1994), 205.

81. Augustine, letter to Marcellinus, 210; Augustine, letter to Nectarius, in Augustine, *Political Writings*, 204.

82. *CAF*, vol. 6, 233.

83. *CAF*, vol. 6, 216.

84. For a discussion of Antifederalist opposition to the ban on religious tests for office, see Isaac Kramnick and R. Laurence Moore, *The Godless Constitution*

(New York: W.W. Norton, 1997). Kramnick and Moore note that, "the 'no religious test' clause was perceived by many [Antifederalists] to be the gravest defect of the Constitution" (32).

85. Tocqueville, *Democracy*, 298.

86. Herbert Storing, *What the Anti-Federalists Were For* (Chicago: University of Chicago Press, 1981), 23.

87. *CAF*, vol. 4, 221.

88. *CAF*, vol. 5, 264.

89. *CAF*, vol. 5, 263–64.

90. Hamilton et al., *The Federalist Papers*, 54.

91. Hamilton et al., *The Federalist Papers*, 26.

92. James Madison, Virginia Convention Speech, June 20, 1788, in *Selected Writings of James Madison*, ed. Ralph Ketcham (Indianapolis, IN: Hackett, 2006), 157.

93. Tocqueville, letter to Claude-Francois de Corcelle, 294.

94. Tocqueville, letter to Hippolyte de Tocqueville, December 4, 1831, in *Selected Letters*, 66.

95. Tocqueville, *Democracy*, 240.

96. As Michael Lienesch puts it, "Antifederalists were not opponents of popular government. In fact, they had an extreme, perhaps excessive faith in the people. Antifederalists spoke often, and in glowing terms, of the virtue of republican citizens." At the same time, Lienesch notes, the Antifederalists "feared degeneration." Worried about "corruption," the Antifederalists sometimes made gloomy statements that can be misunderstood as anti-democratic, Lienesch helpfully explains. See Michael Lienesch, *New Order of the Ages: Time, the Constitution, and the Making of Modern American Political Thought* (Princeton: Princeton University Press, 1988), 152.

97. Kenyon, "Men of Little Faith," 33.

98. *CAF*, vol. 4, 202.

99. *CAF*, vol. 3, 61–62.

100. *CAF*, vol. 3, 198.

101. Storing, *What the Anti-Federalists Were For*, 83.

102. Plato, *The Republic*, 283.

103. Burns, *Leadership*, 452.

104. Tocqueville, *Democracy*, 156.

105. Tocqueville, *Democracy*, 88.

106. Tocqueville, *Democracy*, 87.

107. McWilliams, "Democracy and the Citizen," 96. Specifically, McWilliams suggests that Tocqueville shares with the Antifederalists a belief in the importance of the *small* state.

108. Tocqueville, of course, carefully studied *The Federalist*. For a helpful reconstruction of *The Federalist*'s direct influence on Tocqueville, see Schleifer, *The Making of Democracy in America*, 117–34. See also the more speculative essay by Bernard E. Brown, "Tocqueville and Publius," in *Tocqueville's Democracy in America Revisited*, ed. Abraham S. Eisenstadt (New Brunswick, NJ: Rutgers University Press, 1988), 43–74. I disagree with Brown's claim that Tocqueville was a crypto-monarchist, and I also think that he is wrong to argue that Publius

and Tocqueville shared essentially the same goals and concepts. I find more persuasive the view of Richard Krouse that Tocqueville's science of politics was fundamentally different from Madison's, for whereas the latter broke with the republican tradition by building his system on nonparticipation and the pursuit of interest, Tocqueville's science is founded on democratic participation and the transcendence (at least some of the time) of self-interest. See Krouse, "'Classical' Images of Democracy," 73.

109. Tocqueville, letter to Mill, *Memoirs, Letters, and Remains*, vol. II, 19.

110. Walter Berns points out that "the Federalists made no secret of the fact that they wanted uncommon men to be elected. . . . The persons elected to public office should not reflect the people who choose them," but rather should be superior to them in "wisdom," "patriotism," and "love of justice," as Madison states in *Federalist* 10. See Walter Berns, "Does the Constitution 'Secure these Rights'?" in *How Democratic is the Constitution?*, 67–68.

111. Hamilton et al., *The Federalist Papers*, 347.

112. Martin Diamond, "Democracy and *The Federalist*: A Reconsideration of the Framers' Intent," *American Political Science Review* LIII (1959): 67.

113. Arendt, *On Revolution*, 239.

114. For comparisons of Arendt and Tocqueville, see Pitkin, *The Attack of the Blob*, 115–27 and Suzanne Jacobitti, "Individualism and Political Community: Arendt and Tocqueville on the Current Debate in Liberalism," *Polity* XXIII (1991): 585–604.

115. Arendt, *On Revolution*, 239.

116. Robert Putnam, *Bowling Alone: The Collapse and Revival of American Community* (New York: Simon & Schuster, 2000).

117. Bellah et al., *Habits of the Heart*. Because the Antifederalists believed that the framers aimed to create a regime marked by the spirit of commerce, they would also not be surprised by Sheldon Wolin's claim that America has now seen "the collapse of politics into economics and the emergence of a new form, the economic polity." See Sheldon Wolin, *Tocqueville between Two Worlds: The Making of a Political and Theoretical Life* (Princeton, NJ: Princeton University Press, 2001), 571. Wolin writes that the result of the "economic polity" is "the disappearance of the culture of participation" (570). This disappearance is, of course, exactly what both the Antifederalists and Tocqueville hoped to avoid.

118. Storing, *What the Anti-Federalists Were For*, 76.

119. Tocqueville, *Democracy*, 433.

120. Tocqueville, Speech in the Chamber of Deputies, January 27, 1848, in appendix III of *Democracy*, 750.

121. Tocqueville, Speech in the Chamber of Deputies, 752.

Chapter 3. Lincoln and Tocqueville on Democratic Leadership and Self-Interest Properly Understood

1. Harry Jaffa, *Crisis of the House Divided: An Interpretation of the Issues in the Lincoln-Douglas Debates* (Chicago: University of Chicago Press, 1959), 342–46.

2. John Diggins, *The Lost Soul of American Politics* (New York: Basic Books, 1984), chap. 9; Brian Danoff, "Lincoln, Machiavelli, and American Political Thought," *Presidential Studies Quarterly* XXX (2000): 290–311; David Siemers, "Principled Pragmatism: Abraham Lincoln's Method of Political Analysis," *Presidential Studies Quarterly* XXXIV (2004): 804–27.

3. Sean Mattie, "Prerogative and the Rule of Law in John Locke and the Lincoln Presidency," *Review of Politics* LXVII (2005): 77–111.

4. Joseph Fornieri, *Abraham Lincoln's Political Faith* (DeKalb: Northern Illinois University Press, 2003), 24–28.

5. Allen Guelzo, *Abraham Lincoln: Redeemer President* (Grand Rapids, MI: Wm. B. Eerdmans Publishing, 1999), 119–20.

6. William Lee Miller, *Lincoln's Virtues* (New York: Random House, 2002), 195, 219, 225–26, 438.

7. See Winger, *Lincoln, Religion, and Romantic Cultural Politics* (DeKalb: Northern Illinois University Press, 2003), 94.

8. Fornieri, *Abraham Lincoln's Political Faith*, 24.

9. Other Lincoln scholars have made references to Tocqueville, but again in a rather attenuated way. For instance, Jaffa makes three references to Tocqueville in his two masterworks on Lincoln, but the references are brief and do not deal directly with the issue of democratic leadership. See Jaffa, *Crisis of the House Divided*, 79, 144; Harry Jaffa, *A New Birth of Freedom* (Lanham, MD: Rowman & Littlefield, 2000), 529. Miller briefly notes that the young Lincoln's upward mobility was partly the result of a culture that celebrated the "individualism" that Tocqueville famously described (*Lincoln's Virtues*, 23).

10. Michael Rogin, *Ronald Reagan, The Movie and Other Episodes in American Political Demonology* (Berkeley: University of California Press, 1987), 86.

11. Tocqueville, *Democracy in America*, 12.

12. One measure of Lincoln's effectiveness is that he managed to win the popular vote in the 1858 Senate race; this was a stunning achievement given the wide renown of Senator Stephen Douglas. Ultimately, though, by calling Lincoln "effective" I do not primarily intend to call attention to his success in gaining votes. Instead, by calling Lincoln an effective leader, I mean to suggest that Lincoln was a great educator of his fellow citizens.

13. Tocqueville, letter to Pierre-Paul Royer-Collard, August 20, 1837, in *Selected Letters*, 118.

14. Tocqueville, *Democracy*, 448.

15. Lincoln, Speech on the Sub-Treasury, December 26, 1839, in Abraham Lincoln, *Speeches and Writings 1832–1858*, ed. Donald Fehrenbacher (New York: Library of America, 1989), 51–52 (emphasis in original).

16. Lincoln, Speech on the Sub-Treasury, in *Speeches and Writings 1832–1858*, 52.

17. Hamilton et al., *The Federalist Papers*, 316.

18. Lincoln, Lecture on Discoveries and Inventions, February 11, 1859, in Abraham Lincoln, *Speeches and Writings 1859–1865*, ed. Donald Fehrenbacher (New York: Library of America, 1989), 11.

19. Lincoln, Opinion on the Draft, c. mid-September 1863, in *Speeches and Writings 1859–1865*, 504–5.

20. Lincoln's emphasis on self-interest is also discussed by Guelzo, who goes so far as to argue that Lincoln's "intricate vocabulary of motives, necessity, and self-interest" echoes the utilitarianism of Bentham (*Abraham Lincoln: Redeemer President*, 119). In contrast, Winger suggests that Lincoln is actually a staunch critic of utilitarianism who believed that "the dictates of conscience must ultimately be heeded *apart from moral calculus of self-interest and personal happiness* . . ." (*Lincoln, Religion, and Romantic Cultural Politics*, 10) (emphasis in original). I agree with Winger that Lincoln is ultimately an opponent of utilitarianism, but I think that Guelzo is right to point out that interest-based arguments are an important aspect of Lincoln's thought.

21. Lincoln, Address on Colonization to a Committee of Colored Men, August 14, 1862, in *Speeches and Writings 1859–1865*, 356.

22. Tocqueville, *Democracy*, 527 (emphasis added).

23. Tocqueville, *Democracy*, 527.

24. Tocqueville, *Democracy*, 525.

25. Lincoln, Temperance Address, February 22, 1842, in *Speeches and Writings 1832–1858*, 89 (emphasis added).

26. Lincoln, Speech on the *Dred Scott* Decision, June 26, 1857, in *Speeches and Writings 1832–1858*, 402 (emphasis added).

27. For an illuminating discussion of Lincoln's advocacy of colonization, see Donald Fehrenbacher, *Lincoln in Text and Context: Collected Essays* (Palo Alto, CA: Stanford University Press, 1987), 110–11.

28. Lincoln, "On Sectionalism," c. July 1856, in *Speeches and Writings 1832–1858*, 372.

29. Lincoln, Speech at New Haven, March 6, 1860, in *Speeches and Writings 1859–1865*, 134–35.

30. Tocqueville quoted in Schleifer, *The Making of Tocqueville's Democracy in America*, 302.

31. Lincoln, Speech at Kalamazoo, August 27, 1856, in *Speeches and Writings 1832–1858*, 377.

32. Lincoln, Seventh Lincoln-Douglas Debate, October 15, 1858, in *Speeches and Writings 1832–1858*, 804.

33. Lincoln, Speech on the Kansas-Nebraska Act, October 16, 1854, in *Speeches and Writings 1832–1858*, 334.

34. Lincoln, On Pro-slavery Theology, 1858?, in *Speeches and Writings 1832–1858*, 685–86. "Dr. Ross" refers to the Revered Frederick Ross, author of the 1857 book *Slavery Ordained of God*. For an excellent discussion of Lincoln's views on Ross and other defenders of slavery, see Fornieri, *Abraham Lincoln's Political Faith*, chap. 3.

35. For a thorough attack on the "natural limits" theory, see Jaffa, *Crisis of the House Divided*, 387–99.

36. Lincoln, letter to George Robertson, August 15, 1855, in *Speeches and Writings 1832–1858*, 359.

37. Lincoln, Address to the Young Men's Lyceum of Springfield, January 27, 1838, in *Speeches and Writings 1832–1858*, 35.

38. Lincoln, Lyceum Address, 35.

39. Lincoln, Lyceum Address, 36.

40. On the status of reason in Lincoln's thought, I agree with Lucas Morel, who writes: "To be sure, [Lincoln] closes the Lyceum and Temperance Addresses with tributes to reason as all-powerful to solve political problems. But these statements suggest more in the way of rhetorical flourish than serious reflection on the power of reason to check or curb the public passions." See Lucas Morel, *Lincoln's Sacred Effort* (Lanham, MD: Lexington Books, 2000), 164.

41. Lincoln, Speech on the Kansas-Nebraska Act, 315.

42. Lincoln, Address to the Wisconsin State Agricultural Society, September 30, 1859, in *Speeches and Writings 1859–1865*, 98.

43. Richard Hofstadter, *The American Political Tradition and the Men Who Made It* (New York: Alfred A. Knopf, 1948), 105.

44. Lincoln, Seventh Lincoln-Douglas Debate, 806. Lincoln made similar arguments in speeches at Peoria, Kalamazoo, Cincinnati, and New Haven. See *Speeches and Writings 1832–1858*, 331, 379; *Speeches and Writings 1859–1865*, 85–86, 145. Gabor Boritt (*Lincoln and the Economics of the American Dream* [Memphis, TN: Memphis State University Press, 1978]) notes that Lincoln made arguments against slavery expansion on the grounds that the territories needed to remain free for the interest of white upward mobility. However, Boritt suggests that this "was not a major ingredient of [Lincoln's] argument, however important it might have been to his Illinoisans" (164). I think that Boritt goes too far in downplaying the significance of Lincoln's interest-based argument. I agree with Boritt that in Lincoln's view, slavery should be opposed above all because it is simply immoral. However, Lincoln knew that as a democratic leader his task was to educate and elevate his audience. By starting with what is base, and with what is common—that is, by starting with the interest-based argument—Lincoln sought to hold the attention of his entire audience, so that he could then try to elevate gradually his audience. As Jaffa puts it, "Men may be led toward higher purposes of which they are scarcely conscious, if those who hold these purposes first show concern for and an ability to gratify their less noble demands" (*Crisis of the House Divided*, 199).

45. George Fitzhugh, *Cannibals All! Or, Slaves without Masters* (Cambridge, MA: Belknap/Harvard University Press, 1960), 199.

46. Lincoln, Address to the Wisconsin State Agricultural Society, 97.

47. Tocqueville, *Democracy*, 344, 346–47. As Eric Foner demonstrates, the Republican Party as a whole offered a similar cultural critique of the South. See Eric Foner, *Free Soil, Free Labor, Free Men: The Ideology of the Republican Party before the Civil War* (New York: Oxford University Press, 1970), especially chapters 1 and 2.

48. Lincoln, Speech on the Kansas-Nebraska Act, 331–32. Lincoln made essentially the same argument at Kalamazoo. See *Speeches and Writings 1832–1858*, 379.

49. For an excellent discussion of the concept of the Slave Power, see Foner, *Free Soil, Free Labor, Free Men*, 87–102. Foner notes that Salmon P. Chase argued in 1845 that as a result of the three-fifths clause, "an aristocracy of slaveholders" had seized control of the federal government (89).

50. Lincoln, Speech at New Haven, 135 (emphasis added).

51. Lincoln, Draft of a Speech, c. late December 1857, in *Speeches and Writings 1832–1858*, 414.

52. Lincoln, Speech on the Kansas-Nebraska Act, 339.

53. Lincoln recognized that another way to try to justify slavery would be to argue that African-Americans are not human beings at all. Lincoln argued, though, that to assert this is to engage in what one might call bad faith, for white people who are honest with themselves all recognize the humanity of African-Americans. At Peoria, Lincoln brilliantly detailed a number of ways in which Southerners implicitly conceded the humanity of their slaves. See Lincoln, Speech on the Kansas-Nebraska, 326–27.

54. Lincoln, Draft of a Speech, c. August 1858, in *Speeches and Writings 1832–1858*, 494.

55. Lincoln, letter to Samuel Galloway, July 28, 1859, in *Speeches and Writings 1859–1865*, 27.

56. Lincoln, Speech at Edwardsville, September 11, 1858, in *Speeches and Writings 1832–1858*, 585 (emphasis in original).

57. Cf. Winger, *Lincoln, Religion, and Romantic Cultural Politics*, 137; Jaffa, *Crisis of the House Divided*, 205; Miller, *Lincoln's Virtues*, 279.

58. Lincoln, Speech on the Kansas-Nebraska Act, 315.

59. Lincoln, Fragment on Slavery, 1854?, in *Speeches and Writings 1832–1858*, 303.

60. Tocqueville, *Democracy*, 526.

61. Lincoln, Speech on the Kansas-Nebraska Act, 334, 346.

62. I have emphasized here that in his struggle against slavery expansion, Lincoln sought to foster and to cultivate the moral impulses of the citizenry. However, it should also be noted that Lincoln was, at the same time, wary of moral fanaticism. As Glen Thurow (*Abraham Lincoln and American Political Religion* [Albany: State University of New York Press, 1976]) notes, Lincoln not only feared that "people would forsake the principle of justice"; Lincoln also feared, according to Thurow, "that the people, acting on principle, would become a fanatical, mob-like beast deaf to the voice of prudence" (xii–xiii).

63. Tocqueville, letter to Pierre-Paul Royer-Collard, August 20, 1837, in *Selected Letters*, 118.

64. See Tocqueville, *Democracy*, 512.

65. Lincoln, Fragments on Government, 1854?, in *Speeches and Writings 1832–1858*, 302.

66. Herndon is quoted in David Greenstone, *The Lincoln Persuasion: Remaking American Liberalism* (Princeton, NJ: Princeton University Press, 1993), 12. Greenstone is one commentator who *has* noted that Lincoln himself publicly admitted his ambition: "Lincoln readily acknowledged," writes Greenstone, "the importance of his own and other people's self-regarding, ulterior motives" (12).

67. Lincoln, Speech in Springfield, October 30, 1858, in *Speeches and Writings 1832–1858*, 827.

68. Lincoln, Draft of a Speech, c. August 1858, in *Speeches and Writings 1832–1858*, 488.

69. Jefferson quoted in Yarbrough, *American Virtues*, 146.

70. Lincoln, Temperance Address, 81.

71. Lincoln, Temperance Address, 83.

72. Lincoln, Temperance Address, 83. For a study of the role of friendship in Lincoln's own life, see David Herbert Donald, *We Are Lincoln Men: Abraham Lincoln and His Friends* (New York: Simon & Schuster, 2003).

73. This is a point that Bruce Miroff has emphasized. As Miroff puts it, Lincoln "began from the premise of mutuality, always regarding ordinary citizens as capable of everything that he himself had achieved" (*Icons of Democracy*, 123).

74. Tocqueville, *Democracy*, 433.

75. Lincoln, Speech at Columbus, September 16, 1859, in *Speeches and Writings 1859–1865*, 56.

76. Stephen Douglas, Second Lincoln-Douglas Debate, August 27, 1858, in *Speeches and Writings 1832–1858*, 555.

77. Douglas, Second Lincoln-Douglas Debate, 555–56.

78. Douglas, Sixth Lincoln-Douglas Debate, October 13, 1858, in *Speeches and Writings 1832–1858*, 763.

79. Lincoln, Notes for Speeches, c. September 1859, in *Speeches and Writings 1859–1865*, 28.

80. Lincoln, letter to Joseph Hooker, January 26, 1863, in *Speeches and Writings 1859–1865*, 434.

81. Lincoln, On Stephen Douglas, c. December 1856, in *Speeches and Writings 1832–1858*, 384.

82. Tocqueville, *Democracy*, 532.

83. Tocqueville, *Democracy*, 533, 534.

84. Lincoln, Address to the Wisconsin State Agricultural Society, 92. Similarly, Lincoln suggested that "the mineral resources" of the territories "ought to be developed as rapidly as possible." See Lincoln, Annual Message to Congress, December 1, 1862, in *Speeches and Writings 1859–1865*, 396.

85. Lincoln, Speech on the Kansas-Nebraska Act, 337 (emphasis added).

86. Lincoln, Speech at Columbus, 58. Lincoln also brilliantly criticized the materialism of American culture (and, in particular, the materialism of the "Young America" movement) in his Lecture on Discoveries and Inventions. For an excellent discussion of the ideas found in the Lecture, see Winger, *Lincoln, Religion, and Romantic Cultural Politics*, chap. 1.

87. Lincoln would have likely agreed with Martin Diamond's claim that, "Those who wish to improve American life—specifically, those who would improve the relationship between ethics and politics in America—must base such improvement upon the American foundation. . . . [I]f the aim is improvement, it must be improvement that accepts the limits imposed by the 'genius' of the particular political order; it must be improvement that makes America her better self, but still her own self." See Martin Diamond, "Ethics and Politics: The American Way," in *The Moral Foundations of the American Republic*, ed. Robert Horwitz (Charlottesville: University Press of Virginia, 1986), 95.

88. In the conclusion to *What the Anti-Federalists Were For*, Storing also connects Lincoln's ideas to those of the Antifederalists, insofar as both believed

that "the passage of time would magnify the difficulty of preserving the American republic" (75). Storing does not, though, make the connection that I make between Lincoln and the Antifederalists regarding the need for leaders who are close to the people.

89. Tocqueville, *Democracy*, 267.

90. As discussed in chapter 1, for a brief moment in *Democracy in America*, Tocqueville *does* begin to move toward the idea that democratic leadership is most successful when the leaders remain close to the people; specifically, Tocqueville notes that the clergy in America "try to improve their contemporaries but do not quit fellowship with them" (449).

91. Tocqueville quoted in Pierson, *Tocqueville in America*, 608.

92. Lincoln, letter to the Editor of the Sangamo Journal, March 9, 1832, in *Speeches and Writings 1832–1858*, 5.

93. Lincoln, First Lincoln-Douglas Debate, August 21, 1858, in *Speeches and Writings 1832–1858*, 525.

94. Jaffa, *Crisis of the House Divided*, especially 377.

95. Tocqueville, *Democracy*, 257.

96. James McPherson, *Abraham Lincoln and the Second American Revolution* (New York: Oxford University Press, 1991), 52.

97. Lincoln, Speech on the *Dred Scott* Decision, 397.

98. Winger, *Lincoln, Religion, and Romantic Cultural Politics*, 148.

99. Phillips quoted in Hofstadter, *The American Political Tradition*, 150.

100. Lincoln, Speech on the Kansas-Nebraska Act, 316.

101. The phrase "dogma of the sovereignty of the people" first appears in vol. 1, chap. 4, of *Democracy* (58). Tocqueville is not explicitly critical of the "dogma" in this chapter, but later in the book he implies that the dogma can lead to the "tyranny of the majority."

102. Tocqueville, *Democracy*, 250.

103. Tocqueville, *Democracy*, 250.

104. Lincoln, First Inaugural Address, March 4, 1861, in *Speeches and Writings 1859–1865*, 220.

105. Tocqueville, *Democracy*, 294.

106. Tocqueville, *Democracy*, 292.

107. Tocqueville, *Democracy*, 292; Tocqueville, *"The European Revolution" and Correspondence with Gobineau*, 191.

108. Tocqueville, *Democracy*, 294.

109. Tocqueville, *Democracy*, 433–34.

110. Lincoln, Speech at Chicago, July 10, 1858, in *Speeches and Writings 1832–1858*, 456.

111. William Galston, *The Practice of Liberal Pluralism* (Cambridge, UK: Cambridge University Press, 2005), 165–66 (emphasis added). Galston also discusses the purposes of the Preamble in Galston, *Public Matters: Politics, Policy, and Religion in the 21st Century* (Lanham, MD: Rowman & Littlefield, 2005), 163.

112. Galston, *The Practice of Liberal Pluralism*, 4–5.

113. Lincoln, Speech at Chicago, 456–57 (emphasis added).

114. Jaffa, *Crisis of the House Divided*, 201–3.

115. Lincoln, Address at Cooper Institute, February 27, 1860, in *Speeches and Writings 1859–1865*, 129.

116. Jaffa, *Crisis of the House Divided*, 203.

117. Tocqueville, *Democracy*, 47.

118. Tocqueville, *Democracy*, 292.

119. Tocqueville, *Democracy*, 47, 292.

120. Mark Reinhardt, *The Art of Being Free: Taking Liberties with Tocqueville, Marx, and Arendt* (Ithaca, NY: Cornell, 1997), 85.

121. Patrick Deneen, "Chasing Plato," review of *Corrupting Youth*, by J. Peter Euben, *Political Theory* XXVIII (2000): 427.

122. Alfred North Whitehead, *Symbolism: Its Meaning and Effect* (Bronx, NY: Fordham University Press, 1985), 88.

123. To take just one example, Lincoln said that the "chief and real purpose of the Republican party is eminently conservative. It proposes nothing save and except to restore this government to its original tone in regard to this element of slavery. . . ." See Lincoln, Speech at Columbus, 35.

124. Alasdair MacIntyre, *After Virtue* (Notre Dame, IN: Notre Dame University Press, 1981), 222.

125. Jaffa writes that for Lincoln, "all men are created equal" was "a transcendental affirmation of what [civil society] *ought* to be." See Jaffa, *Crisis of the House Divided*, 321.

126. Jaffa, *Crisis of the House Divided*, 316.

127. Tocqueville, *Democracy*, 547–48.

128. Lincoln, Speech on the Kansas-Nebraska Act, 328.

129. Lincoln, On Slavery and Democracy, 1858?, in *Speeches and Writings 1832–1858*, 484.

130. As Thurow points out, "the Declaration is indifferent to forms of government except, possibly, in excluding absolute monarchy and tyranny; rather, it explicitly says that the People, in instituting a new government, have the right of 'laying its foundations on such principles and organizing its powers in such form, as to them shall seem most likely to effect Safety and Happiness.' Further, in listing the tyrannical actions of George III, it implies that his would be a legitimate government if he had not overstepped the bounds of limited monarchy. The fact that he was a king is not one of the objections made to him." See Thurow, *Abraham Lincoln and American Political Religion*, 55. For an opposing (but ultimately less persuasive) argument, see Arendt, *On Revolution*, 129–30.

131. Lincoln, First Inaugural Address, 220.

132. Lincoln, Speech on the Kansas-Nebraska Act, 328.

133. Thurow, *Abraham Lincoln and American Political Religion*, 55.

134. It was actually not Lincoln, but Douglas who first defined the signers of the Constitution as "our fathers." At Cooper Union, Lincoln accepts this definition for the sake of argument; Lincoln then proceeds to demonstrate that Douglas was wrong to suggest that "our fathers" would have supported Douglas's "popular sovereignty," for many of the framers themselves were plainly willing to use the federal government to ban slavery in the territories. See Lincoln, Address at Cooper Institute, 111–30.

135. Garry Wills, *Lincoln at Gettysburg: The Words That Remade America* (New York: Simon & Schuster, 1992); Willmoore Kendall, "Equality: Commitment or Ideal?," *Intercollegiate Review* XXIV (1989): 25–33.

136. Lincoln, Fragment, 1860?, in Abraham Lincoln, *The Language of Liberty: The Political Speeches and Writings of Abraham Lincoln*, ed. Joseph Fornieri (Washington, DC: Regnery Gateway, 2004), 562.

137. Lincoln, letter to James N. Brown, October 18, 1858, in *Speeches and Writings 1832–1858*, 822 (emphasis added).

138. Lincoln, Address at Cooper Institute, 126–27.

139. Lincoln, Speech at Chicago, 457 (emphasis added).

140. Lincoln, Reply to Committee of the National Union Convention, June 9, 1864, in *Speeches and Writings 1859–1865*, 598.

141. Lincoln, Response to Serenade, February 1, 1865, in *Speeches and Writings 1859–1865*, 670 (emphasis added).

142. Lincoln, Address at Sanitary Fair, April 18, 1864, in *Speeches and Writings 1859–1865*, 589.

143. Lincoln, letter to Henry L. Pierce and Others, April 6, 1859, in *Speeches and Writings 1859–1865*, 19.

144. Herbert Storing, "Slavery and the Moral Foundations of the Republic," in *The Moral Foundations of the American Republic*, ed. Robert Horwitz (Charlottesville: University Press of Virginia, 1986), 324–25.

145. Herbert Storing, "Slavery and the Moral Foundations of the Republic," 325–26.

146. Greenstone and McPherson also argue that Lincoln sometimes articulated a "positive" conception of liberty, but they each use the term in a somewhat different way from the way I am using it. Thus, in *The Lincoln Persuasion*, Greenstone discusses how Lincoln sought to move away from a liberalism that is concerned with the mere satisfaction of interests and preferences, and toward a liberalism that is concerned with the development of human capacities. According to Lincoln's "positive" notion of liberty, people can only be free if they are provided with the conditions for self-improvement (233–40). McPherson, for his part, argues that Lincoln sought to articulate a new "positive" definition of freedom according to which governmental power has the potential to not only repress—but also to augment—human liberty (*Abraham Lincoln and the Second American Revolution*, 62–64, 131–52). Most obviously, Lincoln used the power of the Union Army to liberate African-Americans. In the next chapter, we shall see that Wilson further developed Lincoln's idea that national power is required to liberate the American people.

147. Lincoln, Speech on the Kansas-Nebraska Act, 342.

148. James P. Young also suggests that Lincoln's notion of freedom is related to that of Winthrop. See Young, *Reconsidering American Liberalism: The Troubled Odyssey of the Liberal Idea* (Boulder, CO: Westview, 1996), 124.

149. Lincoln, Speech at Chicago, 449.

150. Lincoln, Address at Sanitary Fair, 589.

151. Howard B. White, "Comment on Morgenthau's 'Dilemmas of Freedom,'" *American Political Science Review* LI (1957): 725.

152. Lincoln, Final Emancipation Proclamation, January 1, 1863, in *Speeches and Writings 1859–1865*, 425, 424.

153. Lincoln, letter to Salmon P. Chase, September 2, 1863, in *Speeches and Writings 1859–1865*, 501.

154. As Lincoln explained, "We can not have free government without elections; and if the rebellion could force us to forego, or postpone a national election, it might fairly claim to have already conquered and ruined us." See Lincoln, Response to Serenade, November 10, 1864, in *Speeches and Writings 1859–1865*, 641.

155. Tocqueville, *Democracy*, 483.

Chapter 4. Wilson and Tocqueville on Leadership and the "Character Foundations of American Democracy"

1. Isaac Kramnick notes that, "Every president since Dwight D. Eisenhower has quoted *Democracy in America*." See Isaac Kramnick, introduction to *Democracy in America*, by Alexis de Tocqueville (New York: Penguin, 2003), ix. Kramnick does not mention, though, that Woodrow Wilson not only quoted Tocqueville, but also carefully studied his works.

2. Woodrow Wilson, "Wilson's Critique of De Tocqueville's *Democracy in America*," c. January 19, 1883, in *The Papers of Woodrow Wilson*, ed. Arthur Link, 69 vols. (Princeton, NJ: Princeton University Press, 1966–1994), 2:295. Hereafter cited as *PWW*.

3. Woodrow Wilson, "De Tocqueville," January 10, 1896, in *PWW*, 9:374–77. Wilson also delivered his "Lectures on Great Leaders of Political Thought" in 1901. See "A News Item," January 12, 1901, in *PWW*, 12:71.

4. Wilson also read and wrote a memorandum on Tocqueville's *Recollections*. As an academic who harbored political ambitions, Wilson used Tocqueville's *Recollections* as an occasion to reflect upon the relationship between theory and practice. Wilson concluded that during the period of time discussed in the *Recollections*, Tocqueville was a "Seer, but no guide." See Woodrow Wilson, "Notes on Tocqueville's *Recollections*," April 11, 1897, in *PWW*, 10:214. This comment is indicative of Wilson's belief that Tocqueville was a great theorist, but not a great leader. See Woodrow Wilson, "A News Report of a Lecture," March 19, 1901, in *PWW*, 12:111. This matched Tocqueville's own self-assessment, for Tocqueville wrote that he "completely lacked the art of holding men together and leading them as a body." See Tocqueville, *Recollections*, 82.

5. Brief references to Tocqueville can be found in Ronald Pestritto, *Woodrow Wilson and the Roots of Modern Liberalism* (Lanham, MD: Rowman & Littlefield, 2005), 87 and Niels Aage Thorsen, *The Political Thought of Woodrow Wilson, 1875–1910* (Princeton, NJ: Princeton University Press, 1988), 37, 62, 167, 210.

6. Thorsen also notes "Wilson's insistence on the primacy of political leadership" and suggests that, "Wilson's contribution to American political theory may be assessed in light of the virtual absence of any sustained reflection upon the notion of leadership within the liberal tradition." See Thorsen, *The Political*

Thought of Woodrow Wilson, 64, 63. Thorsen, though, does not connect Wilson's ideas on leadership to Tocqueville.

7. Woodrow Wilson, "Memoranda," c. September 10, 1899, in *PWW*, 11:239.

8. Woodrow Wilson, "Memoranda," 239. Similarly, in his notes on *Democracy*, Wilson wrote, "Political institutions presuppose a particularly moral and sentimental state of the community, one of [Tocqueville's] valuable reflections." See Wilson, "Wilson's Critique of De Tocqueville's *Democracy in America*," 295.

9. Woodrow Wilson, *Constitutional Government* (New York: Columbia University Press, 1908), 52.

10. Wilson, "Memoranda," 239.

11. Woodrow Wilson, *The State: Elements of Historical and Practical Politics* (Boston: D.C. Heath, 1898), 592–93. In an 1852 speech, Tocqueville used very similar language as he suggested that, "The political sciences form a sort of intellectual atmosphere breathed by both governors and governed in society, and both unwittingly derive from it the principles of their action." See Alexis de Tocqueville, "The Art and Science of Politics," *Encounter* XXXVI (1971): 30.

12. For instance, Wilson denounced "the French revolutionary philosophy" as "radically evil and corrupting. . . . For it holds that government is a matter of contract and deliberate arrangement, whereas in fact it is an institute of habit, bound together by innumerable threads of association. . . ." See Woodrow Wilson, "Interpreter of English Liberty," in *Mere Literature and Other Essays* (1896; Port Washington, NY: Kennikat Press, 1965), 155. Tocqueville's criticism of the philosophy that undergirded the French Revolution can be found in *The Old Regime*. In that work, Tocqueville denounces the *philosophes* for promoting "a kind of abstract, literary politics" that was divorced from "the realities of public life" (138, 139).

13. Tocqueville, *Democracy*, 307.

14. Tocqueville argues that, "By making men pay attention to things other than their own affairs," juries "combat that individual selfishness which is like rust in society." See Tocqueville, *Democracy*, 274.

15. Wilson, *The State*, 12, 11.

16. Pestritto, *Woodrow Wilson and the Roots of Modern Liberalism*.

17. Hartz, *The Liberal Tradition in America*, 207, 230.

18. Sandel, *Democracy's Discontent*. Sandel suggests that Wilson had a republican concern for the "political economy of citizenship" (221). This chapter can be seen, in part, as building upon Sandel's claim that Wilson's thought contains an important republican strand.

19. Rogers Smith, "Beyond Tocqueville, Myrdal, and Hartz: The Multiple Traditions in America," *American Political Science Review* LXXXVII (1993): 549–66; Rogers Smith, *Civic Ideals: Conflicting Views of Citizenship in American History* (New Haven, CT: Yale University Press, 1997).

20. Stephen Skowronek, "The Reassociation of Ideas and Purposes: Racism, Liberalism, and the American Political Tradition," *American Political Science Review* C (2006): 385–401. Skowronek criticizes Smith's "multiple traditions" approach because it fails to reveal, in Skowronek's view, how the "different

strands" of American political thought "intertwine and fuse in ways that are themselves culturally formative" (386). Whether this is a fully accurate assessment of Smith's work is a question that I do not attempt to resolve here. It should be noted, though, that Smith has emphasized that he does find important "linkages" in American political thought between liberal, republican, and ascriptive ideologies. See Rogers Smith, "Response" to Jacqueline Stevens, "Beyond Tocqueville, Please!," *American Political Science Review* LXXXIX (1995): 991.

21. Woodrow Wilson, "The Annual Convention of the Western Association of Princeton Clubs," May 26, 1906, in *PWW*, 16:408. In an address at Swarthmore, Wilson invoked Tocqueville as he discussed the importance of educational reform: "De Tocqueville used to say of our institutions that they required a variety of information and a nicety of discrimination on the part of the citizen unparalleled anywhere else. How, therefore, are we to enable this nation to maintain her freedom? By clarifying her knowledge. Only as we know shall we live." Woodrow Wilson, "The University and the Nation," December 15, 1905, in *PWW*, 16:269.

22. Woodrow Wilson, "President Wilson's Address to the Board of Trustees," c. June 10, 1907, in *PWW*, 17:200.

23. Woodrow Wilson, "Report on the Social Coordination of the University," c. June 6, 1907, in *PWW*, 17:182.

24. Wilson, "Report on the Social Coordination of the University," 183.

25. Tocqueville, *Democracy*, 506.

26. Wilson, "President Wilson's Address to the Board of Trustees," 201.

27. Wilson, "Report on the Social Coordination of the University," 185.

28. Wilson, "President Wilson's Address to the Board of Trustees," 200.

29. Wilson, *The State*, 633. Like Wilson, Tocqueville believed that modern societies should strive for the self-development of *all* of their members. Thus, Tocqueville was deeply troubled by the possibility that under the new "industrial aristocracy," only an elite few would experience full self-development: "While the workman confines his intelligence more and more to studying one single detail," Tocqueville laments, "the master daily embraces a vast field in his vision, and his mind expands as fast as the other's contracts." See Tocqueville, *Democracy*, 556.

30. Wilson, "Report on the Social Coordination of the University," 182, 181.

31. Tocqueville, *Democracy*, 534. Tocqueville's ultimate fear about materialism is that the Americans (and other modern peoples) might give up their political freedom in exchange for "petty and banal pleasures," as he puts it in his chapter on "What Sort of Despotism Democratic Nations Have to Fear" (692).

32. Wilson, "Report on the Social Coordination of the University," 184.

33. Wilson, "The Annual Convention," 410.

34. Wilson, "The Annual Convention," 410.

35. Wilson, "The Annual Convention," 411.

36. Woodrow Wilson, "The Spirit of Learning," July 1, 1909, in *PWW*, 19:280.

37. Wilson, "Report on the Social Coordination of the University," 180.

38. Woodrow Wilson, "Spurious versus Real Patriotism in Education," October 13, 1899, in *PWW*, 11:258.

39. Tocqueville was, of course, ambivalent about the "equality of conditions" that struck him as the "basic fact" about the United States. See Tocqueville, *Democracy*, 10. On the one hand, it is equality of conditions that can produce such dangers as individualism and the tyranny of the majority. On the other hand, Tocqueville finds that equality of conditions also helps produce the widespread political and civic participation that is necessary if *liberté* is to be preserved in the modern world. As Amy Fried puts it, for Tocqueville, equality "can develop participatory skills and a largeness of conception, or it can limit freedom and control the human spirit." See Fried, "The Strange Disappearance of Alexis de Tocqueville in Putnam's Analysis of Social Capital," in *Social Capital: Critical Perspectives on Community and "Bowling Alone,"* eds. Scott L. McLean, David A. Schultz, and Manfred B. Steger (New York: New York University Press, 2002), 27.

40. Woodrow Wilson, "What is a College For?," August 18, 1909, in *PWW*, 19:345–46.

41. Unlike his "quad plan," Wilson successfully enacted his proposed preceptorial system.

42. Wilson, "The Annual Convention," 407.

43. Woodrow Wilson, "The Princeton Preceptorial System," c. June 1, 1905, in *PWW*, 16:108, 109. According to Benjamin Barber, a good teacher can provide us with a model of "facilitating leadership," a type of leadership that is consistent with "strong democracy." See Barber, "Neither Leaders nor Followers," 103–4. Wilson's ideal "preceptor" is precisely a "facilitating leader."

44. Wilson, "The Princeton Preceptorial System," 109.

45. Consistent with this claim, Wilson tried to deal with Congresspeople in a spirit of mutuality. As Cooper notes, whereas some presidents have tried to dominate Congress, Wilson (at least in his first term) "eschewed a driving, cajoling personal assertiveness." Wilson, writes Cooper, saw himself as "the lead horse of a team rather than a coach driver." See John Milton Cooper Jr., *The Warrior and the Priest: Woodrow Wilson and Theodore Roosevelt* (Cambridge, MA: Belknap Press, 1983), 236.

46. In the dialogue sought by Wilson, the democratic leader can be considered *primus inter pares*, for as Wilson explains in "Leaders of Men," it is the leader who has the capacity to "interpret" public opinion. The great task of "interpretation" involves both "read[ing] the common thought" as well as molding—to a degree—that thought. See Woodrow Wilson, "Leaders of Men," June 17, 1890, in *PWW*, 6:659.

47. Woodrow Wilson, "A Speech to Businessmen in Columbus, Ohio," September 20, 1912, in *PWW*, 25:198.

48. Woodrow Wilson, "A Labor Day Address in Buffalo," September 2, 1912, in *PWW*, 25:76.

49. Woodrow Wilson, "An Inaugural Address," March 4, 1913, in *PWW*, 27:152.

50. As Clor succinctly puts it, for Wilson, "Democracy is a massive discussion or dialogue." See Harry Clor, "Woodrow Wilson," in *American Political Thought*, eds. Morton Frisch and Richard Stevens (Itasca, IL: F.E. Peacock, 1983), 273.

51. Woodrow Wilson, *Congressional Government: A Study in American Politics* (1885; Baltimore, MD: Johns Hopkins University Press, 1981), 71, 198.

52. Tocqueville, *Democracy*, 270–76.

53. As a young man, Wilson advocated a constitutional amendment that would allow Congresspeople to serve in the president's cabinet. See Woodrow Wilson, "Cabinet Government in the United States," August 1879, in *PWW*, 1:498–99.

54. As discussed later in this chapter, Wilson did eventually come to endorse, albeit in a lukewarm manner, the initiative, referendum, and recall. He did so largely to secure the crucial support of William Jennings Bryan and his followers. Notably, though, Wilson never came to defend the initiative, referendum, and recall as positive goods, but only as necessary evils which would, he hoped, "rarely need to be actually exercised." Moreover, he never came to endorse proposals for judicial recall. See Woodrow Wilson, *The New Freedom*, ed. William Leuchtenberg (1913; Englewood Cliffs, NJ: Prentice-Hall, 1961), 140–41.

55. Wilson, *Constitutional Government*, 104–5.

56. Wilson's criticisms of the initiative and referendum were prescient. One of the sad ironies of the Progressive Era is that whereas Progressives hoped to create a more deliberative democracy, the reforms that they promoted led to what Philip J. Ethington calls "the plebiscitary advertising campaign that reigns supreme today." See Philip J. Ethington, "The Metropolis and Multicultural Ethics: Direct Democracy versus Deliberative Democracy in the Progressive Era," in *Progressivism and the New Democracy*, eds. Sidney Milkis and Jerome M. Mileur (Amherst: University of Massachusetts Press, 1999), 193.

57. Wilson, *The New Freedom*, 70.

58. Tocqueville, *Democracy*, 61–84. Tocqueville found that Americans were engaged in constant political discussion. Tocqueville writes that, "To take a hand in the government of society and to talk about it is [an American's] most important business and, so to say, the only pleasure he knows" (243).

59. Wilson, *The New Freedom*, 68.

60. On the social center movement, see Kevin Mattson, *Creating a Democratic Public: The Struggle for Urban Participatory Democracy During the Progressive Era* (University Park: Pennsylvania State University Press, 1998).

61. Tocqueville, *The Old Regime*, xiv.

62. Tocqueville, *The Old Regime*, xi.

63. Wilson, *The New Freedom*, 65.

64. Tulis, *The Rhetorical Presidency*. See also James W. Ceaser et al., "The Rise of the Rhetorical Presidency," *Presidential Studies Quarterly* XI (1981): 158–71.

65. Sedgwick, "Executive Leadership and Administration," 429, 427.

66. Sedgwick, "Executive Leadership and Administration," 428, 430.

67. My argument here complements that of Terri Bimes and Stephen Skowronek. In their view, Tulis and others are mistaken when they suggest that Wilson's vision of presidential leadership promotes demagogic appeals to popular opinion. Through an analysis of Wilson's historical writings, Bimes and Skowronek demonstrate that Wilson actually "uniformly condemned presidents who would electrify the people to overcome the inertia of the constitutional system." Bimes and Skowronek conclude that Wilson's vision of leadership was a largely conservative

one, for Wilson greatly feared demagoguery, and thus wanted "popular appeals" by presidents to be "limited to matters of war and peace." They also find that in his own practice as president, Wilson "eschewed Roosevelt-style confrontations over domestic issues in favor of a congressionally centered process of deliberation." See Terri Bimes and Stephen Skowronek, "Woodrow Wilson's Critique of Popular Leadership: Reassessing the Modern-Traditional Divide in Presidential History," *Polity* XXIX (1996): 43, 62.

68. In *The Old Regime*, Tocqueville laments that the French people "had come to regard the ideal social system as one . . . in which an all-powerful bureaucracy not only took charge of affairs of State but controlled men's private lives." Because "the individual citizen was kept in strictest tutelage," the French character was corrupted, with the result that "many Frenchmen have lost their taste for freedom" (167–68).

69. Woodrow Wilson, "Self-Government in France," September 4, 1879, in *PWW*, 1:519 (emphasis added).

70. Wilson, "Self-Government in France," 534. Tocqueville uses the term "habit of servitude" [l'usage de la servitude] in *Democracy*, 317.

71. Wilson, *The New Freedom*, 122.

72. Wilson, *The New Freedom*, 48.

73. Tocqueville, *Democracy*, 692.

74. Wilson, *Constitutional Government*, 183.

75. Sidney Milkis, introduction to *Progressivism and the New Democracy*, 19.

76. Morone notes that Wilson also created "commissions on shipping, the tariff, and Federal employee compensation." See James Morone, *The Democratic Wish: Popular Participation and the Limits of American Government* (New York: Basic Books, 1990), 117.

77. Wilson defined expediency as "the wisdom of circumstances." Wilson quoted in Cooper, *The Warrior and the Priest*, 265.

78. Wilson, "Interpreter of English Liberty," 158.

79. Philippa Strum, *Brandeis: Beyond Progressivism* (Lawrence: University Press of Kansas, 1993), 87.

80. Wilson quoted in Cooper, *The Warrior and the Priest*, 236.

81. Cooper, *The Warrior and the Priest*, 235.

82. Schleifer, *The Making of Tocqueville's Democracy in America*, 176.

83. It is also actually possible to consider institutions such as the FTC to be examples of what Tocqueville called *governmental* centralization. In *Democracy*, Tocqueville argues that governmental centralization is generally salutary, whereas administrative centralization "only serves to enervate the peoples that submit to it." Tocqueville asserts that governmental centralization involves "common authority" over "matters of common interest" (88). By 1912, the problems of large-scale industrial capitalism were certainly affecting the "common interest," and so some economic regulation by the federal government—the "common authority"—perhaps fell under the rubric of governmental centralization. It should also be noted that Wilson argued for what he sometimes called administrative "concentration," in contrast to "[c]omplete centralization." See Woodrow Wilson, "Notes for Two

Classroom Lectures at the Johns Hopkins," c. February 24, 1888, in *PWW*, 5:693. One can argue that with his term "concentration," Wilson means something similar to Tocqueville's term "governmental centralization."

84. Woodrow Wilson, "The Study of Administration," c. November 1, 1886, in *PWW*, 5:363.

85. Cooper, *Warrior and the Priest*, 234.

86. Tocqueville describes the key role played by the *intendants* in the administrative centralization of pre-Revolutionary France in *The Old Regime*, 35–72.

87. Wilson, "Notes for Two Classroom Lectures at the Johns Hopkins," 693.

88. Woodrow Wilson, "A Special Message to Congress," May 20, 1919, in *PWW*, 59:291. Wilson's call for industrial democracy lacked specificity. Brandeis, on the other hand, wrote and thought about this issue in more depth, although even he, as Strum notes, "did not advocate a specific system of worker-management." See Philippa Strum, *Louis D. Brandeis: Justice for the People* (Cambridge, MA: Harvard University Press, 1984), 185.

89. Reinhardt, *The Art of Being Free*, 53.

90. Reinhardt, *The Art of Being Free*, 53–54.

91. Lively, *The Social and Political Thought of Alexis de Tocqueville*, 251.

92. For an illuminating discussion of how commerce and industrialization pose a threat, in Tocqueville's view, to the proper education of democratic citizens, see Laura Janara, *Democracy Growing Up: Authority, Autonomy, and Passion in Tocqueville's Democracy in America* (Albany: State University of New York Press, 2002), 99–128. Moreover, James Schleifer has recently pointed out that the drafts of *Democracy* reveal that Tocqueville considered industrialization to be "'the great fact of our time,' second only to the march of equality." See Schleifer, "Tocqueville's *Democracy in America* Reconsidered," in *The Cambridge Companion to Tocqueville*, 132–33. While the final version of *Democracy* does not lay as much stress on industrialization as do the drafts, Schleifer notes that "the published text . . . does, after all, contain several chapters on the development of manufacturing" and other economic matters (133). Even Schleifer concedes, though, that while Tocqueville may have been deeply interested in the transformations wrought by industrialization, he "chose to leave the full elaboration of that theme to others" (134). It is my argument that Wilson is one thinker who took up the challenge of elaborating precisely upon this theme.

93. Lively, *The Social and Political Thought of Alexis de Tocqueville*, 251.

94. Tocqueville, *Recollections*, 75.

95. Wilson, *The New Freedom*, 32.

96. Wilson, *The New Freedom*, 20.

97. Wilson, *The New Freedom*, 30.

98. Wilson, *The New Freedom*, 23.

99. Tocqueville, *Democracy*, 556–57.

100. Woodrow Wilson, "An Inaugural Address [as New Jersey Governor]," January 17, 1911, in *PWW*, 22:347.

101. Lincoln, letter to Henry L. Pierce and Others, April 6, 1859, in *Speeches and Writings 1859–1865*, 18; Wilson, *The New Freedom*, 159.

102. Tocqueville, *Democracy*, 691.

103. Wilson, *The New Freedom*, 127.

104. Leuchtenberg, introduction to *The New Freedom*, 16–17.

105. Daniel Stid, *The President as Statesman: Woodrow Wilson and the Constitution* (Lawrence: University of Kansas Press, 1998), 111.

106. Lincoln, First Lincoln-Douglas Debate, August 21, 1858, in *Speeches and Writings 1832–1858*, 525.

107. Wilson, "Leaders of Men," 658.

108. Wilson, "Leaders of Men," 658.

109. Wilson, *The New Freedom*, 47.

110. Woodrow Wilson, confidential journal, December 28, 1889, in *PWW*, 6:462–63.

111. Stid, *The President as Statesman*, 73–74.

112. Wilson, letter to Howard Allen Bridgman, September 8, 1913, in *PWW*, 28:265.

113. Stid, *The President as Statesman*, 100.

114. Wilson quoted in Daniel Tichenor, "The Presidency, Social Movements, and Contentious Change: Lessons from the Woman's Suffrage and Labor Movements," *Presidential Studies Quarterly* XXIX (1999), 17.

115. Tichenor, "The Presidency, Social Movements, and Contentious Change," 18.

116. Wilson, *The State*, 576.

117. Wilson, *The State*, 555.

118. Wilson, "Leaders of Men," 663.

119. Woodrow Wilson, "A Lecture on Democracy," December 5, 1891, in *PWW*, 7:359.

120. Wilson quoted in Leuchtenberg, introduction to *The New Freedom*, 9.

121. John Milton Cooper, *Breaking the Heart of the World: Woodrow Wilson and the Fight for the League of Nations* (New York: Cambridge University Press, 2001), 426. Cooper notes that although Wilson failed to gain majority support, the isolationists also failed in this regard. In Cooper's view, majority opinion actually "occupied a broad middle ground" somewhere between "diehard Wilsonianism" and "staunch isolationism" (425).

122. Wilson quoted in Cooper, *The Warrior and the Priest*, 345.

123. Morone, *The Democratic Wish*, 333.

124. Wilson, "The Study of Administration," 149.

125. Woodrow Wilson, "The Ideals of America," December 26, 1901, in *PWW*, 12:210.

126. Woodrow Wilson, "Democracy and Efficiency," October 1, 1900, in *PWW*, 12:17.

127. "Character of Democracy in the United States," in Woodrow Wilson, *An Old Master and Other Political Essays* (New York: Charles Scribner's Sons, 1893), 136.

128. Wilson, "Democracy and Efficiency," 17.

129. Schleifer, *The Making of Tocqueville's Democracy in America*, 177.

130. Tocqueville, *Democracy*, 384.

131. Tocqueville, *Democracy*, 389.

132. Bernard Bailyn, *The Ideological Origins of the American Revolution* (Cambridge, MA: Harvard University Press, 1967).

133. Thomas Paine, *Common Sense and The Crisis* (Garden City, NY: Anchor Books, 1973), 13.

134. Wilson, *Constitutional Government*, 106.

135. Lincoln, Fragments on Government, *Speeches and Writings 1832–1858*, 301.

136. McPherson, *Abraham Lincoln and the Second American Revolution*, 137.

137. Wilson, *The New Freedom*, 164.

138. Woodrow Wilson, "The Road Away From Revolution," c. July 27, 1923, in *PWW*, 68:395.

139. Woodrow Wilson, "The Bible and Progress," May 7, 1911, in *PWW*, 23:20.

140. Woodrow Wilson, Address at Carnegie Hall, New York, December 7, 1911, in *PWW*, 23:586.

141. Wilson, *The State*, 583.

142. Wilson, *The State*, 627.

143. Woodrow Wilson, "The Young People and the Church," October 13, 1904, in *PWW*, 15:512.

144. Pestritto, *Woodrow Wilson and the Roots of Modern Liberalism*, 271.

145. Pestritto has also criticized the subfield of American Political Development for its alleged historicism. See Ronald Pestritto, "Politics and History," review of *The Search for American Political Development*, by Karen Orren and Stephen Skowronek, *The Review of Politics* LXVII (2005): 581–82.

146. See Jaffa, *A New Birth of Freedom*, 84–85.

147. This normative argument is implicit in Pestritto's book on Wilson, and is made more explicit in Ronald Pestritto, "What America Owes to Woodrow Wilson," *Society* XLIII (2005): 57–66.

148. Eileen McDonagh, "Race, Class, and Gender in the Progressive Era: Restructuring State and Society," in *Progressivism and the New Democracy*, 155.

149. I do not mean to suggest that Hegel had *no* influence on Wilson. In particular, the mode of analysis in Wilson's book *The State* is sometimes reminiscent of Hegel's thought. That said, it is my contention that Pestritto exaggerates to a significant degree the influence of Hegel on Wilson. My argument that Pestritto overstates Wilson's Hegelianism is consistent with the claim of Karen Orren and Stephen Skowronek that Wilson's "*Congressional Government* conjured an assessment [of American politics] that was the mirror image of that provided by the German idealists," such as John Burgess. See Karen Orren and Stephen Skowronek, *The Search for American Political Development* (Cambridge, MA: Cambridge University Press, 2004), 42–43.

150. As part of his effort to link Wilson to Hegel, Pestritto also argues that through his graduate studies at Johns Hopkins, Wilson was influenced by Hegel, since Wilson's professors "were educated in Germany and in the tradition of German state theory and philosophy of history." See Pestritto, *Woodrow Wilson and the Roots of Modern Liberalism*, 8. But while Hegel may have influenced Wilson's teachers, Tocqueville surely influenced them as well. For instance, Herbert Baxter Adams—designated by Pestritto as one of the most influential professors on Wilson—was, as Matthew Mancini points out, "a Tocqueville scholar . . . and the author of a still-valuable monograph on the relationship between [Jared] Sparks and Tocqueville," published in 1898. See Pestritto, *Woodrow Wilson and the Roots of Modern Liberalism*, 8 and Matthew Mancini, *Alexis de Tocqueville and American Intellectuals: From His Times to Ours* (Lanham, MD: Rowman & Littlefield, 2006), 111. Moreover, Daniel Coit Gilman, the founding president of Johns Hopkins, was the editor and the author of the introduction for an 1898 edition of *Democracy in America*. As Mancini notes, through professors such as Gilman and Adams, "the legacy of Tocqueville remained vibrant at Johns Hopkins up to and beyond the beginning of the twentieth century" (115). The strong interest of Wilson's teachers in Tocqueville is striking, although it should also be noted that Adams and Gilman published their works on Tocqueville after Wilson had left Johns Hopkins; this means that I cannot go so far as to claim that Tocqueville was necessarily in the forefront of the minds of Wilson's teachers while Wilson was in graduate school.

151. Noting that the science of administration only emerged once the vast problems of the industrial age themselves emerged, Wilson writes, "The philosophy of any time is, as Hegel says, 'nothing but the spirit of that time expressed in abstract thought.'" See Wilson, "The Study of Administration," 361.

152. While arguing against what he labels "false talk about 'a woman's right to live her own life,'" Wilson alludes to Hegel: "An old German philosopher, who used to search for—and in most cases *find*, it seems to me—the fundamental psychological facts of society, used to maintain the apparent paradox that no one ever fully realized his own identity until he lost it in the service of love for another." See Wilson, letter to Ellen Louise Axson, March 1, 1885, in *PWW*, 4:317.

153. Catherine Zuckert, "Political Sociology versus Speculative Philosophy," in *Interpreting Tocqueville's Democracy in America*, ed. Ken Masugi (Lanham, MD: Rowman & Littlefield, 1991), 122–23.

154. Catherine Zuckert, "Political Sociology versus Speculative Philosophy," 124.

155. Pestritto, *Woodrow Wilson and the Roots of Modern Liberalism*, 34.

156. Ellen Axson, letter to Wilson, May 9, 1884, in *PWW*, 3:171; Wilson, letter to Axson, May 13, 1884, in *PWW*, 3:177; Wilson, letter to Axson, May 25, 1884, in *PWW*, 3:191–92.

157. For instance, in 1877, the prominent Harvard Professor Francis Bowen used Alexander Pope's phrase "whatever is, is right" to describe what Bowen calls Hegel's "system of fatalism." See Francis Bowen, *Modern Philosophy, from Descartes to Schopenhauer and Hartmann* (New York: Scribner, Armstrong, and Company, 1877), 382–83.

158. Wilson, *The State*, 13 (emphasis added).
159. Tocqueville quoted in Zuckert, "Political Sociology versus Speculative Philosophy," 126. The passage is from Tocqueville, *Democracy*, 163.
160. Dana Villa, "Hegel, Tocqueville, and 'Individualism,'" *Review of Politics* LXVII (2005): 682.
161. Woodrow Wilson, "When a Man Comes to Himself," c. November 1, 1899, in *PWW*, 11:264.
162. Wilson, *Constitutional Government*, 150 (emphasis added).
163. Pestritto, *Woodrow Wilson and the Roots of Modern Liberalism*, 6.
164. Pestritto, *Woodrow Wilson and the Roots of Modern Liberalism*, 7.
165. Woodrow Wilson, "The Author and Signers of the Declaration of Independence," July 4, 1907, in *PWW*, 17:256 (emphasis added).
166. Jean Yarbrough, "Theodore Roosevelt and the Stewardship of the American Presidency," in *History of American Political Thought*, eds. Bryan-Paul Frost and Jeffrey Sikkenga (Lanham, MD: Lexington Books, 2003), 544–47.
167. Stid, *The President as Statesman*, 72.
168. Bimes and Skowronek, "Woodrow Wilson's Critique of Popular Leadership," 62.
169. Yarbrough, "Theodore Roosevelt and the Stewardship of the American Presidency," 546.
170. Yarbrough, "Theodore Roosevelt and the Stewardship of the American Presidency," 547.
171. Wilson, "Democracy and Efficiency," 8 (emphasis added).
172. Wilson, *Constitutional Government*, 3.
173. Wilson, *Constitutional Government*, 17–18.
174. Wilson, *Congressional Government*, 79 (emphasis added).
175. Granted, Wilson sometimes suggested that limits on government were eroding over the course of American political development. For instance, Wilson writes in *The State* that *"government does now whatever experience permits or the times demand"* (651). However, as Skowronek notes, Wilson viewed the modern erosion of limits on government as a dangerous trend that needed to be controlled and shaped, rather than a trend which should simply be endorsed. See Skowronek, "The Reassociation of Ideas and Purposes," 391–92.
176. Hartz, *The Liberal Tradition in America*, 207.
177. Hartz, *The Liberal Tradition in America*, 230.
178. Sandel, *Democracy's Discontent*, 6.
179. Wilson, "When a Man Comes to Himself," 271.
180. Wilson, "When a Man Comes to Himself," 272.
181. Wilson, "When a Man Comes to Himself," 264.
182. Wilson, "When a Man Comes to Himself," 271.
183. Hartz, *The Liberal Tradition in America*, 62.
184. Wilson, "When a Man Comes to Himself," 272.
185. Tocqueville writes of modern individualists: "Such folk owe no man anything and hardly expect anything from anybody. They form the habit of thinking of themselves in isolation and imagine that their whole destiny is in their own hands." See Tocqueville, *Democracy*, 508.

186. Hartz, *The Liberal Tradition in America*, 140.

187. Wilson, *The State*, 12–13.

188. Link et al., "Editorial Note: Wilson's Lectures on Great Leaders of Political Thought," in *PWW*, 9:326–27.

189. In part because he disliked ahistorical social contract thinking, Wilson was not an admirer of Jefferson's natural rights philosophy. Although Wilson claimed to be a Jeffersonian in 1912, in 1896 Wilson wrote that Jefferson was "not a great American" because his thought was "speculative," "abstract" and "rationalistic." In Wilson's view, Jefferson failed to recognize that "Liberty, among us, is . . . a product of experience; its derivation is not rationalistic, but practical." See Wilson, "A Calendar of Great Americans," in *Mere Literature and Other Essays*, 198.

190. Wolin, *Tocqueville between Two Worlds*, 41.

191. Thomas West (who has coedited a series of books with Pestritto) criticizes Tocqueville precisely for his abandonment of social contract theory. According to West, *Democracy in America* "is an impressive book," but it is "grossly deficient" insofar as "Tocqueville never mentions the Declaration of Independence anywhere in his two volumes. He never discusses the social compact theory of the founding. Whether that is because he did not understand it, or because he chose not to talk about it, does not matter." See Thomas G. West, "Jaffa versus Mansfield: Does America Have a Constitutional or a 'Declaration of Independence' Soul?" *Perspectives on Political Science* XXXI (2002): 242. West also criticizes Tocqueville in Thomas West, "Misunderstanding the American Founding," in *Interpreting Tocqueville's Democracy in America*, 155–77.

192. See Mansfield and Winthrop, editors' introduction to *Democracy in America*, xxvii.

193. Cheryl Welch, introduction to *The Cambridge Companion to Tocqueville*, 8. Welch here paraphrases ideas from Harvey Mansfield and Delba Winthrop, "Tocqueville's New Political Science," in *The Cambridge Companion to Tocqueville*, 81–107.

194. Tocqueville, *Democracy*, 701.

195. Wilson, *The State*, 582.

196. Wilson, *Constitutional Government*, 17–18.

197. Woodrow Wilson, "The Reconstruction of the Southern States," March 2, 1900, in *PWW*, 11:466. Tocqueville also suggested that the experience of slavery badly damaged the character of African-Americans. Just as Wilson claimed that freed slaves were "unpracticed in liberty," Tocqueville argued that freed slaves were unskilled in "the art of being free." Tocqueville wrote that when a slave "becomes free, he often feels independence as a heavier burden than slavery itself, for his life has taught him to submit to everything, except to the dictates of reason. . . . Desires are masters against whom one must fight, and he has learned nothing but to submit and obey. So he has reached this climax of affliction in which slavery brutalizes him and freedom leads him to destruction." See Tocqueville, *Democracy*, 354, 318. Although Tocqueville and Wilson agreed that freed slaves were "unschooled in self-control," as Wilson put it, it must be emphasized that unlike Wilson, Tocqueville never concluded that freed slaves should

be excluded from full citizenship. In contrast to Wilson, who signed legislation segregating federal employees, Tocqueville plainly finds it unjust that free blacks in the North "cannot share the rights, pleasures, labors, griefs, or even the tomb" of whites (343). In particular, Tocqueville was disturbed to find that African-Americans were prevented from voting in the North (252–53). Wilson, for all his interest in Tocqueville, plainly did not absorb the critical insights into the issue of race that are offered by the French thinker. For appreciative discussions of Tocqueville's understanding of race in America, see Margaret Kohn, "The Other America: Tocqueville and Beaumont on Race and Slavery," *Polity* XXXV (2003): 169–94 and Alvin Tillery, "Tocqueville as Critical Race Theorist: The Perverse Effects of Whiteness as Property in Jacksonian America" (paper presented at the annual meeting for the Western Political Science Association, Albuquerque, New Mexico, March 16–18, 2006).

198. Wilson, letter to Allen Wickham Corwin, September 10, 1900, in *PWW*, 11:573.

199. Wilson, "The Ideals of America," 223.

200. Uday Singh Mehta, *Liberalism and Empire* (Chicago: University of Chicago, 1999), 69–70, 49.

201. Wilson, "Democracy and Efficiency," 17 (emphasis added).

202. Of course, Tocqueville himself abandoned his anti-paternalist ideas when he defended French imperialism in Algeria. As Jennifer Pitts and Melvin Richter have discussed, Tocqueville hoped that imperial expansion could serve as a great national project that would elevate, unify, and energize a French citizenry that was mired in apathy and petty pursuits. See Jennifer Pitts, introduction to Alexis de Tocqueville, *Writings on Empire and Slavery*, by Alexis de Tocqueville (Baltimore, MD: Johns Hopkins University Press, 2001); Melvin Richter, "Tocqueville on Algeria," *Review of Politics* XXV (1963): 362–98. See also Cheryl Welch, "Colonial Violence and the Rhetoric of Evasion: Tocqueville on Algeria," *Political Theory* XXXI (2003): 235–64 and Roger Boesche, "The Dark Side of Tocqueville: On War and Empire," *Review of Politics* LXVII (2005): 737–52. On the whole, Tocqueville failed to appreciate how his support of imperialism violated his own ideals and goals. In *Democracy,* Tocqueville brilliantly analyzed how slavery deforms the character of the white masters. Echoing Jefferson's ideas in *Notes on Virginia,* Tocqueville wrote that when young whites in the South are taught that they are "born to command," they become "haughty, hasty [and] irascible" (*Democracy,* 375). Cf. Thomas Jefferson, *Notes on Virginia,* Query XVIII, in *Writings,* ed. Merrill D. Peterson (New York: Library of America, 1984), 288. Tocqueville did not acknowledge, though, that imperialism is likely to have a similarly damaging effect on character, for imperialism, like slavery, violates democratic mores by teaching that the strong have a right to dominate the weak. Furthermore, it is difficult to see how imperialism could teach Europeans to rise above the petty politics of self-interest, for imperialism itself is patently motivated by a narrow conception of national self-interest. Similarly, it is difficult to see how imperialism can teach people to rise above materialism, when imperialism itself involves the domination of another people for economic gain.

203. Tocqueville, letter to Gobineau, January 24, 1857, 347.

204. Wilson, *Constitutional Government*, 18–19 (emphasis added).

205. Skowronek, "The Reassociation of Ideas and Purposes."

206. Skowronek, "The Reassociation of Ideas and Purposes," 390–91.

207. Skowronek, "The Reassociation of Ideas and Purposes," 396. The Wilson quote is from Woodrow Wilson, "Peace without Victory," January 22, 1917, in *PWW*, 40:533–39.

208. In "The Reassociation of Ideas and Purposes," Skowronek highlights Wilson's racist goals, but elsewhere Skowronek draws out other aspects of Wilson's thought, especially his ideas on leadership and constitutional development. See, for instance, Terri Bimes and Stephen Skowronek, "Woodrow Wilson's Critique of Popular Leadership: Reassessing the Modern-Traditional Divide in Presidential History," and Orren and Skowronek, *The Search for American Political Development*, 42–45.

209. Sandel, *Democracy's Discontent*, 319.

210. Wilson, *Constitutional Government*, 52.

Chapter 5. The Vocation of the Democratic Moralist

1. For useful anthologies on civil society, see Don Eberly, ed., *The Essential Civil Society Reader* (Lanham, MD: Rowman & Littlefield, 2000), and E.J. Dionne, ed., *Community Works: The Revival of Civil Society in America* (Washington, DC: Brookings Institution, 2000).

2. Putnam, *Bowling Alone*, 292.

3. According to Robert Gannett, Tocqueville paid more attention than Putnam does to the political context of civic engagement. See Gannett, "Bowling Ninepins in Tocqueville's Township," *American Political Science Review* XCVII (2003): 1–16. Amy Fried, John Ehrenberg, and David Schultz all suggest that unlike Tocqueville, Putnam does not genuinely help us understand the egalitarian preconditions of a democratic civil society. See Fried, "The Strange Disappearance of Alexis de Tocqueville in Putnam's Analysis of Social Capital," in *Social Capital: Critical Perspectives on Community and "Bowling Alone,"* eds. Scott L. McLean, David A. Schultz, and Manfred B. Steger (New York: New York University Press, 2002), 21–49; Ehrenberg, "Equality, Democracy, and Community from Tocqueville to Putnam," in *Social Capital: Critical Perspectives*, 50–73; Schultz, "The Phenomenology of Democracy: Putnam, Pluralism, and Voluntary Associations," in *Social Capital: Critical Perspectives*, 74–98. I also ask whether Putnam is genuinely following in Tocqueville's footsteps, but my focus is on determining whether Putnam's use of "self-interest properly understood" is consistent with Tocqueville's ideas about this "doctrine."

4. Tocqueville, *Democracy*, 525.

5. Fried and Ehrenberg each briefly mention the connection between Putnam and Tocqueville's doctrine of self-interest properly understood, but neither scholar explores in depth the meaning of Tocqueville's doctrine nor the implications of Putnam's use of it. See Fried, "The Strange Disappearance of Alexis de Tocqueville," 26 and Ehrenberg, "Equality, Democracy, and Community," 53.

6. On "moralists," see Tocqueville, *Democracy,* 259, 525–28, 548, 632.

7. At one point in *Democracy,* Tocqueville refers to "philosophers" and then quickly shifts to the term "moralist" (548). The context makes it clear that for Tocqueville, the "moralist" is a widely known author who aims to shape the moral views of "his contemporaries" (548).

8. On the concept of the public intellectual, see Richard Posner, *Public Intellectuals: A Study in Decline* (Cambridge, MA: Harvard University Press, 2001) and Amitai Etzioni and Alyssa Bowditch, eds., *Public Intellectuals: An Endangered Species?* (Lanham, MD: Rowman & Littlefield, 2006).

9. Tocqueville, *Democracy,* 632.

10. Tocqueville, *Democracy,* 547–48.

11. One could argue that Tocqueville sees not just "moralists" as democratic leaders, but also women. After all, in *Democracy,* he writes that, "There have never been free societies without mores, and . . . it is woman who shapes these mores" (590). Because Tocqueville views women as moral educators, one might claim that Tocqueville places them in the category of leaders who must "educate democracy." On the other hand, it is highly problematic to suggest that Tocqueville assigns a leadership role to women, given his insistence that women be excluded from the public realm. Tocqueville notes with approval that "public opinion" in America "carefully keeps woman within the little sphere of domestic interests and duties and will not let her go beyond them" (592). Tocqueville argues that women play a crucial role in shaping morality, but he also believed, as Pitkin notes, that "women's domestic submission" was "essential to American *liberté.*" See Pitkin, *Attack of the Blob,* 126. For an insightful analysis of Tocqueville's argument that women should be excluded from both civil and political life, see Welch, *De Tocqueville,* 190–207. I have argued in this book that Tocqueville offers a highly stimulating and valuable theory of leadership. I have also suggested, though, that his account of leadership should not be viewed as definitive. Tocqueville's exclusion of women from public leadership is clearly an aspect of his theory of leadership that demands rethinking. For discussions of the role of gender in Tocqueville's thought, see Jill Locke and Eileen Hunt Botting, eds., *Feminist Interpretations of Alexis de Tocqueville* (University Park: Pennsylvania State University Press, 2009).

12. Tocqueville, *Democracy,* 44.

13. Tocqueville, *Democracy,* 243.

14. Tocqueville, *Democracy,* 513.

15. Putnam, *Bowling Alone,* 402.

16. Putnam, *Bowling Alone,* 272.

17. Putnam, *Bowling Alone,* 46.

18. I find Putnam's claim that associational life has declined to be largely persuasive; some scholars, though, are skeptical. For an argument that Putnam may have missed new forms of associational life that have replaced those that are disappearing, see Everett C. Ladd, "Bowling with Tocqueville: Civic Engagement and Social Capital," *The Responsive Community* IX (1999): 11–21.

19. Welch, *De Tocqueville,* 53.

20. Tocqueville, *Democracy,* 525, 527.

21. Putnam, *Bowling Alone,* 287, 290.

22. Tocqueville, *Democracy*, 525.

23. Putnam, *Bowling Alone*, 414 (emphasis added).

24. Putnam, *Bowling Alone*, 20, 27, 290.

25. For critiques of Putnam's use of economistic language, see Michael Forman, "Social Rights or Social Capital? The Labor Movement and the Language of Capital," in *Social Capital: Critical Perspectives*, 238–59, and Stephen Samuel Smith and Jessica Kulynych, "Liberty, Equality, and . . . Social Capital?," in *Social Capital: Critical Perspectives*, 127–46.

26. Putnam, *Bowling Alone*, 20.

27. Putnam, *Bowling Alone*, 19.

28. Putnam, *Bowling Alone*, 18–19.

29. Tocqueville, *Democracy*, 525.

30. Robert Putnam, *Making Democracy Work* (Princeton, NJ: Princeton University Press, 1993), 86–91.

31. Putnam, *Making Democracy Work*, 86–88.

32. Skinner quoted in Putnam, *Making Democracy Work*, 88 (emphasis added). The Skinner quotation is from Quentin Skinner, "The Idea of Negative Liberty: Philosophical and Historical Perspectives," in *Philosophy in History: Essays on the Historiography of Philosophy*, eds. Richard Rorty, Jerome B. Schneewind, and Quentin Skinner (Cambridge: Cambridge University Press, 1984), 218.

33. Putnam, *Making Democracy Work*, 88.

34. Tocqueville, *The Tocqueville Reader*, 51.

35. McLean, Schultz, and Steger, introduction to *Social Capital: Critical Perspectives*, 10.

36. Schultz, "The Phenomenology of Democracy," 83.

37. Tocqueville, *Democracy*, 512.

38. Putnam, *Bowling Alone*, 287.

39. Putnam, *Bowling Alone*, 338.

40. Is it truly the case that civic and political participation leads people to have a "habit and taste" for further civic and political engagement? Those who advocate experiential "service-education" programs often suggest that the answer to this question is yes. Assessing the empirical research on this question, Galston concludes that, "On balance . . . the evidence suggests that students who participate in high-quality programs that integrate community service with systematic reflection on their experience are more likely . . . to become civically and politically engaged" later in life as compared to students who do not participate in "service-learning" programs. See William Galston, "Political Knowledge, Political Engagement, and Civic Education," *Annual Review of Political Science* IV (2001): 230.

41. Tocqueville, *Democracy*, 526 (emphasis added).

42. Putnam, *Bowling Alone*, 118.

43. Tocqueville, *The Old Regime*, 169.

44. Tocqueville, *The Old Regime*, 169.

45. Tocqueville, *The Old Regime*, 169. As Sanford Kessler helpfully notes, "Tocqueville believed that in difficult cases, when virtue required sacrifice or clearly conflicted with self-interest, enlightened self-love ill served the cause of freedom." More specifically, Kessler argues that Tocqueville found "self-interest

properly understood" to be "wholly inadequate to deal with the country's griev-
ous racial problem." See Sanford Kessler, *Tocqueville's Civil Religion: American
Christianity and the Prospects for Freedom* (Albany: State University of New
York Press), 139, 130.

46. Jaffa, *Crisis of the House Divided*, 204–5.
47. Tocqueville, *The Tocqueville Reader*, 51.
48. Bellah et al., *Habits of the Heart*, 33–34.
49. Bellah et al., *Habits of the Heart*, 77.
50. Bellah et al., *Habits of the Heart*, 6.
51. Bellah et al., *Habits of the Heart*, 8.
52. Bellah et al., *Habits of the Heart*, 298, 6.
53. MacIntyre, *After Virtue*.
54. See Barack Obama, "Democratic National Convention Keynote
Address," July 27, 2004, http://www.americanrhetoric.com/speeches/convention2004/
barackobama2004dnc.htm and Barack Obama, "Commencement Address at Knox
College," June 4, 2005, http://www.knox.edu/x9803.xml.
55. Obama, "Democratic National Convention Keynote Address."
56. Obama, "Commencement Address at Knox College."
57. Obama, "Commencement Address at Knox College."
58. George W. Bush, First Inaugural Address, January 20, 2001, http://www.
yale.edu/lawweb/avalon/presiden/inaug/gbush1.htm.
59. Tocqueville, *The Old Regime*, 275.
60. Bush, First Inaugural Address.
61. George W. Bush, Second Inaugural Address, January 20, 2005, http://
www.whitehouse.gov/news/releases/2005/01/20050120–1.html.
62. Lawrence Kaplan notes that Bush's "rhetoric entails no obligation to
act;" tellingly, Bush "has yet to devote a speech merely to urging young Americans
to consider the benefits of military service." See Lawrence Kaplan, "American
Idle," *The New Republic*, September 12, 2005, 21.
63. Robert Putnam, "Bowling Together," *The American Prospect*, February
12, 2002, 22.
64. George W. Bush, Speech at the Georgia World Congress Center in Atlanta,
November 8, 2001, http://archives.cnn.com/2001/US/11/08/rec.bush.transcript/.
65. Bush said, "We cannot let the terrorists achieve the objective of frightening
our nation to the point where we don't conduct business, where people don't
shop. That's their intention." See "President Holds Prime Time News Conference,"
October 11, 2001, http://archives.cnn.com/2001/US/11/08/rec.bush.transcript/.
66. George W. Bush, State of the Union Address, January 29, 2002, http://
www.whitehouse.gov/news/releases/2002/01/20020129–11.html.
67. David Gergen, "A Nation in Search of Its Mission," *New York Times*,
June 17, 2002.
68. Galston, "Some Arguments for Universal Service," in *Public Matters*,
74, 68.
69. Bruce Ackerman and James Fishkin, *Deliberation Day* (New Haven,
CT: Yale University Press, 2004), 219, 179.
70. Tocqueville, *Democracy*, 506.

71. Bruce Frohnen, "Compassionate Conservatism Rightly Understood: Self-Interest in a Humane Economy," *Intercollegiate Review* (Fall/Spring 2000–2001): 38.

72. Villa, "Tocqueville and Civil Society," 225. Villa's analysis reveals what he calls the "*expansive* character of Tocqueville's idea of civil society." According to Villa, Tocqueville had a "political conception of civil society," a conception that included "the townships, municipalities, and counties that Tocqueville identifies with local administration" (225).

73. Suzanne Mettler's study of the civic consequences of the G.I. Bill lends support to the claim that government can sometimes enhance civil society, for according to Mettler, this large-scale federal educational program produced a sense of reciprocity and a sense of inclusion that made its participants significantly more likely to engage in civic and political activities later in life. See Suzanne Mettler, "Bringing the State Back In to Civic Engagement: Policy Feedback Effects of the G.I. Bill for World War II Veterans," *American Political Science Review* XCVI (2002): 351–65. If properly designed, other governmental programs can no doubt similarly foster civic habits. As Putnam notes, "Many of the most creative investments in social capital in American history—from county agents and the 4–H to community colleges and the March of Dimes—were the direct result of government policy." Putnam also argues that "civic disengagement" is not caused by the rise of "big government and the growth of the welfare state," for "differences in social capital appear essentially uncorrelated with various measure of welfare spending or government size." See *Bowling Alone*, 413, 281.

74. Tocqueville, *Democracy*, 239.

75. Lincoln, Speech at Chicago, July 10, 1858, in *Speeches and Writings 1832–1858*, 456.

76. Sandel, *Democracy's Discontent*, 318.

77. Sandel, *Democracy's Discontent*, 321.

78. Tocqueville, *Democracy*, 434.

79. Jean Bethke Elshtain and Christopher Beem, "Can this Republic Be Saved?" in *Debating Democracy's Discontent*, eds. Anita Allen and Milton Regan (New York: Oxford University Press, 1998), 194.

80. MacIntyre, *After Virtue*, 6. In MacIntyre's view, the contemporary United States is a pluralistic society in which different groups hold "incommensurable" beliefs; in such a world, a shared conception of virtue will almost certainly never be revived (8). Hence, unlike Putnam, Bellah, and Sandel, MacIntyre does not call for any society-wide change, for he seems to think that major societal change for the better can never take place. MacIntyre thus pins his remaining hopes onto small pockets of community that would separate themselves from the pluralistic world of the "barbarians," as he puts it in his famous analogy at the end of *After Virtue* (263).

81. This "discussion," Tushnet writes, "*is* the project of the United States." See Mark Tushnet, "Federalism as a Cure for Democracy's Discontent?" in *Debating Democracy's Discontent*, 315.

Bibliography

Ackerman, Bruce, and James Fishkin. *Deliberation Day*. New Haven, CT: Yale University Press, 2004.

Arendt, Hannah. *On Revolution*. New York: Penguin, 1963.

Aristotle. *The Politics*. Trans. Ernest Barker. New York: Oxford University Press, 1958.

Augustine. *Political Writings*. Trans. Michael Tkacz and Douglas Kries. Indianapolis, IN: Hackett, 1994.

Bailyn, Bernard. *The Ideological Origins of the American Revolution*. Cambridge, MA: Harvard University Press, 1967.

Barber, Benjamin. *A Passion for Democracy*. Princeton, NJ: Princeton University Press, 1998.

Bathory, Peter Dennis. *Leadership in America: Consensus, Corruption, and Charisma*. New York: Longman, 1978.

Bellah, Robert, Richard Madsen, William M. Sullivan, Ann Swidler, and Steven M. Tipton. *Habits of the Heart: Individualism and Commitment in American Life*. Berkeley: University of California Press, 1985.

Berns, Walter. "Does the Constitution 'Secure these Rights'?" in *How Democratic is the Constitution?* Washington: American Enterprise Institute for Public Policy Research, 1980.

Bimes, Terri, and Stephen Skowronek. "Woodrow Wilson's Critique of Popular Leadership: Reassessing the Modern-Traditional Divide in Presidential History." *Polity* 29 (Autumn 1996): 27–63.

Boesche, Roger. "The Dark Side of Tocqueville: On War and Empire." *Review of Politics* 67 (Fall 2005): 737–52.

———. *The Strange Liberalism of Alexis de Tocqueville*. Ithaca, NY: Cornell University Press, 1987.

Boritt, Gabor. *Lincoln and the Economics of the American Dream*. Memphis, TN: Memphis State University Press, 1978.

Bowen, Francis. *Modern Philosophy, from Descartes to Schopenhauer and Hartmann*. New York: Scribner, Armstrong, and Company, 1877.

Brown, Bernard E. "Tocqueville and Publius." In *Reconsidering Tocqueville's Democracy in America*, ed. Abraham S. Eisenstadt. New Brunswick, NJ: Rutgers University Press, 1988.

Burns, James MacGregor. *Leadership*. New York: Harper & Row, 1978.

Bush, George W. First Inaugural Address, January 20, 2001. http://www.yale.edu/lawweb/avalon/presiden/inaug/gbush1.htm.

———. "President Holds Prime Time News Conference," October 11, 2001. http://archives.cnn.com/2001/US/11/08/rec.bush.transcript/.

———. Second Inaugural Address, January 20, 2005. http://www.whitehouse.gov/news/releases/2005/01/20050120–1.html.

———. Speech at the Georgia World Congress Center in Atlanta, November 8, 2001. http://archives.cnn.com/2001/US/11/08/rec.bush.transcript/.

———. State of the Union Address, January 29, 2002. http://www.whitehouse.gov/news/releases/2002/01/20020129–11.html.

Ceaser, James W., Glen E. Thurow, Jeffrey Tulis, and Joseph M. Bessette. "The Rise of the Rhetorical Presidency." *Presidential Studies Quarterly* 11 (Spring 1981): 158–71.

Clor, Harry. "Woodrow Wilson." In *American Political Thought*, eds. Morton Frisch and Richard Stevens. Itasca, IL: F.E. Peacock, 1983.

Cooper, John Milton. *Breaking the Heart of the World: Woodrow Wilson and the Fight for the League of Nations*. New York: Cambridge University Press, 2001.

———. *The Warrior and the Priest: Woodrow Wilson and Theodore Roosevelt*. Cambridge, MA: Belknap Press, 1983.

Cornell, Saul. *The Other Founders: Anti-Federalism and the Dissenting Tradition in America, 1788–1828*. Chapel Hill: North Carolina University Press, 1999.

Craiutu, Aurelian. "Tocqueville's Paradoxical Moderation." *The Review of Politics* 67 (Fall 2005): 599–629.

Deneen, Patrick. "Chasing Plato." Review of *Corrupting Youth*, by J. Peter Euben. *Political Theory* 28 (June 2000): 421–39.

———. *Democratic Faith*. Princeton, NJ: Princeton University Press, 2005.

Diamond, Martin. "Democracy and *The Federalist*: A Reconsideration of the Framers' Intent." *American Political Science Review* 53 (March 1959): 52–68.

———. "Ethics and Politics: The American Way." In *The Moral Foundations of the American Republic*, ed. Robert Horwitz. Charlottesville: University Press of Virginia, 1986.

Diggins, John P. *The Lost Soul of American Politics*. New York: Basic Books, 1984.

———, and Mark E. Kann. Introduction to *The Problem of Authority in America*. Eds. Diggins and Kann, 3–9. Philadelphia, PA: Temple University Press, 1981.

Dionne, E.J., ed. *Community Works: The Revival of Civil Society in America*. Washington, DC: Brookings Institution, 2000.

Donald, David Herbert. *We Are Lincoln Men: Abraham Lincoln and His Friends*. New York: Simon & Schuster, 2003.

Duncan, Christopher. *The Anti-Federalists and Early American Political Thought*. DeKalb: Northern Illinois University Press, 1995.

Dworetz, Steven. *The Unvarnished Doctrine: Locke, Liberalism, and the American Revolution*. Durham, NC: Duke University Press, 1990.

Eberly, Don, ed. *The Essential Civil Society Reader*. Lanham, MD: Rowman & Littlefield, 2000.

Edelberg, Jacqueline. "Justice Here? Alexis De Tocqueville and the Role of the Jury in the American Judicial Process and Republican Democracy." *The Tocqueville Review/La Revue Tocqueville* 17 (1996): 67–97.

Ehrenberg, John. "Equality, Democracy, and Community from Tocqueville to Putnam." In *Social Capital: Critical Perspectives on Community and "Bowling Alone,"* eds. Scott L. McLean, David A. Schultz, and Manfred B. Steger. New York: New York University Press, 2002.

Elshtain, Jean Bethke, and Christopher Beem. "Can this Republic Be Saved?" In *Debating Democracy's Discontent*, eds. Anita Allen and Milton Regan. New York: Oxford University Press, 1998.

Ethington, Philip. "The Metropolis and Multicultural Ethics: Direct Democracy versus Deliberative Democracy in the Progressive Era." In *Progressivism and the New Democracy*, eds. Sidney Milkis and Jerome M. Mileur. Amherst: University of Massachusetts Press, 1999.

Etzioni, Amitai, and Alyssa Bowditch, eds. *Public Intellectuals: An Endangered Species?* Lanham, MD: Rowman & Littlefield, 2006.

Faulkner, Robert. *The Case for Greatness: Honorable Ambition and Its Critics*. New Haven, CT: Yale University Press, 2007.

Fehrenbacher, Donald. *Lincoln in Text and Context: Collected Essays*. Palo Alto, CA: Stanford University Press, 1987.

Fitzhugh, George. *Cannibals All! Or, Slaves without Masters*. Cambridge, MA: Belknap/Harvard University Press, 1960.

Foner, Eric. *Free Soil, Free Labor, Free Men: The Ideology of the Republican Party before the Civil War*. New York: Oxford University Press, 1970.

Forman, Michael. "Social Rights or Social Capital? The Labor Movement and the Language of Capital." In *Social Capital: Critical Perspectives on Community and "Bowling Alone,"* eds. Scott L. McLean, David A. Schultz, and Manfred B. Steger. New York: New York University Press, 2002.

Fornieri, Joseph. *Abraham Lincoln's Political Faith*. DeKalb: Northern Illinois University Press, 2003.

Fried, Amy. "The Strange Disappearance of Alexis de Tocqueville in Putnam's Analysis of Social Capital." In *Social Capital: Critical Perspectives on Community and "Bowling Alone,"* eds. Scott L. McLean, David A. Schultz, and Manfred B. Steger. New York: New York University Press, 2002.

Frohnen, Bruce. "Compassionate Conservatism Rightly Understood: Self-Interest in a Humane Economy." *Intercollegiate Review* (Fall/Spring 2000–2001): 34–39.

Galston, William. "Political Knowledge, Political Engagement, and Civic Education." *Annual Review of Political Science* 4 (2001): 217–34.

———. *The Practice of Liberal Pluralism*. Cambridge, UK: Cambridge University Press, 2005.

———. *Public Matters: Politics, Policy, and Religion in the 21st Century.* Lanham, MD: Rowman & Littlefield, 2005.

Gannett, Robert. "Bowling Ninepins in Tocqueville's Township." *American Political Science Review* 97 (February 2003): 1–16.

Gergen, David. "A Nation in Search of Its Mission." *New York Times*, June 17, 2002.

Grazia, Sebastian de. "What Authority is Not." *American Political Science Review* 53 (June 1959): 321–31.

Greenstone, David. *The Lincoln Persuasion: Remaking American Liberalism.* Princeton, NJ: Princeton University Press, 1993.

Guelzo, Allen. *Abraham Lincoln: Redeemer President.* Grand Rapids, MI: Wm. B. Eerdmans Publishing, 1999.

Hamilton, Alexander, James Madison, and John Jay. *The Federalist Papers.* New York: Bantam, 2002.

Hartz, Louis. *The Liberal Tradition in America.* New York: Harcourt Brace, 1955.

Hofstadter, Richard. *The American Political Tradition and the Men Who Made It.* New York: Alfred A. Knopf, 1948.

Huntington, Samuel. "The United States." In *The Crisis of Democracy.* New York: New York University Press, 1975.

Jacobitti, Suzanne. "Individualism and Political Community: Arendt and Tocqueville on the Current Debate in Liberalism." *Polity* 23 (Summer 1991): 585–604.

Jaffa, Harry. *Crisis of the House Divided: An Interpretation of the Issues in the Lincoln-Douglas Debates.* Chicago: University of Chicago Press, 1959.

———. *A New Birth of Freedom.* Lanham, MD: Rowman & Littlefield, 2000.

Janara, Laura. *Democracy Growing Up: Authority, Autonomy, and Passion in Tocqueville's Democracy in America.* Albany: State University of New York Press, 2002.

Jefferson, Thomas. *Writings.* Ed. Merrill D. Peterson. New York: Library of America, 1984.

Kaplan, Lawrence. "American Idle." *The New Republic*, September 12, 2005.

Kendall, Willmoore. "Equality: Commitment or Ideal?" *Intercollegiate Review* 24 (Spring 1989): 25–33.

Kenyon, Cecilia. Introduction to *The Antifederalists*, ed. Cecilia Kenyon, xxi–cxvi. Indianapolis, IN: Bobbs-Merrill, 1966.

———. "Men of Little Faith: The Antifederalists on the Nature of Representative Government." *William and Mary Quarterly* 12 (1955): 3–43.

Kessler, Sanford. *Tocqueville's Civil Religion: American Christianity and the Prospects for Freedom.* Albany: State University of New York Press, 1976.

Ketcham, Ralph. Introduction to *The Antifederalist Papers and the Constitutional Convention Debates*, ed. Ralph Ketcham, 1–23. New York: Mentor, 1986.

Kohn, Margaret. "The Other America: Tocqueville and Beaumont on Race and Slavery." *Polity* 35 (December 2002): 169–94.

Kramnick, Isaac. Introduction to *Democracy in America*, by Alexis de Tocqueville, ix–xlviii. New York: Penguin, 2003.

——, and R. Laurence Moore. *The Godless Constitution.* New York: W.W. Norton, 1997.

Krouse, Richard. "Classical Images of Democracy in America: Madison and Tocqueville." In *Democratic Theory and Practice,* ed. Graeme Duncan. New York: Cambridge University Press, 1983.

Ladd, Everett C. "Bowling with Tocqueville: Civic Engagement and Social Capital." *The Responsive Community* 9 (1999): 11–21.

Landy, Marc, and Sidney Milkis. *Presidential Greatness.* Lawrence: University Press of Kansas, 2000.

Leuchtenberg, William. Introduction to *The New Freedom,* by Woodrow Wilson, 1–17. Englewood Cliffs, NJ: Prentice-Hall, 1961.

Lienesch, Michael. *New Order of the Ages: Time, the Constitution, and the Making of Modern American Political Thought.* Princeton, NJ: Princeton University Press, 1988.

Lincoln, Abraham. *The Language of Liberty: The Political Speeches and Writings of Abraham Lincoln.* Ed. Joseph Fornieri. Washington, DC: Regnery Gateway, 2004.

——. *Speeches and Writings 1832–1858.* Ed. Donald Fehrenbacher. New York: Library of America, 1989.

——. *Speeches and Writings 1859–1865.* Ed. Donald Fehrenbacher. New York: Library of America, 1989.

Lively, Jack. *The Social and Political Thought of Alexis de Tocqueville.* London: Oxford University Press, 1962.

Locke, Jill, and Eileen Hunt Botting, eds. *Feminist Interpretations of Alexis de Tocqueville.* University Park: Pennsylvania State University Press, 2009.

Locke, John. *Two Treaties of Government.* Ed. Peter Laslett. New York: Cambridge University Press, 1960.

Lucas, John. *The Principles of Politics.* New York: Oxford University Press, 1985.

Machiavelli, Niccolo. *The Prince and the Discourses.* Trans. C. Detmold. New York: Random House, 1950.

MacIntyre, Alasdair. *After Virtue.* Notre Dame, IN: Notre Dame University Press, 1981.

Madison, James. *Selected Writings of James Madison.* Ed. Ralph Ketcham. Indianapolis, IN: Hackett, 2006.

Main, Jackson Turner. *The Antifederalists.* Chapel Hill: University of North Carolina Press, 1961.

Mancini, Matthew. *Alexis de Tocqueville and American Intellectuals: From His Times to Ours.* Lanham, MD: Rowman & Littlefield, 2006.

Mansfield, Harvey, and Delba Winthrop. Editors' introduction to *Democracy in America,* by Alexis de Tocqueville, xvii–xciii. Chicago: University of Chicago Press, 2000.

——. "Tocqueville's New Political Science." In *The Cambridge Companion to Tocqueville,* ed. Cheryl Welch. New York: Cambridge University Press, 2006.

Mattie, Sean. "Prerogative and the Rule of Law in John Locke and the Lincoln Presidency." *Review of Politics* 67 (Fall 2005): 77–111.

Mattson, Kevin. *Creating a Democratic Public: The Struggle for Urban Participatory Democracy During the Progressive Era.* University Park: Pennsylvania State University Press, 1998.

McDonagh, Eileen. "Race, Class, and Gender in the Progressive Era: Restructuring State and Society." In *Progressivism and the New Democracy*, eds. Sidney Milkis and Jerome M. Mileur. Amherst: University of Massachusetts Press, 1999.

McLean, Scott, David A. Schultz, and Manfred B. Steger. Introduction to *Social Capital: Critical Perspectives on Community and "Bowling Alone,"* eds. Scott L. McLean, David A. Schultz, and Manfred B. Steger, 1–17. New York: New York University Press, 2002.

McPherson, James. *Abraham Lincoln and the Second American Revolution.* New York: Oxford University Press, 1991.

McWilliams, Wilson Carey. "Democracy and the Citizen: Community, Dignity, and the Crisis of Contemporary Politics in America." In *How Democratic is the Constitution?* Washington, DC: American Enterprise Institute for Public Policy Research, 1980.

———. *The Idea of Fraternity in America.* Berkeley: University of California Press, 1973.

———. "Tocqueville and Responsible Parties." In *Challenges to Party Government*, eds. John Kenneth White and Jerome Mileur. Carbondale: Southern Illinois University Press, 1992.

Mehta, Uday Singh. *Liberalism and Empire.* Chicago: University of Chicago, 1999.

Mettler, Suzanne. "Bringing the State Back In to Civic Engagement: Policy Feedback Effects of the G.I. Bill for World War II Veterans." *American Political Science Review* 96 (June 2002): 351–65.

Milkis, Sidney. Introduction to *Progressivism and the New Democracy*, eds. Sidney Milkis and Jerome M. Mileur, 1–39. Amherst: University of Massachusetts Press, 1999.

Miller, William Lee. *Lincoln's Virtues.* New York: Random House, 2002.

Miroff, Bruce. *Icons of Democracy: American Leaders as Heroes, Aristocrats, Dissenters, and Democrats.* New York: Basic Books, 1993.

Morel, Lucas. *Lincoln's Sacred Effort.* Lanham, MD: Lexington Books, 2000.

Morone, James. *The Democratic Wish: Popular Participation and the Limits of American Government.* New York: Basic Books, 1990.

———. *Hellfire Nation.* New Haven, CT: Yale University Press, 2003.

Obama, Barack. "Commencement Address at Knox College," June 4, 2005. http://www.knox.edu/x9803.xml.

———. "Democratic National Convention Keynote Address," July 27, 2004. http://www.americanrhetoric.com/speeches/convention2004/barackobama2004dnc.htm.

Orren, Karen, and Stephen Skowronek. *The Search for American Political Development.* New York: Cambridge University Press, 2004.

Paine, Thomas. *Common Sense and The Crisis.* Garden City, NY: Anchor Books, 1973.

Pestritto, Ronald J. "Politics and History." Review of *The Search for American Political Development*, by Karen Orren and Stephen Skowronek. *The Review of Politics* 67 (Summer 2005): 581–82.

———. "What America Owes to Woodrow Wilson," *Society* 43 (November 2005): 57–66.

———. *Woodrow Wilson and the Roots of Modern Liberalism*. Lanham, MD: Rowman & Littlefield, 2005.

———, and Thomas West, eds. *Challenges to the American Founding: Slavery, Historicism, and Progressivism in the Nineteenth Century*. Lanham, MD: Lexington Books, 2004.

Pierson, George Wilson. *Tocqueville in America*. New York: Oxford University Press, 1938.

Pitkin, Hanna. *The Attack of the Blob: Hannah Arendt's Concept of the Social*. Chicago: University of Chicago Press, 2000.

Pitts, Jennifer. Introduction to *Writings on Empire and Slavery*, by Alexis de Tocqueville, ix–xxxviii. Baltimore, MD: Johns Hopkins University Press, 2001.

Plato. *Gorgias*. Trans. W.C. Helmbold. New York: Macmillan, 1952.

———. *Republic*. Trans. Allan Bloom. New York: Basic Books, 1968.

Posner, Richard. *Public Intellectuals: A Study in Decline*. Cambridge, MA: Harvard University Press, 2001.

Putnam, Robert. *Bowling Alone: The Collapse and Revival of American Community*. New York: Simon & Schuster, 2000.

———. "Bowling Together." *The American Prospect*, February 12, 2002.

———. *Making Democracy Work*. Princeton, NJ: Princeton University Press, 1993.

Raz, Joseph. *The Authority of Law*. New York: Oxford University Press, 1979.

Reinhardt, Mark. *The Art of Being Free: Taking Liberties with Tocqueville, Marx, and Arendt*. Ithaca, NY: Cornell University Press, 1997.

Richter, Melvin. "Tocqueville on Algeria," *Review of Politics* 25 (1963): 362–98.

———. "The Uses of Theory: Tocqueville's Adaptation of Montesquieu." In *Essays in Theory and History: An Approach to the Social Sciences*, ed. Melvin Richter. Cambridge, MA: Harvard University Press, 1970.

Rogin, Michael. *Ronald Reagan, The Movie and Other Episodes in American Political Demonology*. Berkeley: University of California Press, 1987.

Rousseau, Jean-Jacques. *The Social Contract*. Trans. Maurice Cranston. New York: Penguin Books, 1968.

Ruscio, Kenneth. *The Leadership Dilemma in Modern Democracy*. Cheltenham, UK: Edward Elgar, 2004.

Sabl, Andrew. "Community Organizing as Tocquevillean Politics: The Art, Practices, and Ethos of Association." *American Journal of Political Science* 46 (January 2002): 1–19.

———. *Ruling Passions: Political Offices and Democratic Ethics*. Princeton, NJ: Princeton University Press, 2002.

The Saguaro Seminar. "Social Capital Community Benchmark Survey Executive Summary." Kennedy School of Government, Harvard University. http://www.hks.harvard.edu/saguaro/communitysurvey/results2.html.

Sandel, Michael. *Democracy's Discontent: America in Search of a Public Philosophy.* Cambridge, MA: Belknap Press of Harvard University Press, 1996.

———. "The Procedural Republic and the Unencumbered Self," *Political Theory* 12 (February 1984): 81–96.

Schaar, John. *Escape from Authority.* New York: Basic Books, 1961.

———. "Liberty/Authority/Community in the Political Thought of John Winthrop," *Political Theory* 19 (November 1991): 493–518.

Schleifer, James. *The Making of Tocqueville's Democracy in America.* Indianapolis, IN: Liberty Fund, 2000.

———. "Tocqueville's *Democracy in America* Reconsidered." In *The Cambridge Companion to Tocqueville,* ed. Cheryl Welch. New York: Cambridge University Press, 2006.

Schultz, David. "The Phenomenology of Democracy: Putnam, Pluralism, and Voluntary Associations." In *Social Capital: Critical Perspectives on Community and "Bowling Alone,"* eds. Scott L. McLean, David A. Schultz, and Manfred B. Steger. New York: New York University Press, 2002.

Sedgwick, Jeffrey Leigh. "Executive Leadership and Administration: Founding versus Progressive Views." *Administration and Society* 17 (February 1986): 411–32.

Siemers, David. "Principled Pragmatism: Abraham Lincoln's Method of Political Analysis," *Presidential Studies Quarterly* 34 (December 2004): 804–27.

Simon, Yves. *Freedom and Community.* Bronx, NY: Fordham University Press, 1968.

Skinner, Quentin. "The Idea of Negative Liberty: Philosophical and Historical Perspectives." In *Philosophy in History: Essays on the Historiography of Philosophy,* eds. Richard Rorty, Jerome B. Schneewind, and Quentin Skinner, 193–224. Cambridge: Cambridge University Press, 1984.

Skowronek, Stephen. "The Reassociation of Ideas and Purposes: Racism, Liberalism, and the American Political Tradition." *American Political Science Review* 100 (August 2006): 385–401.

Smith, Rogers. "Beyond Tocqueville, Myrdal, and Hartz: The Multiple Traditions in America." *American Political Science Review* 87 (September 1993): 549–66.

———. *Civic Ideals: Conflicting Views of Citizenship in American History.* New Haven, CT: Yale University Press, 1997.

———. "Response to Jacqueline Stevens." *American Political Science Review* 89 (December 1995): 987–95.

Smith, Stephen Samuel, and Jessica Kulynych. "Liberty, Equality, and . . . Social Capital?" In *Social Capital: Critical Perspectives on Community and "Bowling Alone,"* eds. Scott L. McLean, David A. Schultz, and Manfred B. Steger. New York: New York University Press, 2002.

Stid, Daniel. *The President as Statesman: Woodrow Wilson and the Constitution.* Lawrence: University of Kansas Press, 1998.

Storing, Herbert, ed. *The Complete Anti-Federalist*. 7 vols. Chicago: University of Chicago Press, 1981.

——. "Slavery and the Moral Foundations of the Republic." In *The Moral Foundations of the American Republic*, ed. Robert Horwitz. Charlottesville: University Press of Virginia, 1986.

——. *What the Anti-Federalists Were For*. Chicago: University of Chicago Press, 1981.

Strum, Philippa. *Brandeis: Beyond Progressivism*. Lawrence: University Press of Kansas, 1993.

——. *Louis D. Brandeis: Justice for the People*. Cambridge, MA: Harvard University Press, 1984.

Thorsen, Niels Aage. *The Political Thought of Woodrow Wilson, 1875–1910*. Princeton, NJ: Princeton University Press, 1988.

Thurow, Glen. *Abraham Lincoln and American Political Religion*. Albany: State University of New York Press, 1976.

Tichenor, Daniel. "The Presidency, Social Movements, and Contentious Change: Lessons from the Woman's Suffrage and Labor Movements." *Presidential Studies Quarterly* 29 (March 1999): 14–25.

Tillery, Alvin. "Tocqueville as Critical Race Theorist: The Perverse Effects of Whiteness as Property in Jacksonian America." Paper presented at the annual meeting for the Western Political Science Association, Albuquerque, New Mexico, March 16–18, 2006.

Tocqueville, Alexis de. "The Art and Science of Politics." Trans. J.P. Mayer. *Encounter* 36 (January 1971): 27–35.

——. *De la démocratie en Amérique*. Ed. Eduardo Nolla. 2 vols. Paris: Librairie Philosophique J. Vrin, 1990.

——. *Democracy in America*. Trans. George Lawrence. New York: Harper & Row, 1966.

——. *"The European Revolution" and Correspondence with Gobineau*. Ed. John Lukacs. Gloucester, MA: Peter Smith, 1968.

——. *Journeys to England and Ireland*. Trans. George Lawrence and J.P. Mayer. London: Faber & Faber, 1958.

——. *Memoirs, Letters, and Remains of Alexis de Tocqueville*. 2 vols. London: Macmillan, 1861.

——. *The Old Regime and the French Revolution*. Trans. Stuart Gilbert. New York: Anchor, 1955.

——. *Recollections: The French Revolution of 1848*. Ed. J.P. Mayer. New Brunswick, NJ: Transaction Books, 1987.

——. *Selected Letters on Politics and Society*. Ed. Roger Boesche. Berkeley: University of California Press, 1985.

——. *The Tocqueville Reader*. Eds. Olivier Zunz and Alan S. Kahan. Oxford, UK: Blackwell, 2002.

——. *Writings on Empire and Slavery*. Ed. Jennifer Pitts. Baltimore, MD: Johns Hopkins University Press, 2001.

Tulis, Jeffrey. *The Rhetorical Presidency*. Princeton, NJ: Princeton University Books, 1987.

Tushnet, Mark. "Federalism as a Cure for Democracy's Discontent?" In *Debating Democracy's Discontent*, eds. Anita Allen and Milton Regan. New York: Oxford University Press, 1998.

Villa, Dana. "Hegel, Tocqueville, and 'Individualism,'" *The Review of Politics* 67 (Fall 2005): 659–86.

———. "Tocqueville and Civil Society." In *The Cambridge Companion to Tocqueville*, ed. Cheryl Welch. New York: Cambridge University Press, 2006.

Welch, Cheryl. "Colonial Violence and the Rhetoric of Evasion: Tocqueville on Algeria." *Political Theory* 31 (2003): 235–64.

———. Introduction to *The Cambridge Companion to Tocqueville*, ed. Cheryl Welch, 1–20. New York: Cambridge University Press, 2006.

———. *De Tocqueville*. New York: Oxford University Press, 2001.

West, Thomas. "Jaffa versus Mansfield: Does America Have a Constitutional or a 'Declaration of Independence' Soul?" *Perspectives on Political Science* 31 (2002): 235–46.

———. "Misunderstanding the American Founding." In *Interpreting Tocqueville's Democracy in America*, ed. Ken Masugi. Lanham, MD: Rowman & Littlefield, 1991.

White, Howard B. "Comment on Morgenthau's 'Dilemmas of Freedom.'" *American Political Science Review* 51 (September 1957): 724–33.

Whitehead, Alfred North. *Symbolism: Its Meaning and Effect*. Bronx, NY: Fordham University Press, 1985.

Wills, Garry. *Lincoln at Gettysburg: The Words That Remade America*. New York: Simon & Schuster, 1992.

Wilson, Woodrow. *Congressional Government: A Study in American Politics*. Baltimore, MD: Johns Hopkins University Press, 1981.

———. *Constitutional Government*. New York: Columbia University Press, 1908.

———. *Mere Literature and Other Essays*. Port Washington, NY: Kennikat Press, 1965.

———. *The New Freedom*. Ed. William Leuchtenberg. Englewood Cliffs, NJ: Prentice-Hall, 1961.

———. *An Old Master and Other Political Essays*. New York: Charles Scribner's Sons, 1893.

———. *The Papers of Woodrow Wilson*. Ed. Arthur Link. 69 vols. Princeton, NJ: Princeton University Press, 1966–1994.

———. *The State: Elements of Historical and Practical Politics*. Boston: D.C. Heath, 1898.

Winger, Stewart. *Lincoln, Religion, and Romantic Cultural Politics*. DeKalb: Northern Illinois University Press, 2003.

Wolfe, Alan. *One Nation After All*. New York: Viking, 1998.

Wolff, Robert Paul. *In Defense of Anarchism*. New York: Harper & Row, 1970.

Wolin, Sheldon. *The Presence of the Past*. Baltimore, MD: Johns Hopkins University Press, 1989.

———. *Tocqueville between Two Worlds: The Making of a Political and Theoretical Life*. Princeton, NJ: Princeton University Press, 2001.

Yarbrough, Jean. *American Virtues: Thomas Jefferson on the Character of a Free People*. Lawrence: University Press of Kansas, 1998.

———. "Theodore Roosevelt and the Stewardship of the American Presidency." In *History of American Political Thought*, eds. Bryan-Paul Frost and Jeffrey Sikkenga. Lanham, MD: Lexington Books, 2003.

Young, James P. *Reconsidering American Liberalism: The Troubled Odyssey of the Liberal Idea*. Boulder, CO: Westview, 1996.

Zetterbaum, Marvin. "Alexis de Tocqueville." In *The History of Political Philosophy*, eds. Leo Strauss and Joseph Cropsey. Chicago: University of Chicago Press, 1987.

Zuckert, Catherine. "Political Sociology versus Speculative Philosophy." In *Interpreting Tocqueville's Democracy in America*, ed. Ken Masugi. Lanham, MD: Rowman & Littlefield, 1991.

Index

◆⇒◎⇐◆

211